LOWER
MERRIMACK

Puritans and Victorians both suffer from the misconception that certain generations were too "civilized" or restrained to enjoy themselves outdoors or to experience the glories of nature. Individually they walked, rode, swam, and disported themselves in the Valley. View Near The Laurels, *an 1847 lithograph, depicts The Laurels, West Newbury, which was a favorite picnic spot in the 19th century, and who knows how old the tradition was then? Courtesy, Historical Society of Old Newbury, Newburyport, Massachusetts.*

L O W E R
MERRIMACK

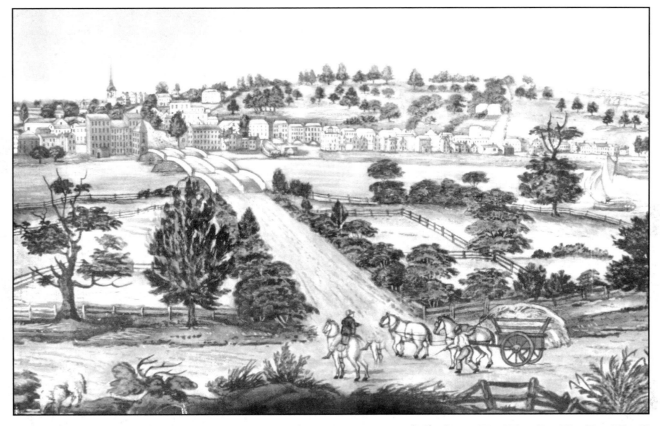

THE VALLEY AND ITS PEOPLES

An Illustrated History
by
Paul Hudon

American Historical Press • Sun Valley, California

For my family, five generations of workers in the Merrimack Valley.

Library of Congress Catalogue Card Number: 2004113064
ISBN: 1-892724-44-8

Bibliography: page 198
Includes Index

Contents

An important feature of the system of industrial capitalism introduced at Lowell was the corporation boardinghouse. In order to ensure a proper home environment for the thousands of single young women who came to work in the textile mills, boardinghouses supervised by matrons were built by the corporation. Merrimack Mills and Boarding-Houses, *an 1848 engraving, shows the brick blocks of the Merrimack Corporation along Dutton Street, with the mill in the background. (MVTM)*

Acknowledgments

Special thanks to the following: Donna Mailloux (Pollard Memorial Library, Lowell); Pam Chicklis (Lowell Historic Preservation Commission); Jeffrey R. Brown (North Amherst, Massachusetts); Ralph Fasanella (Ardsley, New York); Christopher Snow (Newburyport, Massachusetts); Daniel Lombardo, (The Jones Library, Amherst, Massachusetts); Sally Pierce (Boston Athenaeum, Boston); Marsha Rooney (Andover Historical Society); Florence Bartoshevsky (Baker Library, Cambridge, Massachusetts); Louis T. Karabatsos (Lowell, Massachusetts); Martha Mayo (University of Lowell); Nicki Thiras (Addison Gallery of American Art, Andover, Massachusetts); Mary Flinn and Martha Larson (North Andover Historical Society); Ann Farnam, Bettina A. Norton, Dean T. Lahikainen, and Marylou Birchmore (The Essex Institute, Salem, Massachusetts); Julia P. Fogg (Chelmsford Historical Society); Ellie Reichlin (Society for the Preservation of New England Antiquities, Boston, Massachusetts); Howard Curtis and Greg Laing (Haverhill Public Library); Dan Jones (Peabody Museum of Archeology and Ethnology, Cambridge Massachusetts); Mary Allis (Fairchild, Connecticut); Kathy Flynn, John Grimes, and John Nove (The Peabody Museum of Salem); John Roberts (North Andover, Massachusetts); Frederick Johnson and Eugene Winter (Robert S. Peabody Foundation for Archeology, Andover, Massachusetts); Wilhelmina Lunt and D'Arcy G. van Bokkelen (The Historical Society of Old Newbury, Newburyport, Massachusetts); Harriet Ropes Cabot (Cotuit, Massachusetts); Thomas E. Leary (Slater Mill Historic Site, Pawtucket Rhode Island); Eartha Dengler and Jonas Stundza (Immigrant City Archives, Lawrence, Massachusetts); Russell Reeve (Stevens Memorial Library, North Andover, Massachusetts); Ronald Bourgeault (Hampton, New Hampshire); Sue Nault (Merrimack College, North Andover, Massachusetts); Paula Newcomb (Amesbury, Massachusetts); Ernest Price (Rowley, Massachusetts); Regina Tracy (Custom House Maritime Museum, Newburyport, Massachusetts); Arthur L. Eno, Jr. (Lowell, Massachusetts); Patricia O'Malley (Bradford College, Haverhill, Massachusetts); Elizabeth Sholes (Pawtucket, Rhode Island); Marion Hall, Patricia Markey, Jessann Freda, Nancy Leonardi, and Robert Hauser (Merrimack Valley Textile Museum, North Andover, Massachusetts); Mrs. Stuart L. Potter and Charles Steans (Billerica Historical Society); and Richard Koke (New York Historical Society, New York, New York).

In addition, thank you to John Roberts for the topographical information in Chapter I, and the work of Thomas Dublin in the story of Lowell mill girls related in Chapter VI. I am also indebted to Peter Molloy for his research on the construction of the Great Stone Dam at Lawrence. Most especially, I thank Julian S. Miller of Haverhill for his two years of patient work at transforming the manuscript diary of Isaac Merrill into six volumes of typescript. For him, this was a labor of love, no doubt. For us, it retrieves the personality of Merrill and casts a light on this place as it will not be again.

For the revised edition, special thanks go to Paul Marion, Matthew Coggins, Julie Mofford, Robert Forrant, Jay Williamson, Greg Laing, Steve Syverson, Mayor Michael J. Sullivan, David Burke, Jim Beauchesne, Kay Frishman, Pat Jaysane, Carol Majahad, Kathy Szyska, Robert Halpin, and Ahmed Ali.

By 1856 a wider panorama of Lawrence had unfolded. As seen from the Clover Hill residence of Pacific Mills agent William Chapin, this view documents the remarkable growth of the city during its first decade. The farmhouse of John Fallon, who succeeded Chapin in 1871, marks the comfortable retreat of mill management away from the noise and smoke of the factories along the river. This lithograph by John B. Bachelder is one of twenty in the artist's Album of New England Scenery. *(MVTM)*

Preface

There are at present one dozen towns on the lower Merrimack and they're located along the water with unexpected balance, six on either side. Tyngsborough, Dracut, Methuen, Merrimac, Amesbury, and Salisbury lie one next to the other on the northern side, in the direction of the current. In the reverse, upstream direction, West Newbury, Groveland, North Andover, Andover, Tewksbury, and Chelmsford take up the southern side. In addition, there are four cities: Lowell, Lawrence, Haverhill, Newburyport. The oldest of the lower Valley towns was Newbury (1635), and the most recent is Merrimac, which was separated from Amesbury in the year of the Unites States' centenary (1876). As a comparison of maps will show, however, the passing of time not only adds to the inherited stock of the past, it also subtracts. Rowley, Billerica, Dunstable, and Bradford began with frontage on the Merrimack, but each has since been trimmed and shaped to make room for other communities. Bradford, indeed, has disappeared altogether, though it was there on the river for more than two centuries, from the year it was separated from Rowley (1675) to the year it was absorbed into Haverhill (1897). And, if Newbury is still on the map, it no longer touches the water of the Merrimack since the separation of Newburyport (1764) and West Newbury (1819).

These 16 communities, however, do not compose the latest chapter of one, continuous story. Instead, there have been several stories: Pennacook and Puritan and Yankee, each in turn has held the stage and written the lines being told on the lower Merrimack. In more recent times, since the 1800s, the story of the region has unfolded out of the needs of the industrial corporation, whether the purpose was site development or product research or manufacturing. The rise of the corporation has ensured the domination of economics over all other plots and subplots of the last century and a half. So, the later peoples who came to the cities and towns of the lower Merrimack—from every corner of Europe and from the Middle East, or in more recent years from Hispanic America and from southeast Asia—were informed by the rules of economic survival before reaching the American political and social structures.

Beginning, again and again, may be *the* American Dream, and if that is the case the residents of this region have done their share toward keeping it moving. What follows, then, is not *the* story of the lower Merrimack, but a number of stories about displacements and departures. Some of these are local stories mainly (Chapters I, II, III), while some are of national significance, though centered in local events (Chapters IV, V, VI). But in all cases the story tells of change, and each change involved a people to make it happen. In that sense, at least, the current tale of the lower Merrimack, "Finding the Future," is like those that have come before.

It remains only to add that any errors, of fact or fancy, are my own.

— Paul Hudon

I

THE STRONG PLACE

Here were huckleberries still hanging upon the bushes,
where they seem to have slowly ripened for our especial use.
— Henry David Thoreau, *A Week on the Concord
and Merrimack Rivers*, 1849.

All of us now living in the Valley of the lower Merrimack have seen
the stone walls that mark the landscape of its towns. They are as familiar
as the river itself and seem to have grown directly from the soil, as indeed
they have. The walls were made by the hands of English settlers who
farmed the Valley's soil, but the stones lay for 10,000 years, disturbed by
nothing but the frost that heaved and pushed them out of the earth. It
needed the European view of things to arrange them into boundaries,
separating yours from mine. Robert Frost, a Valley poet, passed the word
to us: good fences make good neighbors. As we look at them, however,
some of these walls are in peculiar places; they enclose stands of trees,
separate forest from forest, so it is impossible to say what is being kept in
or why anyone should be kept out.

Henry David Thoreau was delighted by the sight. He was glad, he
said, to see nature reclaim the land from the grubby industry of the

*A Pennacook village on the bank of the Merrimack River in modern Andover, known
as the Shattuck farm site, is depicted in this diorama. Researched by Dr. Frederick
Johnson of the R.S. Peabody Foundation for Archaeology and constructed circa 1950,
it represents typical aboriginal village life of the Late Woodland Period, about AD
1400, just prior to European settlement. Activities shown include drying fish,
grinding corn, and building snowshoes and canoes. Courtesy, R.S. Peabody
Foundation for Archaeology, Andover, Massachusetts.*

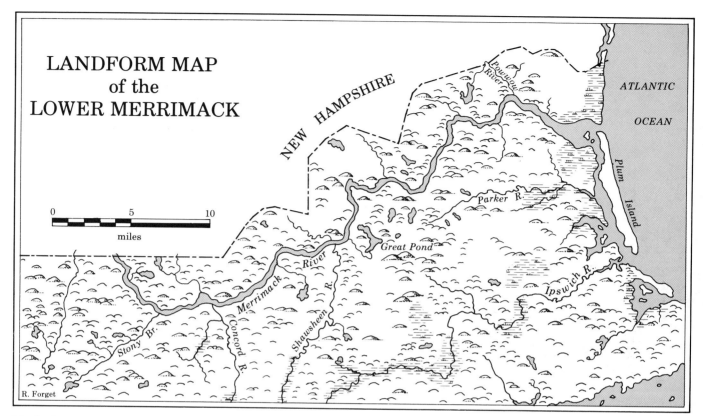

LANDFORM MAP of the LOWER MERRIMACK

The basic structure of the land underlying the Valley settlements is shown in this landform map of the lower Merrimack area. Its numerous hills and ponds are visible, along with the marsh areas around the rivers. Map made by Robert Forget for The Valley and Its Peoples.

Yankee farmer. The spiritual Mr. Thoreau, also a poet of the Valley, found it hard to sympathize with his neighbors, and they returned the compliment. His observation nevertheless is accurate. The stone walls that no longer have a purpose present us with a double exposure of time: they show us where the land used to be farmed. Like the remnants of fruit orchards stranded on the median of our local interstates, or the lilacs we occasionally find in the wild, the stone walls remind us that the use we make of this place does not exhaust its possibilities.

The Valley is littered with the objects of its former tenants. It has been home not only to many people—individuals in the hundreds of thousands. It has been the home also of several peoples—groups large or small, surviving for centuries or merely decades. So what is left now is a multiple exposure rather than a double one, as though four or five family portraits were projected at the same time onto a single screen. Some of these people would be familiar to us; some would look like intruders. And it would be impossible not to have favorites. But all of them belong here. They might not all be in the same focus, some after all being projected over a long distance from the past. Each is a face that at one time was the witness to the river and its Valley. The business of filtering out one image·from

the others begins with objects, things having weight and color, things that resist human manipulation. Objects participate in the response to questions posed to the past, and none will make a grander response than the place itself.

For most of its length, the Merrimack runs directly south toward Massachusetts Bay. In fact, there is geological evidence that the river did at one time empty into the Atlantic in the vicinity of Boston Harbor. That, however, was many thousands of years ago, before Pleistocene glaciation covered the entire northeastern United States with ice and altered the surface of the Valley. Glaciation occurred in this area as long as half a million years ago, but the last glacier began its descent from the north only 70,000 years Before Present. This ice sheet is known as the Wisconsin Glacier and lay over the Valley one mile thick, gray-brown in color, holding a great scattered mass of debris in a frozen clutch. It reached to Cape Cod, then extended west-southwest along the continental shelf across Long Island, New York, New Jersey, and Pennsylvania. About 18,000 years ago, the flow of ice stopped and some 3,000 years after that the glacier began its slow retreat. Ten thousand years ago the Merrimack was finally uncovered, free of ice.

The topography of the Valley was created in the recession of the Wisconsin Glacier. The most prominent result of this process is what geologists call drumlins but the rest of us call hills. We have Powow Hill in Amesbury and Ames Hill in Tewksbury. Ayer in Haverhill, Whortleberry on the line between Tyngsborough and Dracut, Holt in Andover and Robbins in Chelmsford are only a handful among so

Located in the Byfield section of Newbury, the "Haystack" boulder was named in obvious reference to its shape. Deposited by the glacier, this outcropping of quartz hornblende diorite represents an erratic formation in the otherwise gentle, rolling coastal plain of the Merrimack Valley. From John Henry Sears, Geology of Essex County Massachusetts, *1905. Courtesy, Peabody Museum of Salem.*

hill, it spread rather evenly; and because the till contains so much clay it prevents sufficient drainage. These areas are called moraines and today have a wet soil in spring. In other places, the sand and smaller rock debris within the glacier flowed along its fissures, those cracks that develop in any mass of that size. When deposited on the surface of the earth, these materials formed eskers—long, winding hills seeming to cover the remains of prehistoric serpents. Today they are likely subjects of commercial mining for gravel. There are several such systems in the region of the lower Merrimack, and one of them begins near Nickle Mine Hill on the Dracut/Methuen town line.

Some fissures in the glacier must have opened entirely, and this caused large blocks of ice, called dead-ice, to be cut off and left behind as the ice flow retreated north-northwest. These chunks of dead-ice melted in isolation. When this happened in a slight depression of till, a bog or swamp resulted. Great Swamp in Tewksbury and Spruce Swamp in Dracut are examples of this, as is Tadmuck in Westford. Where the depression was deeper and there was a proper bedrock foundation, the same process formed lakes and ponds. Lake Cochichewick in North Andover, the largest body of water in the region, as well as Chadwick in Haverhill and Johnson's Pond in Groveland, may have formed in this way.

Even today, the land of the Valley is reacting to the glacier, or to the absence of it. Freed thousands of years ago from the immense weight of ice 5,000 feet thick, the land is rebounding still. The adjustment this causes in the earth's crust may explain the earthquakes that have been recorded here since the 17th century, and that the Native Americans reported had been part of their relationship with the god of the place.

It is uncertain when exactly the first human inhabitants entered the Valley of the lower Merrimack. We can be sure, however, that the people of the first settlement lived in the Valley for long centuries—for millenia, really—during which time the Valley underwent slow and profound transformations. Spruce forests replaced tundra, and pine subsequently replaced spruce. Temperature was the regulating factor in this process and, in the warming temperatures that began 8,000 years ago, the forest changed again to a variety of hardwoods: oak, hickory, and maple. As one vegetation cover displaced its predecessor, new species of animals came to exploit the new habitat. The change was far from dramatic: the transformation from tundra with its mosses and lichen to hardwood forest took more than 4,000 years. The place changed, and the only constant was the need for humans to change with it. To put it simply, when there were elk and caribou, the aboriginal settlers were hunters of elk and caribou; when the cultivation of beans and corn became possible, they were part-time farmers.

many others. None of them is very impressive, perhaps, few of them rising much more than 400 feet above sea level. Yet all of them together give the lower Merrimack its characteristic rolling landscape. In any season, there is something in them of color or shape or light that leads one to think that beauty can be explained after all. Moreover, these hills and the lakes and ponds between them create those sudden cascades of water, abundant falls that have been so important to the region's economic history. The drumlins or hills are shaped in an oval, with a blunt end where the debris from the glacier was collected in front of some larger obstruction, most likely an outcropping from the solid bedrock. The other end is streamlined, showing that the glacier smoothed the clay as it receded. Because they are oval and not round, the hills have a long and a short axis. The direction of the long axis is the clue that tells the direction in which the ice moved away from the Valley. The combined angles of the glacier and the river amounted at several points to about 90 degrees; their relative movement was at right angles.

The drumlins are made of a material called till, which is a mixture of sand, clay, and boulders. This sediment was deposited directly by the glacier, but in differing configurations. Where there was no obstruction to gather it up into a

The story of these vast stretches of life in the Valley relies on records that offer little hope of achieving an exact picture of its communities. The edges are blurred where, indeed, edges can be found at all. Fossils and pollen borings tell what the flora and fauna of the Valley were through many thousands of years, while artifacts of stone or bone display human skill both in the making of them and in their use.

The people of the first settlement lived in the Valley for 9,000 years, developing more than one culture during that time. It seems clear that settlements were present in the period archeologists call the Middle Archaic Period (8,000-5,000 BP) and probably some occurred before that, in the Early Archaic Period. Through those millenia, and into the three phases of the Woodland Period (2,000-300 BP), the Valley natives underwent the change from an exclusively hunting economy to a partially agricultural one. That change was never totally articulated. The gathering of berries was done in the years before settled fields were planted and harvested, while hunting and fishing remained crucial to the subsistence of the tribes down to the time when the written record begins. The women of these tribes farmed, it seems, and hunting remained a male occupation. The crops consisted of a variety of squashes, beans, and corn. Modern studies have confirmed the legends telling that the cultivation of corn was introduced into this region from the southwest. That direction of the compass was always associated with good things in the minds of the Native Americans. It was the direction, for instance, in which worthy souls of the dead would go to enjoy endless days of delight.

The last Native American people to occupy the lower Merrimack called themselves the Pennacook, but that is somewhat misleading because it applies not only to one particular tribe of that name, but also to a loosely knit confederation of tribes associated by common allegiance to the sachem of the Pennacook. The Pawtuckets (or Wamesits), the Pentuckets, and the Agawams were the principal tribes of this so-called confederation living on the lower river, and they recognized their commonality with the tribes of the upper Valley. The sachem regularly divided his time between a winter residence at Pennacook (now Concord, New Hampshire) and a summer stay at Wickasauke (now Tyng's Island) some few miles upstream from Pawtucket Falls. The Pennacook had no written language and relied solely on oral traditions, on stories told from generation to generation to preserve what they prized of their history. Also, they relied on place for instruction, which demonstrated the continuous cycle of a human history, turning and returning in season with the freeze and the thaw of land and river.

The economy of the Pennacooks, though partially nomadic, had its center in the river they called *Merroh Awke*, meaning Strong Place. (The Massachusets tribe, living to the south of the Pennacooks, called it River of the Sturgeon.) It is difficult to say how far the Pennacooks' treks after game took them, but the broad river with a swift current was always home. True, they did not favor settlement directly on its shores. They preferred rather to locate on or near the smaller streams and creeks, which are tributary to the Merrimack. They especially sought ecotonal zones, areas where two systems of fauna meet and overlap. There was a larger number of species in the ecotones of the Valley, so food might be available on the same site for more than one season. The choice of location, the decision to move or not to move was made for the reason of food. Knowledge of where food was abundant, and when, was the central concern of the Pennacook community. It was the stock of accumulated skill. The primary lesson was to eat when possible. One witness to their habits was amazed to see them able to go for days with little food and some days with none at all. But at other times they would eat "not ceasing till their full bellies leave nothing but empty plates." They lolled at their meals in "the Turkish fashion," he said.

The Pennacooks were powerless to ignore the demands of survival in the Valley, so they naturally saw in *Merroh Awke* the face of strength. They respected power and always were impressed by its display. Some of their leaders were reputed powwows, persons who could make things happen rather than simply suffer them. Part of the authority of their leader Passaconaway was based on the powers they said he had to make water burn, rocks move, or trees dance. They believed he could transform himself into a flame, survive, and return as himself, the Child of the Bear. This attitude toward displays of power may explain why Passaconaway decided not to offer resistance to the English settlers. Their superiority was obvious and to counter their will was as futile as resisting the sleet of winter or the summer drought.

The Pennacooks saw, however, that power was good as well as evil. Evidence of this attitude can be found in the names they used to describe the places around them: The Smile of the Great Spirit, The Beautiful Waters of the High Place, The Beautiful River with the Bright Strong Current and Pebbly Bottom. They seemed to reason that if everything might be withheld, then anything was a gift. The greatest gift, however, was the yearly run of fish that came up the Merrimack: shad, alewives, salmon that came late in winter with the waking of the earth. The tribes of the lower Valley gathered at the Pawtucket Falls to gather the harvest. It was a time of reunion and thanksgiving. Each year the river was at the center of their renewal; each year the river gave proof of concern and paid the tribute that secured the contract between people and place. Now, however, came alien settlers, for whom the river was not the center of life, but its frontier.

Left: *Chief of the Pennacooks Papisseconewa, better known as Passaconaway, was always friendly to European settlers. This mid-19th century lithograph portrays him wearing a conical cap and bear's head, the symbol of Passaconaway and his tribe. Courtesy, Merrimack Valley Textile Museum (MVTM).*

Below: *Sponsored by the Andover Historical Society, a team composed of Massachusetts Historical Commission staff and field school students worked for two summers excavating the site of a Pennacook village. Field school team members expose a hearth during their 1981 excavation. Courtesy, Massachusetts Historical Commission.*

Below: *Long important to the Valley's economy, the Merrimack River salmon,* salmo salar, *provided food for Native Americans and immigrants until the 19th century. Progressive improvements are expected to insure the salmon's return to the river during the 1980s. Courtesy, Peabody Museum of Salem.*

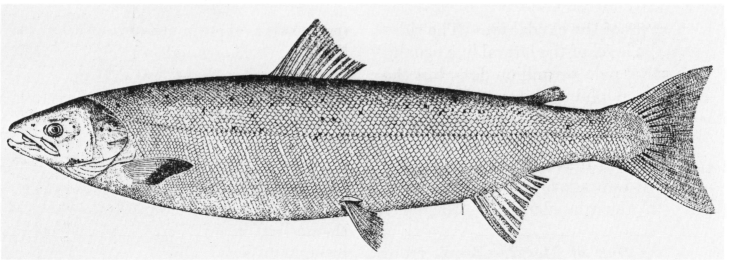

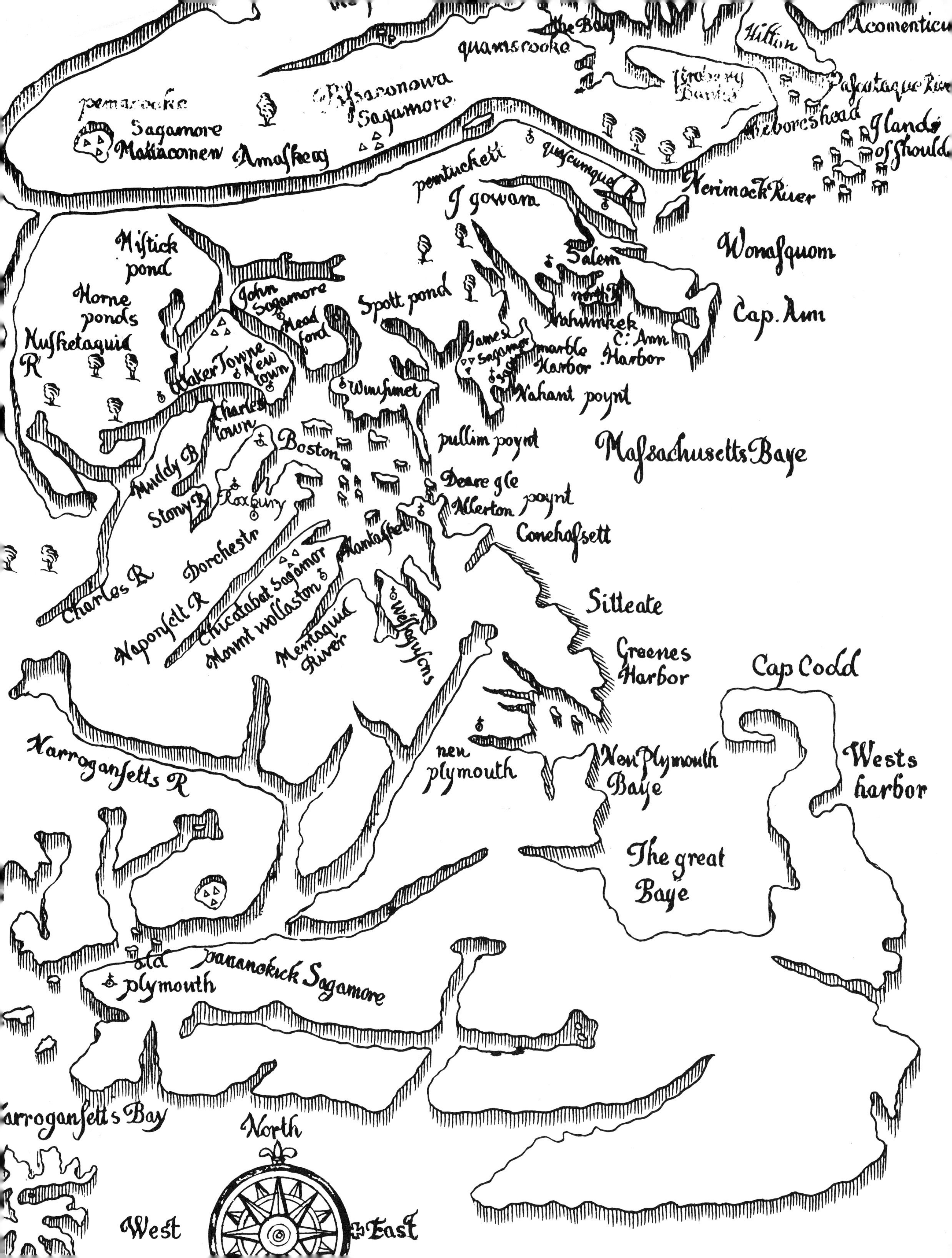

Acomenticu

the Bay

Hilton

quamscooke

Piscaronowa Sagamore

Strabery Danke

Pascataque River

pemaroohe

Sagamore
Mattaconnen

Amaskeg

quscumquen R

Nerimack River

Neboresheard

Ilands
of Should

pentuckett

Igowam

Wonasquom

Mistick pond

Salem

Cap. Ann

Horne ponds

John Sagamore

Spott pond

north R

Nusketaquid R

Mead ford

Nahumkek

C: Ann

Water Towne
New town

James Sagamore

marble Harbor

Harbor

Charles town

Winnisimet

Nahant poynt

Muddy B.

Boston

pullim poynt

Massachusetts Baye

Stony R.

Roxbury

Deare yle
Allerton poynt

Dorchester

Conehassett

Naponsett R.

Chicatabat Sagamor

Nantasket

Sitteate

Mount wollaston

wessaguscus

Greenes Harbor

Cap Codd

Mentaquid River

Narroganfetts R.

new plymouth

New Plymouth Baye

Wests harbor

The great Baye

old plymouth

nannokick Sagamore

Narroganfett's Bay

North

West

East

II

"UNDER THE VISOR OF RELIGION"

[Chelmsford] . . . WHICH BORDERETH UPON MERRIMACK RIVER NEAR TO PAATUCKET, which we do find a very comfortable place to accommodate a company of God's people upon; that may with God's blessing and assistance live comfortably upon and do good in that place for church and commonwealth.

— Petition of the towns of Woburn and Concord "for the erecting of a new Plantacon on Merremacke River," 1653.

The people of the second settlement came over the ocean, from the East, and at that time the mouth of the river was obscured by the sand dunes of an island that lay across it. Voyagers sailing south from the Gulf of Maine or north from Massachusetts Bay could not easily sight the river, particularly as they preferred to sail the safe waters to the east of Cape Ann and the Isles of Shoals. These natural outworks kept strangers at a distance. From the St. Lawrence to the Plata, rivers were a special objective during the 100 years and more when Europe's explorers charted the waters of the New World. The sailors who came, and the

Engraved for William Wood's New England's Prospect, *published in London in 1634, this map was intended to show Europeans what is now eastern Massachusetts and southern New Hampshire. The Merrimack River is identified and runs from left to right across the top portion of the map. Wood's account of the New World is that of a scientific observer, as indicated by this detailed map with its numerous place names. (MVTM)*

princes or merchants who sent them, dreamed of finding a water passage to the Orient. The Orient held treasures of silk and spices, wealth in trade. It was a dream that died hard, but when Europeans awakened to reality they saw that the Merrimack was not a passage but a frontier.

The name and origin of the first European to see and hear the waters of the Merrimack remain unknown. It may be that the river and its valley were visited by travelers from Europe centuries before Columbus made his voyage in 1492. The facts of that tale, however, are thin and uncertain, so we are left with controversy until the opening of the 17th century, when the written record of this story begins.

Even that presents us with debate. In 1613 the French explorer Samuel de Champlain published a map to accompany his account of the voyages he had made to North America. The map clearly shows a large river on what is now the coast of Massachusetts, somewhat north of a place he called Beauport. The river can only be the Merrimack, though the map bears no legend. What is not at all certain is when, and to what extent, Champlain investigated the site. Apparently he was not impressed; he did not return nor did he send others to settle the place. In 1608 he founded the city of Quebec far to the north, and so began the events by which France came to occupy the valleys of North America's great waterways–the St. Lawrence, the Mississippi, and the Ohio. These giants seemed to promise control of the continent, and compared to them the Merrimack was a minor stream indeed. However, it suited the purpose of English Puritans well enough. When Champlain died in 1635, he was the governor of New France. In that same year the English planted their first settlement on the Merrimack.

It was the celebrated John Smith who, in 1614, discovered the Merrimack for the English crown. Smith was a hero in his own day, and he is known for his adventures in Virginia and his storybook rescue by the Indian princess Pocahontas. But Smith traveled elsewhere, and he was a practical man of business as well as a figure of romance. In particular he had a talent for selling an idea. He not only found the river; he also suggested the name "New England" and helped organize the settlement of the region. By 1620 he had marshaled enough support to persuade Parliament to establish a council for that purpose. This body was to act as an agent, a sort of development company, allotting rights and territories in the king's new lands across the sea. Officially it was called the "Council established at Plymouth in the County of Devon for the Planting, Ruling, Ordering, and Governing of New England." However, the key to its enterprise was not in the character of the English who remained by the estuary of the Plym, ordering and ruling. The key to success was in the character of the English who emigrated to New England, to plant. In the

later 1620s there were groups in several parts of England, in the south, in the east, and in London, who began to coordinate a response to the opportunity advertised by the Council. They were not all alike, but they were all charmed by the prospect of New England. Also they were Puritan, though not yet ready to accept that nickname foisted on them by their enemies.

In March 1627 the Council of New England granted the right of colonization to a group of Puritans calling themselves the Dorchester Company. The grant was bounded by the oceans on the east and west, by the Charles River on the south, and by the Merrimack on the north. This made for a rather narrow tract with its western end trailing off into mystery. Nevertheless, only two years later, in March 1629, the same tract was granted a second time, again to a Puritan group—now described as "the governor and company of Massachusetts Bay in New England." It was a trading and colonizing company like the first, but with this difference: the governor and company of Massachusetts were allowed the right to leave England; they were allowed to establish a legal government across the sea. This is a unique exception in the history of English colonies, and it speaks volumes about the amount of influence—and bribes—that Puritans were able to concentrate on the Council and on the king.

Obviously, they had great expectations. Massachusetts Bay was a special place to these Puritans only as they could be, there, what they had it in their souls to be. Today's view of them is obscured by three centuries of commentary, but these English men and women saw themselves in the clear light of their own conviction. They thought and spoke of themselves as the Remnant, the remains of Israel, the Lord God's one chosen beloved. Despite every prejudice of our century we can invoke to deny it, all the evidence forces the conclusion that the Puritans lived in sacred time. Just as we hope to continue the Republic of Jefferson and Madison, they thought to continue the epic of the Old Testament; when they talked of Massachusetts Bay as Zion in the wilderness, it was no metaphor. And, like the ancient Jews, they waited on God's direction. Words and events were messages and signs; the most remote circumstance was a coded transmission of God's intent that only needed deciphering. The discovery of New England, then, the mere fact of its existence, was proof to them that God had reserved it for Puritan rule.

However, God is no democrat, and if he sent the Puritans to settle the Merrimack Valley he was not sending them to rule themselves. There is nothing Puritans spoke so harshly against as democracy. In their opinion, asking for leadership from the people was asking the crew, ignorant of all mathematics, to navigate the ship. Instead, the right to leadership belonged only to those they called the saints, those God had elected to share his vision. Intended for solitary bliss in the next world, the saints were obliged, while still in this one, to contract with one another, and this covenanted society or congregation is what they called the church. The Puritans were at pains always to mark a clear difference between the community of saints, which was the church, and the place of its worship, which was the meetinghouse. The church was a living community of men and women endowed with God's power to teach and rule. Not everyone was delighted with the rule of these saints, so matters of discipline would soon enough disturb the peace of the Valley towns. Lydia Perkins Wardwell of Newbury, for example, was publicly flogged for appearing naked before her judges in protest against their misuse of authority. One author reacted with indignation to the severity of the judgement:

> And this is the discipline of the church of Newbury
> in New England, and this is their religion, and their
> usage of the handmaid of the Lord, who in a great
> cross to her natural temper, came thus among them, a
> sign indeed, significatory enough to them, and
> suitable to their state, who under the visor of religion,
> were thus blinded into cruel persecution.

If instruction and punishment were often confused in the minds of the Puritans, it was because both were taken as legitimate means to rescue mankind from its willful destruction. The word of God would be translated directly into law, to ensure that society would become a great schoolhouse where even the greatest dolt of Christendom might do right provided only that he obey civil law. This way, the state would also guarantee the delivery of truth to future generations, so that the children of Adam and Eve would not live like beasts of the field.

In March 1630 John Winthrop and Thomas Dudley, governor and deputy governor of Massachusetts, gathered with several hundred other Puritans to hear a parting instruction from John Cotton, master of the church at Boston in Lincolnshire, England. Master Cotton went to II Samuel for his text:

> Moreover, I will appoint a place for my people
> Israel, and will plant them that they may dwell in a
> place of their own and move no more.

The entire government of the Massachusetts Company then boarded ship and sailed off to build the New Jerusalem, a city upon a hill as a beacon of direction to mankind, forever.

Such was the vision of the English Puritan. However, he was more certain of the destiny that brought him than of his capacity to live it. For the irony is that the saint was never certain of his sainthood. God gave signs of favor, and wealth was one of them, but no man or woman could ever

be sure of being God's chosen. Constantly under the obligation to survey their lives for signs of election or destruction, the Puritans lived at the edge of doubt. Who can wonder that they feared savages lurking in the wilderness?

The General Court of Massachusetts, sitting at Boston, was anxious to occupy the tract granted by the Council of New England, but it took half a century of persistent effort to secure the frontier of the Merrimack for the Puritan cause. The process began in 1635 with the planting of Newbury at the mouth of the river. Four years later the General Court authorized the settling of Rowley, an unusually large parcel that later was divided to make up the towns of Bradford, Groveland, Georgetown, and Boxford. Also, Rowley was oddly shaped, squeezed between Newbury and Ipswich on the coastal end of town and fanning out to some 18 miles where it fronted on the Merrimack. In 1640 Salisbury and Haverhill were established and six years later, Andover. Chelmsford and Billerica were both settled in 1655, plotted side by side with their northern limit on the river. Billerica at the time included all of contemporary Tewksbury and parts of Lowell and Wilmington; Chelmsford also comprised parts of Lowell and what is now Westford. In 1668 Amesbury became autonomous after 20 years as Salisbury-new-town. Puritan occupation of the lower Merrimack Valley was completed in 1672 with the establishment of Dunstable, an enormous

Grief and mourning were expressed in elaborately carved gravestones, such as this example with its cursive death's head at the top. The Reverend Thomas Barnard was the third minister at Andover, and during his term the North Parish and South Parish divided. These later became the towns of North Andover and Andover. Photo by Gayton Osgood.

area of 200 square miles, equal to an English dukedom, according to one proud local historian. Most of that tract presently lies in the state of New Hampshire, but it also included Tyngsborough, which is now the first town touched by the Merrimack as it flows into Massachusetts. (On May 10, 1643, the General Court organized Middlesex and Essex counties.)

The procedure followed in making these towns was always the same, and it required the approval of the General Court. Whoever occupied the Merrimack Valley would owe political allegiance to the Puritan theocrats; they would have no squatters. A group of families in a town already incorporated—at Charlestown or Ipswich or Woburn—would petition the General Court and argue that crowded conditions required that they move on; their economic survival demanded more land. They then had to show that a qualified minister would go with them to undertake the covenanting of the saints, and to assure that right teaching would guide the new community. Also, there were economic considerations. The free male heads of households, those who signed the petition, were expected to provide the capital to begin the new town. These were constituted the proprietors and shared in the division of common lands in proportion to their contribution. Typically, the larger landowners were also members of the church, so that economic and spiritual power resided in the same individuals. The proprietors might benefit from two and three divisions of land until the entire grant had been put to private use, though that might take more than one generation.

Population was low. Billerica was established by 25 families, and the great expanse of Dunstable was at one time occupied by half a dozen families. Numbers grew moderately through the whole colonial period. At the time of the War of Independence, in 1775, Haverhill had fewer than 2,000 inhabitants, while Newburyport, with over twice that number, was the metropolis of the Valley.

The process of occupying the Valley was not so neat as the recitation of town names and their birthdates seems to indicate. Expansion often brought conflict within the towns and this sometimes led to separation, as in the case of Amesbury. Distance and the difficulty of travel also encouraged subdivision. Thus the northern end of Rowley, fronting on the Merrimack, was chartered as the town of Bradford in 1675. Or, again, in 1709 the farmers in the south end of Andover were allowed their own meetinghouse because the original North Parish (1646) was too distant for their convenience. Squabbles over the location of the meetinghouse led to the same solution in Newbury (1725), in Haverhill (1726), and in Chelmsford (1729).

This wholesale parceling of the Valley's real estate did not go unchallenged by the people who called themselves the proprietors of New Hampshire. The charter of 1629 bounded the authority of the governor and company of Massachusetts Bay at three miles north of the Merrimack but in 1629 everyone assumed that the Merrimack ran out of the west. It was soon found that the river ran from the north and not out of the west. Did the charter still apply? Was the Merrimack still a political frontier? Yes, legally it was, according to the Puritans at Boston, and they insisted that the charter be followed to the last letter of the title. In 1658 Governor John Endicott ordered a survey of the river's course. The surveying party determined that the Merrimack began at the mouth of the Winnepesaukee River, so the official claim of the government at Boston extended to three miles north of that line. In fact, the Bay government ruled the towns of New Hampshire for nearly 40 years, from 1641 to 1679, and in that period planted the town of Dunstable. However, the claims of rival proprietors were revived after 1680, and the political face of the Valley became obscure again for another half century.

Besides marking the political frontier with New Hampshire, the Valley was a physical frontier, separating wilderness from civilization, heathen from Puritan. If the Puritan condemned the wearing of long hair, after the manner of "barbarous Indians," the Pennacook replied in kind against the "bastard Englishman" for his filthy habit of growing hair on his face. Nevertheless, the Pennacook tribes were remarkably unwarlike. The great chief Passaconaway always counseled against resistance to the English, and he repeated this advice in his last meeting with the tribes at Pawtucket Falls in 1660. His son Wannalancet followed the same policy of deference. If the policy was intended to save the Pennacooks from destruction, it failed totally. The Pennacooks disappeared, pressed by the land hunger of the Puritans and ground between the wheel of English ambition and the stone of French rivalry.

Still, while they survived, the Pennacooks were a puzzle to the English newcomer, challenging his need to find a role for them in God's plan. According to one Puritan invention, these savages were the lost tribe of Israel, those cut off from the life of God. Cotton Mather called them "the veriest ruins of mankind," so degenerate that they were barely distinguishable from the forests they inhabited. Obviously decoyed by God for the instruction of his darlings, the Pennacooks were taken as the living example of the Puritans' future should the Remnant ever separate from the saints.

What the Puritans saw as the laziness of the Indians was glaringly offensive. According to the Puritan ethic, labor and toil was a way of social education, the gentlest means to virtue for the majority of mankind (that is, those who are not saints). "Wee heartily pray you," Governor Endicott was advised by the authorities in London, "that all bee kept to labor as the only means to reduce to civil, yea to Godly life; and to keep yough from falling into many enormities, which by nature wee are all too much enclyned into." Besides this moral benefit, labor brought economic dividends. Labor begat property. John Cotton wrote "that in a vacant soyle, hee that taketh possession of it, and bestoweth culture and husbandry upon it, his Right it is." True enough, the "soyle" of the Merrimack Valley was vacant after a fashion because the Pennacook population had been much reduced by a plague several years before the English came to settle. This plague, too, was sign to the Puritans that God intended the Valley for their cause.

Many saw the sin of the naked heathen but few attempted his salvation. One who did was John Eliot. For 60 years this extraordinary man labored to bring the hope of Christianity to the Bay Indians. From the Charles to the Merrimack, the entire breadth of the Puritan grant, Eliot established so-called praying villages where Christianized Indians were gathered on lands reserved for them by the General Court. In 1653, two years before the court sanctioned the bounds of Chelmsford and Billerica, it provided for the establishment of Wamesit, a praying village for Pennacook converts at the junction of the Concord and the Merrimack. There, and at the falls nearby, Eliot preached the good news of the Gospel to the Pennacooks in their own language. He told them of their sin in Adam and of their relation to its redemption by the Christ. He gave what he had, freedom as he found it. Eliot, however, did not expect the Pennacooks to forsake the Valley to live in the sacred time of the Puritan, and his genius was to separate culture from theology. Wamesit was a semiautonomous village ruled in part by the local chief, Numphow, and according to tribal law, in part by General Daniel Gookin, who had been commissioned by the Court to deal with Indian affairs. In the end, isolation from the rising sea of English values was impossible. There is now a church opposite the South Common in Lowell named to honor Eliot, but the Christian community at Wamesit had already vanished before he died in 1690.

The tribal life of the Pennacooks, Christian or not, never recovered from the shocks suffered during King Philip's War. King Philip was a Wampanoag chief—his true name was Pometacom—who led an alliance of tribes in war against the English from July 1675 to August 1676. Most of the conflict was fought on the southern and western ends of Massachusetts and in the towns of Rhode Island, but in March 1676 danger was present and real on the Merrimack. General Daniel Denison makes this clear in a letter to the Secretary of the Commonwealth:

> I received your intelligence the Substance whereof
> I had 2 houers before by ye way of Billerica and
> Andouer, together with certaine intelligence that the
> enemy is passed merrimack their trecks seene

yesterday at wamesit and 2 of their Scouts this morning at Andouer who by 2 posts one in the night & againe this Day about 2 of the clocke importunes for helpe as doth Haueril . . .

None of the river towns was seriously molested, though nearby Groton was reduced to its last outpost. Few of the Pennacook tribes joined Philip, choosing instead to follow Wannalancet and remain friendly to the English. This attempt at neutrality only generated suspicion on both sides, and the Indians at Wamesit, being cultural half-breeds, were the object of particularly strong feelings. In November 1675 a party of Philip's men burned a barn in Chelmsford. The culprits got away, so the inhabitants of the town punished the Indians nearest at hand. That these Indians were neutral did not matter, nor that they were Christian; it did not matter even that most of them were women and children and all were unarmed. Despite the protest of Lieutenant James Richardson, who owned the barn, 14 men of Chelmsford took up their guns and trooped to the wigwams at Wamesit in a cloud of indignation and fear. In the confrontation that followed, two rounds of buckshot wounded five women and children, killing one boy. A murder trial followed the incident, but the two men accused were acquitted.

One incident among so many cannot tell the story of the dissolution of the Pennacook people. Once the English had arrived in the Valley, the native population had no recourse but flight. They had no defense but to put distance between themselves and these intense strangers who were bent on eradicating any deviation from one, absolute ideal.

Wannalancet twice withdrew from contact with the English and both times he returned. Each of these treks left him with less land and fewer followers, so that before his end he had become a relic surrounded by a residue. Some of his tribes deserted him to take up with his nephew Kancamagus in war against the English. The last known about Wannalancet is that in 1696 he was made a ward of Colonel Jonathan Tyng, the redoubtable Indian fighter of Dunstable. Tyng, along with Major Thomas Henchman of Chelmsford, received the lands of the praying Indians at Wamesit from the General Court as payment for military service in maintaining the Merrimack frontier. These two sold shares to 44 others and together they pastured their sheep at the place, behind a proper English stone wall.

A threat like King Philip's depended on the combined efforts of many tribes and on the unlikely chance that any Indian leader could unite them long enough to achieve the destruction of the Puritan towns. By contrast, later military action at the Merrimack frontier relied on the political presence and sustained will of the French in Canada. For decades the French and their Indian allies, operating out of fortified settlements in the district of Maine and elsewhere, did what they could to dislodge the English. The effort was not continual, but when the kings of France and England were at war in Europe, they were at war everywhere. On this continent the contest ended in 1759 when the English took Quebec City, but in the Valley the struggle was most intense in the last decade of the 17th century. Amesbury, Haverhill, Andover, Billerica, Chelmsford, Dunstable: all had crops and barns burned, inhabitants killed or taken prisoner. Each town has its tale of terror and daring, but none more popular than the story of Hannah Duston.

Hannah was taken by Indians during a raid at Haverhill in mid-March 1697, then dragged off into the isolation of their settlements deep within the upper Valley. This was little more than a week after Hannah had given birth to a son—one of 13 children. She was carrying the infant in her arms and was accompanied by Mary Neff, a widowed townswoman who had been acting as her nurse, when both

During the centuries following Hannah Duston's exploit, her legend grew. Artifacts accumulated and, like pieces of the True Cross, were displayed for the public. Here a 19th-century descendant displays the cloth in which the scalps were purportedly wrapped. Courtesy, Trustees of the Haverhill Public Library.

Hannah Duston's exploits are well remembered in the Merrimack Valley. The monument to her erected on June 1, 1861, in Haverhill was the first monument erected to a woman in the United States. That one was replaced in 1879 by this bronze statue designed by Calvin Weeks of Haverhill. Courtesy, Trustees of the Haverhill Public Library.

were captured at Hannah's house. En route, the Indians killed the child and several adult prisoners also from Haverhill. Hannah and Mary were not alone with the Indians, however. An English boy who had been captured at Worcester a year and a half before was also a member of the party. There is no doubt that Hannah was telling the truth when she later claimed to have prayed to her God, but after six weeks of captivity she signed for herself the warrant of her fate. One night near the end of March, she and Mary and the boy, Samuel, killed 10 Indians and removed their scalps. Hannah and her companions took the scalps as proof and returned to Haverhill by canoe, on the current of the Merrimack. Mrs. Duston became the heroine of the Valley. As Robert Caverly wrote in *The Merrimac and Its Incidents* (1866):

> Her noble deeds are held in high renown,
> *Sacred* like *heirloom* in that ancient town;
> And long as Merrimac's bright waters glide
> Shall stand that mother's *fame*, still by its side.

Her action improved morale, no doubt, and the General

Court was happy to give her and her accomplices a bounty of 50 pounds. However, the security of the Valley depended less on the occasional heroic deed and more on the daily tending to business. The primary concern was to keep the towns alive, economically. One town order at Newbury, dated August 7, 1690, proclaimed, "in his majesty's name," that all the "soldiers" of the town "are required to carry their arms and ammunition with them into meadows and places, where they worke, and if any man doe refuse or neglect his dewty as above expressed he shal pay five shillings for every such neglect." In July of the previous year, the "select Men" of Dunstable twice petitioned the General Court, for a supply of meat and for the defense of their gristmill, saying that without its help they "must be forced to draw off and leave the towne." The danger of desertion so alarmed the Bay government at Boston that it warned the inhabitants of Dunstable and Chelmsford in 1694 that they would forfeit the property they left undefended. The court also imposed a heavy fine for evasion of military service. Still, only two years later, two-thirds of the citizens of Dunstable had left the place, and the court itself provided 30 pounds for the minister's salary.

Despite fire, despite death and abduction, the Puritans were still on the Merrimack when the new century began in 1701. Nevertheless, the decade of the 1690s was a watershed in the history of the Valley, separating the story of the Puritan experiment from all the other stories that have been told of this place. The violence of warfare on the frontier was only part of it. The smallpox epidemic of 1691 and 1692 added to the insecurities of daily life. Longer-lasting tensions were generated by the political legacies of the 1680s. The charter of 1629, so prized by the Puritan fathers for the independence it gave them, was revoked in 1684. Worse still, in 1686 the royal government at London made Massachusetts a part of the larger unit, the Dominion of New England, governed by the king's appointed servant, Sir Edmund Andros. The project collapsed in 1689 when James II was replaced by William III in what the English call their Glorious Revolution. It did not escape the notice of the Bay leaders that their deliverance from the tyranny of Andros had relied on the incompetence of James and on the abilities of his son-in-law. God might be made responsible for both, the Puritans reasoned, but how would this help the anxieties that came with the realization that the political future of Massachusetts depended not on law, but on personality and circumstance?

One consequence of the Andros episode was to depress the maritime sector of the Bay economy, and another was to call into question most titles to the land in the agricultural sector. And for the residents of the lower Merrimack, there was worse news still. Robert Mason, who had reactivated his family's claims in New Hampshire, was a political ally of Andros and a member of his Council. Mason had pressed his family's claim to New Hampshire with enough success to whet his appetite for more, and before his death in 1688 he had read his grant to run south beyond the Merrimack. In fact he claimed all the land of Essex County, down to Salemtown, the first jewel in the Puritan Crown of Glory. Mason's claim might have had no legal base, but what of that? Who would have thought that the charter would be taken? And without that charter the Puritans had no more right to the Valley than Mason had; moreover, Mason also had the friendship of King James. Mason died in 1688 and James was harried out of England in the following year, so the Merrimack towns were not cut off from Massachusetts. Still, the 1690s began in confusion and uncertainty.

Enemies were everywhere. The soldier in his red coat, the judge at the land court in his robes, Mason at Portsmouth dispatching his requests to Andros and the king. Why not, then, spectral enemies? God or the Devil, any man might know himself well enough to believe in either, or in both if he accepted the final grace. So when some citizens at Andover in 1692 gave evidence of dealings with the Devil, of witchcraft, that is, some of the town's citizens believed them, while others could not.

The real consequence of the witch hysteria at Andover, as in the other Puritan towns, was to divide the community. "We were all exceedingly astonished, amazed and consternated and affrighted even out of reason," one witness later testified. There were public trials where the gentlefolk of Andover tore at each other with accusations and evidence, and no one was safe. The town's leading citizens, Osgood, Johnson, Faulkner, two of them daughters of the minister, were accused. Goodwife Foster, aged widow of one of the town's original incorporators, died in prison after 21 weeks of ill-treatment. After nearly a year of such conflict the magistrates and the ministers burst the bubble and imposed silence. If enemies were everywhere, they would choose which to confront, and for their purpose the French and the Indians, even the political maneuvers of English royalists, were a better choice of enemy to keep God's Remnant undivided on the frontier.

From the perspective of our century, trained as it is in the vocabulary of psychology, the Puritans might be described as anxiety neurotics. And well they might have been, living as they were in a valley where the wilderness was a constant lesson in the difficulty of subjugating nature, including their own. Also in the language of psychology one can say that they confronted time with the vigor and desperation of a narcissist. However, ultimately as little profit derives from a 20th-century definition as from a 17th-century one. Only one thing can be said of the Puritans with certainty: they knew a prophecy. The entire world might be made fit by nature for the habitation of men, but the Puritans would make the Merrimack Valley a place fit for the habitation of saints.

III

LAND AND RIVER AND SEA

The land was ours before we were the land's.
She was our land more than a hundred years
Before we were her people.
— Robert Frost, "The Gift Outright," 1942.

In *Magnalia Christi Americana*, written in 1702, Cotton Mather tells the story of a Puritan divine who ventured north of the Merrimack during that first decade of settlement. He had gone beyond the bounds of Massachusetts to preach to those other Englishmen, "the inhabitants upon the River Pascataquack," to instruct them in God's holy purpose. They were not having any. When the preacher got to the part about the "main end of Planting this Wilderness," one member of the involuntary congregation objected. "Sir," he cried out, "you are mistaken, you think you are preaching to the People at the Bay; our main end was to catch fish." Not fishers of men, alas, but trawlers after an income. The story became popular, repeated as late as 1825 by Nathaniel Adams in his *Annals of Portsmouth*. Its endurance shows that the Merrimack was a real boundary, fixed in the thinking of the settlers on either side. Those in Massachusetts had a religious purpose and those in New Hampshire an

Governor William Dummer (1677-1761) left land in Byfield to support the academy that bears his name. The son of a silversmith, he served the Commonwealth in several terms as lieutenant governor and governor. Courtesy, Essex Institute, Salem, Massachusetts.

economic one. It would be difficult to decide who was more pleased with the difference, and the convenience of the line between them.

In fact, the religious and economic motives cannot be separated so surely. The Puritans were never angels for want of being saints, never willing to live on air. The leaders at Massachusetts Bay in particular were clearsighted in calculating what the New World might contribute to their incomes. John Winthrop in his native Suffolk was both lord of Groton Manor and a lawyer who competed successfully for preferments. In 1628 he was admitted to the Inner Temple, a closely kept sanctum at the very top of the legal profession. Still, he was hard pressed financially, squeezed between rising demands on his income and the inflation that destroyed his real earnings. When he wrote down the pros and cons of resettlement, before leaving England, he spoke of himself in the third person:

> His meanes heer are so shortened (now 3 of his sonnes being com to age have drawen awaie the one half of his estate) as he shall not be able to continue in that place and imployment where he now iss, his ordinary charg being still as great almost as when his meanes was double.

Winthrop decided on Massachusetts because he could not maintain his scale of living, and his station in society, if he stayed in England. He moved geographically in order to stay in place, economically and socially. Both economics and religion are powerful motives for action. Both, after all, offer rewards. Keeping them distinct and in balance is an equation difficult to maintain, and the resolution is not hereditary. From generation to generation, the need to earn a living pressed hard on the Puritan resolve to establish Zion in the wilderness. That commitment disappeared with the wilderness, and the tamed Valley revealed a new ideal of economic independence and political equality.

Land and its tillage was the chief livelihood of the great majority of the English; it naturally became the chief attraction for those with a thought of removing to Massachusetts Bay. John Smith—a first-rate promoter—knew his audience when he described the advantage of New England to the husbandmen in Old England:

> Here should be no hard landlords to rack us with high rents, or extorted fines to consume us; here every man may be master and owner of his own labor and land in a short time.

Smith wrote this in 1614, the year he explored the coast in both directions from the Merrimack. In 20 years, settlers began arriving in the Valley to test Smith's promise that in this place industry and time would make a man free of all masters.

Like the settlers in other parts of Massachusetts Bay, the settlers of the Valley were attracted first to those areas already cleared by the Indians. They also chose the areas nearest the coast, because these offered rock-weed, kelp, and eel grass in fall and winter as stable bedding and in spring as fertilizer for corn, potatoes, and roots. And like migrants everywhere, the settlers of the Valley at first tried to duplicate as nearly as possible the life-style they had left behind. They sought the security of the familiar.

However, some crops would not adapt well to the conditions of the Merrimack Valley. English wheat in particular was a disappointment, though the other English cereals—oats, barley, and rye—did well. The settlers readily adopted Indian corn as well as the Indian practice of using fish as fertilizer. Fish were plentiful and free to those in the Valley; and, one writer maintained, even the lightest soil would produce 40 bushels of rye to the acre when manured liberally with fish. If any Puritans noticed that they were taking lessons in agriculture from the heathen savages, they were quiet about it.

Not so with fruit trees and orchards. The English needed no instruction on this topic. An apple orchard is mentioned at Salisbury-new-town (Amesbury) as early as 1649, though its stage of maturity is not known. The cultivation of apples was extensive, pursued as much for the cider as for the fruit. By 1764 Middlesex County alone produced 33,436 barrels of cider, or enough to give each family seven barrels. Productivity seems to have been a source of local boasting—and some humor. One historian of Bradford claimed that some apple trees of that town were large enough to yield 8 or 10 barrels of cider. The trees of one citizen reportedly produced a superior cider "which for many years bore the highest price in market of any made in the state." Pears were also prized, though grown in smaller quantities, and Governor William Dummer produced a distinctive variety on his land in Byfield (Newbury). A hardy winter pear was developed at Bradford, which also produced outstanding quantities of peaches and plums throughout the 18th century.

The care and breeding of livestock was a second area in which the English farmer distinguished himself from the native worker of the land. Oxen and horses, cows and sheep each had a particular role in the Valley's economy, and all eventually provided edible flesh to supplement native game and fowl. Oxen were of special value. They extracted boulders and stumps while clearing the fields; they pulled the plow at planting and hauled the grain to the mill after harvest. They drew in hay, apples, and firewood. At Newbury-port, at the mouth of the Merrimack, they were used to move heavily loaded drays from wharf to warehouse and back again. Horses seldom were used for

John Winthrop (1587-1649) typifies the Puritan elite of the first period of settlement. A lawyer and landowner in old England, he practiced both professions in New England and also served as the first governor of Massachusetts. (MVTM)

sheep, because they require a smooth grass pasture rather than the roughage goats can consume. "Until the land be often fed with Cattell, Sheepe cannot live." Goats, cows, and oxen had to prepare the way. Still, the sheep population increased rapidly in the last quarter of the 17th century. In 1660 John Cutting at Newbury had a total of 47 sheep, an enormous number compared to the usual three to twelve in a flock. Near the end of the century the town counted 5,635 sheep. Most of these were gathered into four flocks, and though they belonged to individual farmers in town, they were cared for by municipal shepherds on common land.

Finally, trees growing on the land produced abundant harvests from a variety of species suitable for a number of uses. In *New England's Prospect*, written in 1633, William Wood speaks of the red oak, the white, and the black. "As these are different in kind, so are they chosen for such uses as they are most fit for. One kind being more fit for clapboard, others for sawn board, some fitter for shipping, others for houses." He also described the New England walnut, cedar, fir, and pine, the ash and elms. Pine was doubly valuable, for the rosin, turpentine, and pitch it provided were essential for building and maintaining ships. The pines themselves, of course, were used for masts. Some of these magnificent pines were more than 200 feet tall and 40 inches in diameter.

After 1685 these larger trees were reserved for the use of the Royal Navy, and tree wardens roamed the forests of the Valley marking what pines they chose. The bulk of the lumber business was centered in the upper Valley of the

anything but human transport, so oxen remained crucial to the economy of the Valley, as to the rest of Massachusetts Bay, well into the 19th century.

Cows were few at first; for the first 50 years a herd of 12 was considered large. The ratio of cows to oxen may be used as a measure of the maturity of a settlement. In 1766 Haverhill, already in the second quarter of its second century, counted 716 cows and 252 oxen, while Ashfield, in the Berkshires, settled only 20 years before, counted 35 oxen and 31 milkers. In addition to milk, the cows yielded butter and cheeses. Goats were kept for the same purpose and were valued because they required so little care.

Sheep, on the other hand, demanded a great deal of care. By 1600 the English husbandman had already had more than four centuries of caring for sheep, but conditions in the Valley presented new problems. For one thing, there were the wolves. Unlike pigs and goats, sheep are not fighters and so were helpless against these predators. Even with the bounties offered for wolves—their heads were often nailed to the meetinghouse door—it was not much before 1700 that they were eliminated from the Merrimack towns. Pasturage presented another difficulty in raising

Livestock had an important role in the domestic economy of the Merrimack Valley. Sheep provided wool, a renewable resource, for clothing and blankets, and edible flesh. They required smooth pastureland and protection from predators. (MVTM)

Lumber was an important economic asset in the Merrimack Valley. Numerous local sawmills developed from the 17th century on to mill the wood necessary for buildings and tools. A riverside sawmill of the 18th century is depicted here, with its shipyard at right. Lumber could be floated down the Merrimack to the coastal shipyards. (MVTM)

Merrimack, where scores of sawmills, built on the tributaries of the river, prepared timber products for export. Most of this trade was moved overland toward the coast by teams of oxen, because the Pawtucket Falls at Chelmsford prevented using the river as a means of transportation. The lumber operations below the falls, in the lower Valley, were generally more for home markets than for export, though exports were made as long as a surplus was at hand.

The English fished the Merrimack even before they settled the Valley. Sturgeon were a prized catch, growing, it was claimed by some, to 12 or 14 feet. These great fish were pickled and sent to markets in Europe. Of course, the English were attracted also by the same teeming runs of anadromous fish that had been so vital in the yearly cycles of the Pennacooks' economy. Shad and alewives, salmon and eels were staple fare. Unlike the Pennacooks, however, the Europeans converted fish into cash, feeding a market far beyond the population of the Valley. The quantities taken from the river by Europeans were consequently much larger, and within 50 years of settlement the fish population began its decline. The original stock was so large, however, that even after years of decline the quantity taken was still considerable. As late as 1790, 60 to 100 fish were caught daily at Amesbury during the spring run of the salmon.

Henry David Thoreau, who spent his earliest years at Chelmsford, could still remember in the mid-1840s "the tales of our seniors" who had been "sent on horseback in *their* childhood from the neighboring towns, perched on saddle bags, with instructions to get the one filled with shad, the other with alewives." Finally, a historian of Chelmsford, writing in 1820, tells that the annual catch of salmon, shad, and alewives in that town was 2,500 barrels, and that this was far less than in former times, "so that they are rather desirable as a luxury, than as an article of cheap living."

Trade provided a further source of income for the first generation of Europeans in the Merrimack Valley. The trade for furs with the Pennacooks and other natives was highly lucrative, but it could not survive the destruction of hunting grounds by the advance of European agriculture. Trade on the sea was another matter. Considerable sea fishing was done from the port on the Merrimack side at Newbury, though in absolute numbers the size of this operation never matched the men and ships operating out of the southern ports of Essex County. On the other hand, the Newbury river front was a thriving center of coastal trade with the other British colonies as they developed.

A kind of internal commerce existed for the first decade of Massachusetts Bay, the earlier arrivals providing the necessities of life to those who followed. This market of immigrants was significant, considering that more than 12,000 Puritans arrived during the 1630s.

But the beginning of the English civil wars in 1640 put an abrupt end to this flow of settlers, and a boom economy went bust. The economic necessity this presented was accepted as an opportunity, seen as heaven-sent, of course. "It pleased the Lord to open to us a trade with Barbados and other islands," John Winthrop wrote. Fish, clapboard, planks, and other lumber products became immediately available for ready markets. In 1641 Sam Winslow at Salisbury-new-town contracted to supply 30,000 pipe staves yearly, presumably to make casks used in shipping. The cultivation of hemp and flax was begun and, according to Winthrop, these enterprises prospered. What had seemed at first to be the end of the economy became instead the stimulus for growth and diversification. Pork, beef, and oxen, either salted or on the hoof, were taken from the meadows of Valley towns and transported to the West Indies or to tobacco and sugar plantations in Virginia and the Carolinas. On the return voyage the ships might bring cotton for making yarn and cloth, or sugar and molasses for distilling into rum. There were distilleries at Haverhill and Newbury well before the mid-18th century, and they were quite important to the commerce of the region, since rum was both a commodity and a medium of exchange. The General Court did not fail to control and support this trade by establishing corn, at a fixed price, as the standard of exchange. In 1652 Massachusetts Bay set up its own mint, and transactions could be made in coin rather than in products.

Several Merrimack towns became commercial towns. The river was, and is, navigable by coastal shipping for some 11 miles, to Bradford and Haverhill. Haverhill, on the northern side, was ideally located for trade with upcountry towns; goods were carted by ox team overland to the riverside at Haverhill, avoiding the falls at Amoskeag and Pawtucket that made the Merrimack unsuitable for rafting. In the third quarter of the 18th century, James Duncan, a successful Haverhill merchant, built facilities at Lebanon, New Hampshire, to grind flaxseed and to make linseed oil, and kilns to produce potash used in making glass, soap, and fertilizers. The oil and potash were carted from Lebanon to Haverhill, where they were put on board ship and sent downriver for export. The empty carts were then filled with imported goods that had come upriver to his warehouses. In just over two years the gross value of shipments sent by Duncan into the northern town amounted to $96,000, a considerable amount in the Valley's pre-Revolutionary economy. And he was only one merchant among others with this sort of operation at Haverhill. By this time—about 1750—the economies of British colonies had found specialized products and crops, and these were the source of cash income for whole communities. The towns of Essex County cultivated onions that were exported in large quantities. The towns of northern Middlesex County were noted for the growing of hops; Tewksbury was a particularly large producer. The hops were used at local breweries or sent to other cities, such as the 3,000 pounds shipped to New York on the schooner *Bernard* in February 1763. The towns of the lower Merrimack Valley were rooted, deeply and surely, in the broad estates of the British Empire, from

Barbados and the West Indies to the Carolinas and New York, and of course to the home islands that met their need for manufactured goods—porcelains, cutlery, textiles.

Rather than separating the three sectors of the Valley economy from 1635 to 1763, land and river and sea were combined to support individuals, families, and communities. Once the settlers had survived beyond the first generation of scarcity, even a small farm could turn an extra cow or pig into imported clothing or a teapot or steel cutlery.

The towns of the Valley never were exclusively agricultural. Even pioneers will not live by bread alone, if they are given a choice. The communities required artisans and professionals to duplicate as completely as possible, and as soon as possible, the style of life they had known in Old England. Not having the cash to attract them, the towns offered land and privileges. In 1638, only three years after incorporation, the selectmen at Newbury granted Richard Dummer the right to erect a corn mill, and they agreed to allow no other provided that Dummer could meet the town's need. John Hoitt, brickmaker, was enticed from Ipswich by the townsmen at Haverhill in 1650, seduced by the offer of free land and clay pits, provided he furnish the

The Merrimack River's juncture with the Atlantic was an important connection for trade and commerce. Lumber and agricultural products sent downstream were processed or wholesaled through Newburyport, where incoming foreign goods were marketed and distributed. Imports from faraway lands reached the Valley's hinterland through traffic on the river. (MVTM)

townspeople with bricks. In 1656 the town of Chelmsford gave Samuel Adams 450 acres and the right to build a sawmill, on the condition that he supply the town with boards at three shillings per hundred. In the same year, Chelmsford gave William How 12 acres of meadow and 18 of upland, "provided he set up his trade of weaving and perform the town's work."

The differences in the amount of land granted are evidence that the freemen of Chelmsford valued some services more than others. The bestowing of land and privilege was made to fit the service to the community. Edward Whittington and Walter Wright, weavers at Andover, were granted land in 1673, "for encouragement of erecting a fulling mill, which they promise to set about in the spring." Shipbuilding and commerce were similarly encouraged from Newbury (in 1650) to Haverhill (in 1681). Such arrangements were made for blacksmiths, tanners, carpenters, and other artisans, and of course for ministers, teachers, and physicians. This method of dealing with the shortage of skilled labor resulted in a network of social relations in which individual rights were balanced according to the values of communal obligations.

Puritans had a strong sense of community. This was shown, for instance, in their notion that truth was held by the congregation of saints, and no individual, however august his station, was allowed to claim dispensation to teach or impose discipline unchecked by others. Even Governor Winthrop was reprimanded on this point. Likewise, property was not allowed to be unrelated to communal need and control. In part this came from the practice of centuries that put property at the service of families rather than individuals, and the practice continued in early New England. So in 1640, the General Court of Massachusetts awarded Winthrop's wife, Margaret, 3,000 acres in order to enlarge the Winthrop estate for the benefit of the governor's children.

Some of the economic development in the Valley

Following the capture of Louisburg by the British, the Acadian population was resettled in New England and other British colonies. Some were quartered in Andover with Jonathan Abbot, with whom they developed a friendship. When the Frenchman Jacques Hébert departed for Allenstown, New Hampshire, in 1770, he sent Abbot this elaborately decorated powder horn as a token of esteem and thanks. Courtesy, North Andover Historical Society.

required more than could be given or managed by one individual. In March 1717 Ephraim Foster and six other freemen at Andover addressed a petition to "his Majesties Justices of the Generall sesions of the peace now wholden att Ipswich for the county of Easex." They required "for our selves and in Behalf of our partners,"

> . . . that we may have Libberty to erect a wire [sic] in Marrimick River against henery [Henry] Boddals which we say is much in the Senter of our upper Towns.

The weir was intended, of course, to draw fish from the river. The catch would be sold at profit to the partners, a profit equal to, consistent with, and contained by the service done to the community in growing food at fixed prices. Some undertakings needed the support of whole towns, such as the Great Bridge over the Concord at Billerica, which was built and maintained by Dunstable, Chelmsford, Billerica, and Groton, all the settlements that used it.

The principle of economic cooperation had its political consequences for the towns of the Valley, however, as for all the towns of Massachusetts Bay. Despite strong attachment to a tradition of command, the Puritan fathers found that the participation of all freemen—church members or not—in political decisions was the only way to ensure peace and tranquillity and to prevent dissension from easily destroying the community. Despite themselves, the Puritans became democrats. It was consensus democracy that allowed only one set of values and left no room for minorities, but it was democracy nonetheless. Town meetings became the form of participation and they made it clear that property, not sainthood, should admit individuals to the process of control.

At Rowley in 1674 and 1675, after death had removed the strong hand of the Reverend Ezechial Rogers, the rule of the saints was challenged by a handful of citizens, with Abraham Jewett in the lead. They said it was the town (the freemen), and not the church (the saints), that paid for the minister's salary. It was the town, then, that had "Libberty" to choose the minister. This was contrary to the idea of church rule, at the center of Puritan life during the first generation. The controversy at Rowley was soon lost in the demands of Philip's War, but the trend away from church rule continued until equality and participation, the ideals of secular authority, prevailed against the Puritan virtues of subordination and command. In 1701 Boston celebrated the accession of Queen Anne, as was done throughout the British Empire. The Reverend Samuel Willard was shocked that in these festivities government officials were given a place of honor before the clergy. But it was done, and Boston must have been the last English-speaking city to

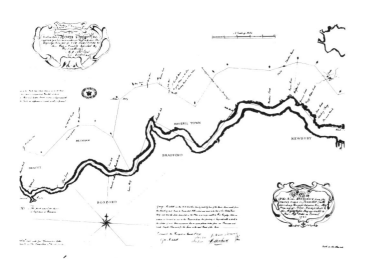

The boundary line between Massachusetts and New Hampshire was disputed until the settlement of 1739. This map, made in 1741, traces the Merrimack River from Pawtucket Falls (now Lowell) to the Atlantic and denotes the New Hampshire boundary following the river's course some three and a half miles to the north. Note that Boxford, rather than Andover, is incorrectly given river frontage. Courtesy, Trustees of the Haverhill Public Library.

think of it as news. The citizens of Massachusetts Bay were beginning to share a common inheritance with the other English colonies, and the inheritance was secular.

Yet one value of the Puritan past survived. The conviction remained that thrift, industry, and perseverance would be rewarded. This notion, often called the Puritan work ethic, was defended even when no longer nurtured by the Puritan theology that had been its matrix. The point is made by the career of the Reverend William Symmes at North Parish in Andover. The good pastor assumed his duties in November 1758 and stayed a rather long time, until death took him in 1807. Through that half century, heavy with change, Symmes preached a liberal version of Puritan doctrine. That is what his congregation expected of him, and why they had "called" him rather than another to be their minister. However liberal his teaching on grace and predestination, he still defended the work ethic. "Beware sloth. Till the land," he said in 1785. "It is not God's ordinary method to rain down bread for the food of man." That wealth indicated God's favor had always been doubtful. On the other hand, it became increasingly certain that wealth won the respect and even the deference of other citizens, and it gave access to political power.

The face of the Merrimack as a frontier aged beyond recognition until even the memory of it was dissolved by time. The frontier against the wilderness and the military frontier against the French—even the political frontier with

New Hampshire—all were gone before the War of Independence in 1775.

The Indians and their French advisors made one final, devastating raid on Haverhill in 1708, killing 16 people, abducting 31. After this, the military operations were carried away from the towns of the Valley, and contributed a share of men and materiel to bring the war to the French in Canada. In 1763 the treaty was signed by which the French king relinquished all his territories and rights on this continent. The lands to the west suddenly became safe—safe from French military attack and safe from the sudden loss of legal title to the land. There was a surge of population, and the frontier began its relentless move westward.

On August 10, 1737, the members of the General Court of Massachusetts gathered at Salisbury, on the Merrimack, while the members of the General Court of New Hampshire met at nearby Hampton. This put both representative assemblies within negotiating distance of the Commission, which was then making another attempt to settle the disputed boundary between them. It was a major effort but, like one made six years before at Newbury, it failed. In desperation, the Commission appealed the question to the highest authority, the king.

Both Massachusetts and New Hampshire hired agents to argue their case before the king's Privy Council, where the decision would be made. It may be that the lords of the Council were predisposed against Massachusetts, which had the reputation among officials at London of being too independent. It may be that New Hampshire's agent, John Thomlinson, was genuinely superior to his rival from Massachusetts in presenting his case. Or it may be that Thomlinson played with the inspiration of a gambler, because he had bought the claims of the Mason family to New Hampshire in 1738.

For whatever reason, when King George made his decision on March 5, 1739, the case went for New Hampshire. The Privy Council decreed a line three miles north of the northern side of the Merrimack, from its mouth to three miles north of Pawtucket Falls, and from there due west until it met with His Majesty's other dominions. At one stroke, Massachusetts lost 28 towns it previously had claimed, some of them in the Merrimack Valley. The men of Massachusetts protested mightily against the decision, but there was no appeal. At this time, in this place, neither the will of God nor the will of the people was substantial enough to challenge the will of the king that fell between them.

The lower Merrimack Valley had acquired its permanent dimensions. The irony is that in 1739, New Hampshire and Massachusetts were more alike than ever before and the difference between them was fading with each passing year, until the populations on both sides saw the need for united action.

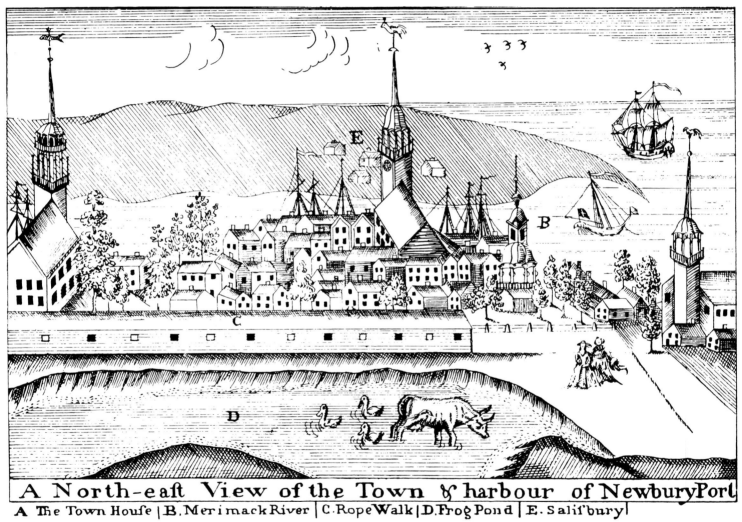

A North-east View of the Town & harbour of Newbury Port

A The Town House | B. Merimack River | C. Rope Walk | D. Frog Pond | E. Salisbury

IV

THE VALLEY IN A CHANGING AMERICA

Every order of things which has a tendency to remove
oppression and meliorate the condition of man, directing his
ambition to useful industry, is, in effect, republican.
— Robert Fulton, *Address to Congress,* 1807.

For a work of this kind will never be perfected by the
abilities and labours of one man.
— Oliver Evans, *The Young Mill-Wright,* 1795.

The spring of 1775 called the men and women of the Valley towns to
another year of labor: preparing of land, the planting of seed, the long
months of care and risk to be outlived. They waited for signs from the
place itself, as the generations had come to know the signs in the nearly
150 springs since the first European tilled the soil of the Valley. The great
flocks of migrating geese had already passed, late in the winter; beavers
left their lodges and returned to the work they had deserted since before
the first snows of the previous year. The river ran with fish. And, more to
the point for the thousands of farmers on the lower Merrimack, the bud
of leaves on the red oak was as big as the ear of a mouse, indicating it was

*Newburyport, the smallest city in Massachusetts, was created out of Newbury land
beginning in 1722, when the Third Parish was set off from the First. The enterprise
of the ''waterside'' people (those living adjacent to the Merrimack) resulted in
Newburyport's successful petition to become a separate, incorporated town in 1764,
and a city in 1851. This engraving shows the importance of maritime economy along
the river—there are more masts than church spires! (MTVM)*

safe to plant the corn.

However, the spring of 1775 was unlike any other, before or since. The farmers at Chelmsford and Amesbury, at Bradford, and Dunstable, scanned the horizons beyond the Valley. They looked to Boston and Philadelphia and London for political signs, and most of them seem to have understood that soon they would reap a harvest of dragon's teeth. For one year now, since March 1774, relations with the king and Parliament had been in their final stage of collapse; a decade of strain was about to break into open conflict. In that month Parliament had ordered the port of Boston closed and in three separate acts had reorganized the government of Massachusetts, investing more power in a governor appointed by the crown. To emphasize the point of these changes, the London government named Major General Thomas Gage, a military man with 20 years of loyal service in America, as its first governor of Massachusetts under the new rules. At issue were commerce and politics, money and authority.

The towns of the Merrimack Valley answered Parliament, measure for measure. To the closing of Boston's port, they responded each in turn with a resolution, voted at meetings and binding on all citizens, not to buy British goods and not to consume them. Closing the ports on the Merrimack was a vital step in making that boycott effective in Massachusetts. To the subversion of the state's royal charter of 1692, the towns responded with defiance: they ignored the legislature convened by Gage at Boston, and instead sent delegates to the assembly of "patriots" that met at Concord and later moved on to Cambridge.

The center and the means of resistance among the people of the Merrimack Valley were the town and town meeting. Town meeting was an institution developed by the townsmen themselves, in the Valley as in other regions of New England. It was not imposed and it was not imported, except that some basis for it came with the English immigrants in the habits of their daily dealing with one another and the needs of agricultural village life in medieval England. In New England the habits of centuries were transformed by the demands of frontier living. Town meeting was used to mediate internal conflict, a way of preventing disagreement among individuals from exploding the community. In short, it set boundaries on aggression, and it made clear to individuals how much aggression the communities could tolerate. Also, since 1632 the towns had elected delegates to the lower chamber of the General Court, and this gave them some measure of control over their own economic and political well-being.

But the events of 1774 transformed the town meeting. In fact, they tempt the use of that ancient phrase *annus mirabilis*, Year of Marvels. For townsmen at Dracut, Tewksbury, and Andover debated not only this incident or that act of Parliament; they debated also the very basis of

society, its nature and capacities. In other words, what a man owed to the public and what he reserved for himself and his own.

The towns of the Valley were not alone in challenging the authority of Parliament. Beyond them, the other towns of Massachusetts and the 12 other British colonies had their backs up. Not that the townsmen of the Merrimack Valley felt they had much in common with the people of the other regions where the drama of political revolt was being played: the coastal plains of the Carolinas, the area of Chesapeake Bay, the Hudson Valley. There were economic ties among the regions, certainly, but they did not hide from these men and women the great variations in social organization, political structure, and religious beliefs that made British colonies so different from any nation on earth.

Why the men of Georgia and Virginia, Pennsylvania and New York, should have overlooked their differences to concentrate attention on one point of community is a question that may have no satisfactory answer. Their one common link was their relationship with England. It was as siblings that they had a bond, and it was as siblings that they united in rebellion against the Mother of Parliaments. Their concentration of purpose achieved its focus at Philadelphia in September 1774 with the meeting of the First Continental Congress. The townspeople of the Merrimack Valley agreed, formally at town meeting, to ally themselves with the decisions of this Congress and to follow a unified direction in their economic and political resistance to Great Britain. The language of the resolution of the Andover townsmen is typical:

> Dec. 26, 1774: The town accepts every article & clause of Continental Congress requesting non-importation, non-exportation and non-consumption of British goods. Anyone over 21 who neglects to sign, shall have his name published in "Essex Gazette" as an enemy to the country.

The language of the resolution incidentally also reveals the underside of the town's freedom. Once a legal vote was taken in due process, there was no room for minority opinion. And God help the individual who, for whatever reason of courage or folly, stood against the town. Though he might not be banished he would be made to feel the crushing weight of exile among his own, a sinner among saints.

Eventually the 13 colonies formed a united political structure, and because they could not rely on a common tradition of place—which, after all, was England—they looked to antiquity for their model. They founded a republic. But the thoughtful men were worried because their trusted authorities said that such a republic was not possible. James Harrington and John Locke, who had defended England's "Glorious Revolution," the venerated French

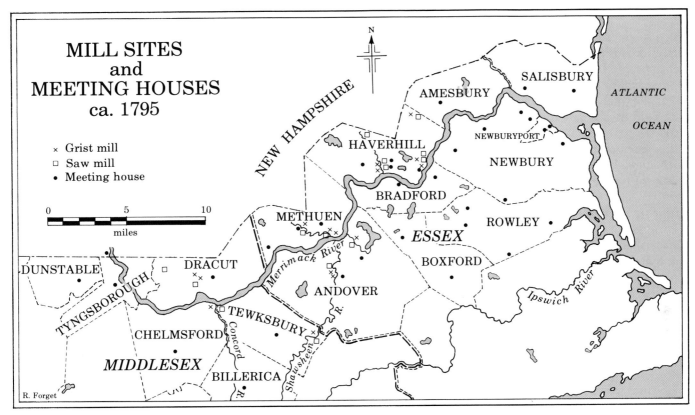

MILL SITES and MEETING HOUSES ca. 1795

× Grist mill
□ Saw mill
• Meeting house

0   5   10
miles

NEW HAMPSHIRE

SALISBURY

AMESBURY

ATLANTIC OCEAN

NEWBURYPORT

HAVERHILL

NEWBURY

BRADFORD

METHUEN

ESSEX

ROWLEY

BOXFORD

DUNSTABLE

DRACUT

ANDOVER

Ipswich River

TYNGSBOROUGH

Merrimack River

TEWKSBURY

CHELMSFORD

Concord

Shawsheen

MIDDLESEX

BILLERICA

R. Forget

Osgood Carleton's 1798 Map of the Commonwealth of Massachusetts, based on individual town surveys of 1794-1795, provided the basis for this map of the Merrimack Valley. Carleton's key, which included numerous symbols, has been reduced here to show gristmills, sawmills, and meetinghouses as primary indicators of settlement patterns within the towns. Map made by Robert Forget for The Valley and Its Peoples.

philosophe Montesquieu, even that strange "young" man from Geneva, Jean Jacques Rousseau, all agreed that republics composed of so various a society as the British colonies, spread as they were over so large an area, could not survive.

On the level of theory, republics were small, composed of persons who enjoyed a near equality of income so that no one might master another. Women and servents, the propertyless in general, were excluded from the *res publica*, the public thing, precisely because in private things they were dependent on those with property. They might be bought. In many cases, they *had* been bought. The freeman was male, over 21, and in charge of his own economic life. Inevitably, this made him a taxpayer. Finally, the theory went, the republic's freemen shared a common reservoir of interests and values: they knew what needed protecting and which means of protection were honorable.

This theory of a republic spelled out what the allied towns of the Merrimack Valley had become in practice. But even here, on a local scale, there were difficulties in making the structure work. For instance, in January 1764, two miles of the waterfront of the Merrimack at Newbury were set off as the town of Newburyport, and the charter of incorporation left no doubt why this was necessary:

. . . the town of Newbury is very large, and the inhabitants of that part of it, who dwell by the water side there, as it is commonly called, are mostly merchants, traders and artificers, and the inhabitants of the other part of the town are chiefly husbandmen, by means whereof many difficulties and disputes have arisen in managing their public affairs.

Those whose livelihood comes from the sea have economic needs different from those who live by the land, so that, at Newbury, it was easier to divorce the two than to live in rancor and misery. How, then, would it be possible to unite more than two million persons living along so many hundreds of miles of the Eastern Seaboard? At least the townsmen of Newbury had a century and a half of experience at the business. What did the inhabitants of the 13 colonies have except their own government and suspicions of all the others? Furthermore, the republic model was drawn from antiquity and there was the example of antiquity itself; all the educated men at the time knew the story of Rome, how power had corrupted the Republic of Rome into the Empire of Rome. So, it was against all reason that participants in the events of 1774 disregarded the voices of the past. They made a republic, and for two centuries Americans have been working at keeping faith with that great gamble.

Those who lived from March 1774 to March 1775, found it difficult to judge when the point of breach was passed, the point at which all the parties, or most of them, agreed that no return was possible—or at least that none was desirable. The thick of battle narrows all points of view and in the end offers only one route of escape. For the king and his minister the breach was discovered in November 1774, when they decided that what the colonials had been naming defense of liberty they would name rebellion. Despite impassioned pleas for conciliation from Edmund Burke and others in the House of Commons, the king's government sent 12,000 troops to Boston. They arrived in March 1775. Eight hundred of these troops were sent by Gage on the historic march into Middlesex County on April 19, 1775, to search out and destroy hidden arms. Neither of the military engagements that resulted, on the green at Lexington and across North Bridge at Concord, had the scale of modern war. But these "embattled farmers," as Longfellow later described them, surely "fired the shot heard round the world." The national leaders, Franklin and Jefferson, later

A rare survival, this Revolutionary War helmet was worn by Michael Titcomb of Newburyport, who served in the Washington Life Guard from 1776 to 1779. Titcomb, trained as a cabinetmaker, also had a mast yard in Newburyport and was appointed first lieutenant of the Merrimack *in 1798. Courtesy, Essex Institute, Salem, Massachusetts.*

claimed that no one had talked of independence before hearing the news of the events at Lexington and Concord. Those events revealed the breach. These British subjects were certainly at the end of one road, so whichever road they now chose would have to be a beginning. The slow waters of the Concord River left the scene of battle at North Bridge, joined the swifter current of the Merrimack at Chelmsford, and rushed, free, toward a destiny in the Atlantic. In April 1775, after a year of continual correspondence, Americans suddenly realized that they had been calling to each other from a common future.

The year of rapid movement was over. Now began the years of tedious work, the slow drudging toward the vision seen in the clear light of spring. Endurance was needed rather than speed, stamina more than outrage. Perhaps, after all, the long generations of contention with the unyielding soil of the Valley were not lost on these farmers become soldiers.

Only the minutemen of Chelmsford, of those from the Valley towns, reached Concord before the battle ended. Others joined in the bloody pursuit of the British as they retreated back to Charlestown. That retreat was the beginning of a siege, for Gage soon found himself surrounded by the people he had come to rule. The first major engagement in the War of Independence, at Breed's Hill and Bunker Hill, was in fact his attempt to loosen that circle. He succeeded, but at a fearful cost. "We have lost some extremely good officers," he reported to London. "The trials we have had show the rebels are not the despicable rabble too many have supposed them to be." He ended with an assessment that became a prediction. "The conquest of this country is not easy; you have to cope with vast numbers. In all their wars against the French, they never showed so much conduct, attention, and perseverance as they do now." But the king and his government could not hear what they chose to ignore. It took six years of war and two of negotiation to bend their willful ignorance into something like accommodation.

Gage was correct nevertheless. There were many in Massachusetts with combat experience, and some had gained the confidence of command in the French wars. One of these was Colonel James Frye of Andover, who rode to Breed's Hill with cheering news for friend and stranger alike. "This day 30 years ago," he told them, "I was at the taking of Louisbourg [Nova Scotia]. This is a fortunate day for Americans. We shall certainly beat the enemy!" There were hundreds from the Valley at Charlestown on this day of battle, June 17, 1775. Nearly 75 came from Haverhill alone, and more than 50 from Amesbury. There were the men of Tewksbury led by John Trull and those of Methuen under John Davis. One company came from Newbury with Captain Jacob Gerrish, and two from Newburyport, led by Captains Erza Lunt and Benjamin Perkins. They did not

Families in the Merrimack Valley were under the constant shadow of death, from infancy through adulthood. In an epidemic of cholera or typhoid in the fall of 1778, multiple deaths occurred among the Fletcher, Swallow, and Woodward families of Dunstable in the space of a week. These stones record the ominous toll to those families. Courtesy, Richard Graber, Andover, Massachusetts.

beat the enemy that day, but they responded with valor to the reminder that they were Americans.

The victory that escaped the men of the Valley so close to home was pursued into the middle and southern states of the Union. For six years the townspeople of the Valley made their contribution to the common effort at independence. This meant not only the soldiers who were sent every year at town charge to serve in the Continental Army. It meant also the supplies of food and clothing Massachusetts required of the towns. Toward the end, for instance, in 1780, Amesbury sent 33 oxen, weighing 900 pounds each, to help feed the army, while in the following year Haverhill contributed more than 16 tons of beef for the same purpose. The women of the Valley were at their spinning wheels and looms, making blankets and clothing for the soldiers of the republic.

The sea also was an arena of battle, one in which the ports on the Merrimack played a significant role. In June 1775, with hostilities just beginning, Bradford, Haverhill, Amesbury, and Newburyport cooperated to block the entrance of the river to British ships. These towns, however, were not satisfied with merely a defensive policy. Following the practice of the 18th century, Congress commissioned private vessels to harass enemy shipping. Thus Congress was able to disrupt enemy commerce at little or

no cost to the public, while the privateers, as they were called, stood to make a handsome income from "prizes" taken on the seas. It is difficult to say how many privateers were commissioned from Newburyport, but it was probably more than 100, for there were 61 in the years from 1780 to the signing of a treaty three years later. These 61 vessels carried 518 guns and just over 2,000 men. Privateers were also commissioned out of Salisbury.

Some of the experienced sailors of the Valley did serve on the vessels of the republic's young and small navy, and they challenged the great warships of His Britannic Majesty on the high seas. Two Newburyporters, cousins of the prominent Lunt family, were aboard the *Bonhomme Richard* as second and third lieutenants at the time of her encounter with *HMS Serapis* in September of 1779.

For two years the course of the war was inconclusive. However, the tide was turned in a series of sharp encounters in and about Saratoga, New York, during the summer and fall of 1777. This clear defeat of the British ruined their hope of dividing the 13 confederated states and, more important still, convinced the French that the Americans could win. In February 1778 the government of Louis XVI gave recognition to the United States of America and signed a military alliance, pledging loans, arms, and men. The French no doubt were motivated by revenge, hoping to return the injury they had received from Britain in 1763. But, whatever their purpose, it served America's well enough. The French alliance proved to be the decisive trick that turned the game in America's favor.

The war ended in October 1781 at Yorktown, Virginia, on a slip of land between the James and York rivers. Maneuvered into a dead end, British general Cornwallis found himself outnumbered by a combined American and

French force on land, and cut off by a French fleet from help by sea. He surrendered without a fight. Britain might have pursued the war, of course. She had by no means exhausted her economic and military resources. But the disaster at Yorktown produced political convulsions at London, which forced Geroge III to deal with the "rebels" he so heartily despised. The result, in 1783, was the Treaty of Paris, and his grudging acceptance of American independence. The republic was sovereign at last.

Winning the War of Independence was not the end of the revolution made by Americans. Looking at what was happening around him, John Adams concluded that people will make revolution only after it has been accomplished in the mind; in other words, there is no completing the design until the design is recognized. For the English king and his government, the design was completed when they conceded to relinquishing sovereignty over the 13 colonies now calling themselves the United States of America. But, for the 13 governments of the United States and for the peoples they represented, the story was only half told, the design only half recognized. With military decisions behind them, Americans now faced the political decisions they had neglected or shunted or escaped during the years of the war. The republic was sovereign but in what way should it rule? What structures would best translate the idea of the republic into reality? And there were conceptual problems as well. How can 13 governments make up one republic? How can sovereignty be shared when sovereignty is indivisible?

Finding solutions to these political riddles was complicated by the economics of the decade. It's not surprising, then, that political debates in the Valley were strongly marked by the commercial character of the region's economy, and particularly by the hard times of the postwar decade. After March 1781 the new republic was ruled by the Articles of Confederation, and the inability of the federal establishment to promote trade under this constitution fueled the demand by merchants that the constitution be changed. In the end they accepted an entirely new one, written at Philadelphia in 1787; they declared themselves satisfied that its provisions would promote commerce and so recognized, in that document, the end of the American Revolution.

Newburyport was the undoubted queen of the Merrimack at this time, but Salisbury, Amesbury, Bradford, and Haverhill were also merchant towns. Together they anchored the northern end of the wide circumference of Essex ports, billowing out into the Atlantic: Gloucester, Ipswich, Marblehead, Manchester, Beverly, and, to anchor the southern end, Salem, the second-largest town in New England. These ports of Essex County constituted commercial interests second only to Philadelphia. The men who controlled this formidable nexus of power were clear about

their objectives and confident of achieving them. The political notions of the Essex men of commerce had a significant impact on the new federal constitution, and two men who were part of the establishment at Newburyport were well placed to make individual contributions.

One of these was Theophilus Parsons. In 1778 he was 28 years old, a young lawyer in practice at Newburyport. In that year Parsons was among the politically minded men from various towns of Essex County who gathered at Treadwell's Tavern in Ipswich to debate a proposed state constitution for Massachusetts. Parsons also wrote the *Essex Result*, a pamphlet that made public the opinions and findings of the meeting. They objected, the *Result* said, to the lack of a bill of rights in the proposed constitution, and they thought that the power of the state—executive, legislative, judicial—ought to be carefully divided and balanced. These changes were needed to safeguard the rights of the individual. Among the many readers of the pamphlet who found the changes sensible and just was John Adams, a friend of Parsons who helped put the views of the *Result* into the Massachusetts constitution of 1780. The structure of the federal establishment, debated and resolved at Philadelphia in 1787, also bears the obvious marks of the *Essex Result.*

The structure of government, however, was only one of the problems addressed by Parsons and his colleagues. The gathering of 1778 also talked about the structure of society because, for the men of Essex, the republic was a form of government in the middle, facing dangers from above—when power was concentrated in one individual—and dangers from below—when power was taken by people "of the lower sort." The men of Essex saw no better remedy against the tendency to drift to either extreme than to put the throttle of power in the hands of the men of wealth. This is done, according to the *Result*, by dividing the legislature into two houses, the one representing the "people," and the other representing property. In this view of things, wealth always indicated wisdom, goodness, education; it demonstrated high moral purpose and rigorous intelligence together with the ability and prudence to handle money.

In 1778 Theophilus Parsons was at the beginning of a long and distinguished career at law, nearly all of it at Newburyport. In 1806, however, he was appointed Chief Justice of the Supreme Judicial Court of Massachusetts in Boston. When he died seven years later, he left behind a number of important precedents, particularly in the field of shipping and insurance. For the men of Essex, 1778 was the beginning of an association, loosely organized but powerful enough over the next generation to affect national politics from time to time. In 1780 Governor John Hancock called them the Essex Junto, not meaning to be friendly. Thirty-two years later, Henry Clay dismissed them as the

dent on the lower Merrimack for 20 years. When he was 12 years old, his merchant father sent Rufus to the Dummer School at Byfield in Newbury where he was instructed by master Samuel Moody, as Parsons had been before him. Later, after four obligatory years at the "colleges at Cambridge," he returned to the Valley, settling at Newburyport and reading law with Parsons. For three years, during the 1780s, King was elected to represent the town in the Massachusetts delegation at the Continental Congress. The Essex Junto could hardly have found anyone more qualified to present and defend its views at Philadelphia.

The next 20 years rewarded those who had wanted to increase the authority of the federal government. With a national trade policy, with public and private credit secure, with the establishment of the Bank of the United States, commerce and business in the young republic flourished. The merchant towns of the lower Merrimack enjoyed a long summer of prosperity.

The shipyards on the Merrimack—at Salisbury and Amesbury, at Bradford and Haverhill, and of course at Newburyport—recovered and surpassed their prewar productivity. In 1772 one witness reported 90 ships launched at Newburyport alone. In the boom years that covered a decade on either side of 1800, the Merrimack yards saw the construction of over 1,000 vessels of all sizes and descriptions. Twelve thousand tons were launched in 1810 alone. And also in 1810, a year of relative decline, Newburyport had 160 vessels in the European and West Indies trade, and 54 more in the Banks fisheries. Fortunes were made, great and small. This prosperity was reflected in Newburyport's appearance. Timothy Dwight, former president of Yale College, traveled widely throughout New England and New York during these years, and he found the town one of the finest on his itinerary. Its High Street became the site of grand mansions in the newest Federal style. The town had a new meetinghouse, and a new courthouse built in 1805 inspired by the famous Charles Bulfinch.

The capital accumulated in this commercial prosperity was put to work, invested in "internal improvement," which was the rage of the era throughout the new republic. Improvement in transportation was a particular favorite, perhaps because results were so immediate and dramatic. No fewer than four bridges were built across the Merrimack, all of them after a design by Timothy Palmer of Newburyport, and some of them built with the help of Palmer's mentor, the engineer Moody Spofford. The first bridge, the Essex-Merrimack, was finished in 1792 at Deer Island, about three miles upstream from the center of Newburyport. In rapid succession there came the great bridge at Haverhill, 650 feet long, 34 feet wide; the third connected Andover and Methuen; and the fourth, at Pawtucket Falls, was built between Chelmsford and Dracut.

One of the great eccentrics of his day, Newburyport's Timothy Dexter gained a fortune through commerce and shipping, although he began his career as a leather dresser. Lord Timothy, as he styled himself, wrote an account of his life entitled A Pickle for the Knowing Ones *and kept a lion in his yard for two weeks in 1795, among other oddities. Newburyport engraver James Akin engraved this likeness in 1805, the year before Dexter died. Courtesy, Essex Institute, Salem, Massachusetts.*

"Jackals of the Essex Kennel." The Essex Junto has had fewer defenders than did their Puritan ancestors, whose temper of mind they inherited. And like their sainted forebears, the Junto became another perfect example of how a point of view held too long becomes a blind spot.

A second Newburyporter played an individual role in this political story of a changing America. Rufus King was born at Scarborough in the District of Maine, but in 1787 he represented Massachusetts at the Constitutional Convention at Philadelphia, and by that time he had been a resi-

The Middlesex Canal

Moving goods on the waters of the Merrimack no doubt began even before Paul White, merchant at Newbury, obtained the town's permission to build a wharf on the river. That was in April 1655, and it was the first grant for such an enterprise on record. The river was used in this commercial way well into the present century when coal, for example, was barged up to Merrimacport, to Haverhill, and to other locations. But it was natural that the heyday of commerce on the Merrimack should coincide with the golden years of prosperity that followed the ratification of the Federal Constitution of 1789. The proof and the symbol of the river's place in this flourishing trade was the Middlesex Canal.

Constructed between 1797 and 1803, the canal left the river at Chelmsford and ran for a distance of 27 miles before reaching Charlestown, its southern terminal. And it was no simple ditch: the course of the canal required building 20 locks, 8 aqueducts, and 48 bridges. The most impressive structure in the canal may have been the aqueduct that carried the canal 30 feet above the Shawsheen River at Billerica. By 1814 the Middlesex was one of a network of canals that connected the capitals of Massachusetts and New Hampshire.

However much a triumph of American finance and engineering, the Middlesex was costly for the region of the lower Merrimack, particularly for the merchants of Newburyport. In 1805 almost 10,000 tons of freight moved south through the canal to the port of Charlestown; nearly 90 percent of that was New Hampshire lumber, and all of it was diverted from the wharves at the mouth of the river. The lower Merrimack was pushed aside by the success of the Boston merchants competing with those of Newburyport, but what the canal took from commerce, it returned as industrial enterprise. Its proximity to the power of Pawtucket Falls made the canal another reason to choose Chelmsford as a site for the industrial production of cotton goods. The development of Lowell after 1821 brought over a decade of prosperous activity on the Middlesex. That ended with the construction of the Lowell-Boston Railroad in 1835; the railroad could move freight faster, and, unlike the canal, it was not stopped by the freeze of winter. The canal corporation struggled through the 1840s, but it did not survive the next decade. It was officially pronounced dead, its charter annulled, by the General Court in 1860.

Painted about 1825, this view shows the Middlesex Canal from the house of William Rogers in Billerica. At left, a man on horseback pulls a canalboat, while another man rides for pleasure at center. Jabez Warren Barton painted this watercolor as a companion piece to his view of Rogers' house. Courtesy, Billerica Historical Society.

Also at Pawtucket Falls, on the Chelmsford side, Newburyport capital created the Proprietors of Locks and Canals on Merrimack River in 1792, still in operation and one of the oldest corporations in the United States. The locks and canals were to provide a way around the falls for the timber that the merchants of Newburyport wanted to divert to their wharves at the mouth of the river. A decade later (1803) Newburyporters incorporated a company to construct the Newburyport-Boston Turnpike. Finished in 1806, the road was 34 miles long and as straight as engineers were able to make it. It cost $500,000 to build, an enormous sum, and included two hotels that the investors added to the original design. The investors obviously expected the route would be heavily traveled, but in this they were disappointed.

Manufacturing attracted less capital investment than transportation, but the need and benefit were widely acknowledged, as is shown in the following resolution passed at town meeting of Newburyport in 1786.

> We exceedingly lament, that in a country abounding with every material, the ingenuity and dexterity of whose people are exceeded by none, the practice of exporting unwrought materials, and importing manufactures, should be general, for we esteem it impolitic and uncommerical to export the former, till wrought to perfection or to import the latter, especially when wrought from materials of our own produce . . .

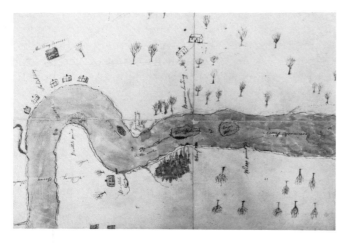

This manuscript map of the Merrimack River shows the bend at Salisbury Point, just below the ferry between Newbury and Amesbury, and continues to the edge of Newburyport. We can date this map at about 1790, since the Rocky Hill Meeting House, built in 1785, is shown at the top left, but Timothy Palmer's bridge, built in 1792 across Deer Island, does not appear. Courtesy, Historical Society of Old Newbury.

The residents of the towns of the lower Merrimack were anxious, as were all Americans, to establish economic independence, especially from the need to import the manufactured goods of England. The Newburyport Woolen Manufactory, the first incorporated textile company in Massachusetts, began operation in 1794. Across the Merrimack in Amesbury, Ezra Worthen also ran a textile operation using the waters of the Powow to turn the wheels of his mill. The ablest local machinist of the period was Jacob Perkins. A native of Newburyport, Perkins invented machines for making nails, milling coin, and making banknotes that could not be counterfeited. His success, however, was never equal to his ambition and the irony is that he eventually moved to London thinking to improve both his reputation and his income. In the meantime, the notes of the Massachusetts banks were for the most part engraved and printed at Newburyport.

Less glamorous, perhaps, but surely another bellwether of prosperity were the investments made by the citizens of the lower Merrimack in the banking and insurance industries so vital to commerce.

Finally, the culture of the town reflected growth. A wide variety of activities made their appearance, from singing schools and dramatic readings to traveling circuses with their wild assortment of educated pigs, acrobats, and ventriloquists. Newspapers began making weekly appearances. There were other publishers and printers at Newburyport. Edmund Blunt published Captain Lawrence Furlong's *American Coastal Pilot* and the *New Practical Navigator* by Nathaniel Bowditch, both signal contributions by native "Porters."

The agricultural sector of the Merrimack's economy shared in the prosperity of its commerce. Newbury, in particular, stimulated by the growing urban market at its back door, experienced a 25 percent increase in population between 1800 and 1810. Newbury farmers responded to the opportunity for a larger volume of sales by increasing the number of plantings, and by increasing the amount of fertilizers they used. The yield per acre of its farms was above average for the period: 40 bushels of corn, 200 of potatoes, 25 of barley, 20 of rye. Wheat as usual was more difficult to grow, yielding only about 10 bushels to the acre.

The towns of the lower Merrimack enjoyed a prosperous economy for 20 years after the Constitution of 1789. Many, perhaps most, of the townfolk enjoyed a happy prospect of plenty. Some leaders, however, reported having political premonitions—nightmares, in their definition of politics. They saw the face of opposition materialize before them, and the face belonged to Thomas Jefferson. By 1800, despite his thousands of acres and his slaves, Jefferson had somehow become accepted as a spokesman of the common man. Also, during the 1790s Jefferson was generally recognized as the most important of several leaders of an emerging po-

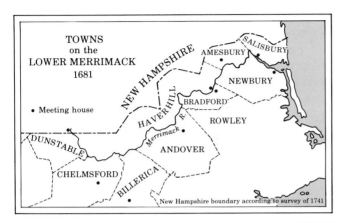

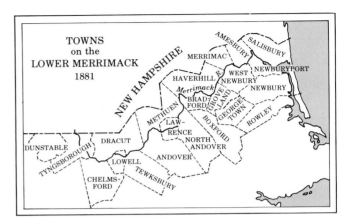

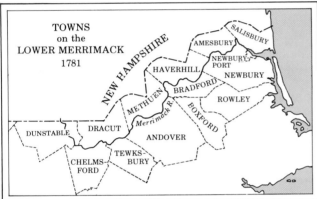

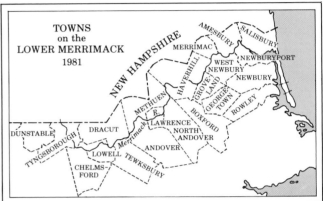

These township maps show the changing boundaries of Valley communities over time. Some towns that bordered on the Merrimack at one period no longer have direct access to the river. Maps made by Robert Forget for The Valley and Its Peoples.

litical party who were called Republicans or Democratic-Republicans. The discovery of the common man was decisive as a prophecy of our political history. The discovery completed a train of thought begun by the previous generation, and it was the final evolution in political ideas of the new republic. It was inevitable as well that the thought produced a revolutionary device, politics by party. James Madison, also among the leaders of the new party, best justified the development of party politics. After all, he said, toleration was not new for Americans who had observed a wide variety of Christian forms without ever coming to open war. In the same way, he thought, political parties would make political toleration possible. Honest differences would lead to controlled opposition: parties were a mechanism to keep the Union together despite radical differences of opinion about how it should be run.

Today parties are accepted as a basic element of political life, but it was a difficult passage for that generation to negotiate. The Federalists, the party in power under Washington and Adams, clung desperately to the claim that the ability to lead was natural to some people only and that the ability could not be conferred by the votes of "people of the lower sort." The Puritans had thought that wealth might indicate the knowledge of God's plan and so confer the obligation to lead. These secular Yankee merchants of Essex were saying that wealth demonstrates superior ability to manage things and men and so bestows the right to govern. The mere fact that another party was emerging to challenge these natural leaders was a clear sign of perversion at the base of the republic. Nevertheless, Jefferson continued his "evil" ways, and the Democratic-Republicans pursued office and displaced Federalists in local and state elections. Finally, in the 1800 election, Jefferson was elected President of the United States.

The American system, the republic, was completed when John Adams, Federalist, peaceably relinquished the office of President of the United States to Thomas Jefferson, Democratic-Republican. Historians have often remarked that Jefferson, in March 1801, walked from his inauguration at the Capitol to a reception at the White House rather than ride in a carriage as Washington and Adams had done. This reportedly symbolized his coming from "the people." And, true enough, as a symbol it remains pleasing, but it ought not obscure the substance: that he was allowed office at all is astounding. There was no precedent, anywhere, for such an orderly transfer of power.

The Essex Junto remained in the forefont of opposition to

Jefferson after his election. Charges and stories were printed about Jefferson and his administration in the *Newburyport Herald and Country Gazette* that now would be considered ridiculous. Jefferson was an atheist, they said, and would bring the collapse of Christian morality; his prattling about the common man would bring the elimination of private property which was, after all, the foundation of the republic. The accusers pointed out that Jefferson was a friend of France and devoted to all the radical political ideas that the French Republic had been spreading to the rest of Europe since 1792. By contrast, feelings against the French ran so high at Newburyport that the town raised $30,000 to build a warship for use by the American navy. Launched on October 12, 1798, it was named the *Merrimack*, a 360-ton vessel carrying 28 guns. In mid-December it sailed to the West Indies to join a squadron under Commodore John Barry. With that, one historian of the town has said, "Newburyport had in effect issued its own declaration of war against France."

It may be that the Junto's diatribe against Jefferson was meant to immunize the voters of the Valley against the seduction of Jeffersonian rhetoric. But concerning trade and Jefferson's policies' detrimental effects on the commercial prosperity of the Valley, there were more than words at issue. The Essex men, and the Federalists in general, accepted the Constitution of 1789 because it gave the federal government the power to promote trade, and it didn't seem possible to them that the power might be used to damage commerce. After all, wasn't that why Americans had rejected the rule of Parliament? Yet, in 1807 Jefferson, with the support of his partisans in Congress, issued an Embargo Act that outlawed trade with both England and France. Jefferson's purpose was political: he wanted to maintain the neutrality of the United States during the intense and prolonged wars in Europe. However, the consequence of Jefferson's policy was economic: it put an immediate end to the years of prosperity that the port towns on the Merrimack had shared with the entire maritime sector of the American economy.

Jefferson's policies delayed American involvement in Europe's wars, but they also put new life in the waning political fortunes of the Essex Junto. When war against England finally came in 1812, under Jefferson's successor, they called it Mr. Madison's war. They thought it had nothing to do with them. How galling it must have been for the Valley Federalists in particular to see their old enemy, Joe Varnum of Dracut, sitting in 1813 as president *pro tem* of the Senate, acting Vice-President of the United States. Joe Varnum, proud of nothing so much as of his 500-acre farm with "more than 10 miles of good stone fence upon it."

The diehard New England Federalists favored secession over submission to this flagrant disregard of their interest. They convened at Hartford, Connecticut, in 1814, but in the end the Hartford Convention did not lead to a rupture in the Union. The majority understood that it was one thing, in 1764, to separate two square miles of river front on the Merrimack because merchants and farmers at Newbury couldn't manage to get along. It was quite another to cast away 40 years of monumental political invention by thousands of individuals and scores of towns.

Forty years lay between the Boston Port Bill (1774) and the Hartford Convention (1814). In that time the towns on the lower Merrimack had made their contributions to the military effort against England and had participated significantly in the political revolution as well. In that time the maritime economy of the region was well served by the power of the Federal establishment, particularly by the voice of the Essex Junto, strident and unreasoning as that voice often was. At the end of the republic's second war with England, in 1815, it seemed that the region had made its last contribution to the evolution of America and that the Valley of the lower Merrimack would become a political backwater.

Sloop-of-war Merrimack *was built at Newburyport in 1798 and was equipped with 28 guns. It typified American war vessels in the period when the Navy was being built. Courtesy, Peabody Museum of Salem.*

V

ENTERING THE INDUSTRIAL AGE

And now when upon the subject of the river, I think it proper to observe, that though in various ways this town in common with others upon its brink derive great advantages from this noble stream, it is obvious to any person who will take the trouble to reflect upon the subject that these advantages are much less than they might, indeed ought to be.
— Gardner Perry, *History of Bradford, Massachusetts*, 1820.

If you wish for increasing prosperity, you must move, like the planetary system, round a common centre, and that with increasing harmony. You must sacrifice at one altar and remember that you are members of one community, and interested in promoting the honor and prosperity of one town.
— Wilkes Allen, *History of Chelmsford*, 1820.

Nathan Appleton tells the story of how he and some others traveled to Chelmsford one day in November 1821, how they inspected the falls

A rare survivor, this throstle-type spinning frame was built by the Locks & Canals machine shop in Lowell during the 1830s. The frame consists of both wood and iron, a transitional feature typical of this period. It has 64 spindles, 32 on each side. Courtesy, Slater Mill Historic Site.

Represented here in its natural state, the river appears as it might have looked before the building of the dam, canals, and factories that would be called Lowell. Painted by Alvan Fisher in 1833, this landscape belies its time and place, as by this date the river was already lined with brick mills. Courtesy, Baker Library, Harvard University.

on the Merrimack at that site, and how in fact they had gone there only because the place offered waterpower. Patrick Tracy Jackson and Paul Moody were, like Appleton himself, natives of the Valley; the other three—John W. Boott, his brother Kirk Boott, and Warren Dutton—were Bostonians. Six men, prospectors as they've been called, in search of power to continue a business project already well under way at Waltham on the Charles. The two rivers, the ancient frontiers of Puritan Massachusetts, were again put to common effort, and like their "sainted" ancestors, these six new colonials came to the Merrimack Valley looking for place but found instead opportunity, an occasion in time.

The visit to Pawtucket Falls opened the industrial chapter in the Valley's story. Yet it was more than a local event, because the success of Appleton and his associates reached national proportions. The textile mills they built on the power of the Merrimack became an example to other Americans, and a proof to the rest of the world that the American republic was coming of age. Those mills were a demonstration that Americans had the technical and financial capacities to be a manufacturing nation. But it was not enough just to prove that Americans could do this; it was important, too, that the mills at Chelmsford prove Americans able to do it better than anyone had done it before, anywhere. Americans would learn from the past. The republic would avoid all the errors of tired old Europe.

England in particular was a model to avoid, and doing better than the English was still a need Americans had not outgrown. The record of British factories and factory cities

was like an omen to be dispelled, for there was no denying that British industry had brought many evils to the English. There were physical evils, such as unsafe workplaces and filthy living conditions, and moral evils such as greed and despair. There were social evils as well, all of them opening vast inequalities of wealth between those who owned the factories and those who labored in them. England might be a fit place for these inequalities, as England's political culture rested on centuries of class divisions. Americans, however, regarded social inequality as distinctly not American. Equality was the very soul of the republic and economic self-reliance was the base of all equality. Twenty years before an English settlement was made in the Valley, John Smith promised that "here every man may be master and owner of his own labor." More recently, Thomas Jefferson had constructed a political movement by glorifying farmers as the Lord's Chosen on earth. The self-sufficiency of farmers was not merely a virtue, it was *the* Virtue on which the republic was founded—its source of power. How, then, could this republic survive the inequalities that industrial production brought with it?

Concern with this question during the first generation after the ratification of the Constitution, for 30 years or so after 1789, is quite apparent. For instance, it was this concern that motivated Bailey Bartlett in 1801. A group of townsmen at Haverhill had petitioned the town "for leave to conduct the water by means of an acqueduct from Round Pond, so-called, into the settled part of town for private and public convenience." The request was referred to a committee with Bailey Bartlett as its chairman. He reported in favor of the petition, but attached conditions to the committee's approval. The first of these was that no one be allowed to buy more than one share of the stock until the subscription had been open for 90 days. At the end of this period, the remaining unsold shares might be taken by any of the shareholders. And, further, the company that built and operated the aqueduct was required to submit its regulations to the town for approval.

Bartlett, who was elected to Congress in his district, reflected the thinking of the citizens of Haverhill and the surrounding towns. The ideals of the common voter were a common inheritance, grown out of the Puritan notion of property and from the experience of two centuries in the Valley. The experience of the place taught that in some final sense all property was communal, and that private gain was not its only purpose. So, again, in 1803, the town of Haverhill granted a petition to erect a hay scales, certainly a useful enterprise in this farming community. But the town also exercised its right to control the price of service: one and a quarter cents per hundredweight for all hay loads over 600 pounds, and eight cents for each load under 600 pounds.

Like most Americans of the period, the citizens of

Haverhill were extremely wary of concentrations of wealth, because wealth generated social and political power, and like the framers of the Constitution, they wanted power distributed, not concentrated. These were the thoughts and fears that Appleton and his friends had to confront and overcome, when they came to build their mills at Chelmsford. They didn't ignore those fears, they didn't pretend to have a technical problem only or a financial problem only. They had a social problem as well, involving nothing less than the character of the American people and the definition of the republic. But they managed to solve it: for nearly 20 years they combined the ideals of republican equality and the needs of industrial production. Or so it seemed, for a time. American statesmen, such as President Andrew Jackson, and foreign celebrities, such as Charles Dickens, came to the Valley and marveled at the accomplishment. The radiance of American Virtue was a promise of hope that in the Merrimack Valley a better future had been found.

Until November 1821, the Valley of the lower Merrimack was like the valleys of scores of other rivers where water-power was providing a new sort of education. In England and in America, sites of falling water acted as a kind of lens, concentrating mechanical experience and mathematics and the hope of profit with a focus intense enough to put a brand on the future. The Puritan and Yankee residents of the Valley had used the waters of the Merrimack's tributaries, from the first decade of settlement, to power the mills—sawmills, gristmills, fulling mills—that the economies of their towns had demanded. But textile mills were different. They required many more workers and so presented managerial problems of organization and control. Also, textile mills were far more complex in their mechanics than even the most sophisticated grist- or fulling mill.

Beginning a textile enterprise meant designing and making an efficient wheel and wheel pit, it meant building an efficient transmission system of shafts, pulleys, and belts. Textile production also meant arranging the machines so the work could move easily from one to the next as each performed a step in a series that transformed fiber into yarn. Besides, each enterprise had to make its own machines. Since there were no machine manufacturers, each mill needed its own machine shop where the good ideas, those that worked, were arrived at collectively. The textile entrepreneur in 1800 or 1810 had to be part machinist, part millwright, part personnel manager, and he had to combine these various skills in himself or find others who would work with him or for him.

The technological demands of textile manufacturing were decidedly more complex than any known before, but there were sites on the tributaries of the Merrimack where the demands were well met. On the Powow at Amesbury

Ezra Worthen, with the help of Paul Moody and Jacob Perkins, began to operate a cotton-spinning mill in 1812. At Chelmsford, the following year, Phineas Whiting and Josiah Fletcher built a mill 60 feet long by 50 feet wide and 40 feet high "for a cotton manufactory" powered by the Concord River. Five years later, in 1818, Thomas Hurd bought their mill and fitted it with an impressive assortment of machines for making woolens. The choice of location was natural for Hurd, who came from Charlestown. Chelmsford and Charlestown lay at opposite ends of the Middlesex Canal, a waterway that Hurd no doubt hoped would link his mill with the Boston markets. Meanwhile, Moses Hale and Oliver Whipple were also developing the site on the Concord, complete with a power canal that they

Before Lowell and Lawrence were built, individual mills utilized the power of waterfalls. The Methuen Company's cotton mill, shown in this circa 1837 lithograph of the falls and mills on the Spigot River, represented the style of building typical in Lowell. Individual operations like this one persisted alongside the Lowell model until well into the 19th century. (MVTM)

began in September 1821.

None of this work was done in isolation; each site relied on news from other places where textile technology was being pursued aggressively, and no machinist scrupled at using the discoveries of others. Chance played a role in establishing these contacts. How quickly one could get news, how quickly it could be analyzed and adapted, whether, indeed, there was anyone able to decipher the news, all these factors depended as much on chance as on effort. But there were efforts made, and no contacts were sought out more eagerly than those with English mechanics, particularly those with managerial experience. Nearly all innovations in textile technology originated in England in the 25 or so years before 1800. Any Englishman who could dem-

Newbury native Paul Moody (1779-1831), an excellent machin-
ist, trained first as a weaver with the Scholfields in the 1790s,
and later as a machine maker with Jacob Perkins of New-
buryport. After working as superintendent of the machine shop
at Waltham, he transferred to Lowell along with his staff, tools,
and patterns to make the necessary machinery for the new mills
on the Merrimack. Moody's skill was an important component
of the ultimate success of the Boston Associates. (MVTM)

onstrate firsthand knowledge of machines was respected for his high skills and sometimes as a business partner. In 1802 James Scholfield, a British immigrant, was first in the Merrimack Valley to card wool by machine. He used the waters of Cochichewick Brook in Andover's North Parish. Though a small stream, the brook offered a drop of more than 70 feet in little more than a mile; the Pennacooks were accurate in calling it "Place of Cascades." Scholfield stayed long enough to help Nathaniel Stevens, a native of the town, begin his enterprise of woolen manufacture in 1813. That operation was also located on Cochichewick Brook on a site formerly occupied by a gristmill. Stevens learned from Scholfield as well as from Moses Hale of Chelmsford, who became his father-in-law in 1815.

In Andover's South Parish, Abraham Marland, another English immigrant, began his cotton-spinning mill in 1804 at a site on the Shawsheen River. Only six years later he refitted for woolen manufacturing and so helped spawn a firm of machine builders who later—and again on

Cochichewick Brook—became the renowned Davis and Furber Machine Company, maker of woolen machinery down to the present. But, in the early years, it was the technology of cotton manufacturing that was on the cutting edge of a revolution, and by far the greatest contribution made by an Englishman to the American textile industry was made by Samuel Slater.

Nathaniel Stevens (1786-1865) was born and raised in Andov-
er's North Parish, where he established his woolen mill in a for-
mer gristmill on the Cochichewick Brook in 1813. The business
he founded was carried on by his family at that site until 1972.
The Stevens' company eventually acquired other mills in the
Merrimack Valley, including two at Haverhill, one at Andover,
and one at Dracut, in addition to those in other New England
locations. The mills made woolen flannels and suitings, and
during the Civil War they prospered with orders for blankets
and uniforms. (MVTM)

Slater was an early arrival from England, coming in the first year of the republic, 1789, and during his 22nd year. He carried only his indenture to document his seven years of experience at the cotton-spinning mill of Jedediah Strutt. Strutt himself was a former partner of Richard Arkwright, the inventor of the spinning frame, so while Slater was a first-generation American, he was a third-generation machinist of impressive pedigree. Within months of his arrival, Slater was in partnership with Moses Brown, merchant of Providence, Rhode Island, and in less than two years they organized the first successful cotton-spinning

Abraham Marland (1771-1849) was born in Lancashire, England, and immigrated to the United States in 1801. After an initial foray into cotton manufacture at Beverly and Lynnfield, Marland settled at Andover in the business of wool manufacture. The Marland Mills were known for their fine flannels and continued for 30 years after the death of the founder. In 1879 the mill was purchased by Stevens, who ran it until the early 1960s. Abraham Marland was instrumental in establishing the Episcopal Church in Andover. (MVTM)

mill in America. Located on the Blackstone River at Pawtucket, Rhode Island, the mill and others like it that Slater built in the Blackstone Valley were for two decades the most advanced model of cotton manufacturing in America.

While Slater led, others followed. In 1803 Charles Robbins, trained by Slater at Pawtucket, moved to New Ipswich, New Hampshire, and there, by the end of 1804, he operated a mill of 500 spindles, the first spinning mill of the Slater type outside the Blackstone Valley. Nathan Appleton was a native of New Ipswich, and though he had left the town when still a boy, he was well acquainted with Charles Barrett and the other locals involved in the project. He had this chance to take a close look at a cotton manufactory, especially after 1810 when his brother Samuel bought a

quarter interest in the mill. Nathan was not impressed, not, at least, with what he saw at New Ipswich. Slater's of course was not the only model, and though a potent one to its generation, it was not the model that came to dominate the Valley of the Merrimack. Rather, the mills at Chelmsford, established by Appleton and his friends after 1821, became the prototype, and those were organized on a model tested and proved at Waltham.

The mills at Waltham were organized by the Boston Manufacturing Company, and the story is reasonably familiar of how Francis Cabot Lowell, merchant of Boston, became, according to Appleton, the "animating spirit" of this most revolutionary enterprise. Indeed, his personal efforts were considerable, though none of them succeeded unaided. To reinvent the power loom he used what his memory was able to pirate from English designs. Lowell also used his very considerable ability at mathematics to synchronize four separate alternating motions of the power loom, while deriving all four from the simple rotary motion of a waterwheel. However, for mechanical experience and skill Lowell relied on Paul Moody, with the added consultation of Moody's own mentor, Jacob Perkins. Work on the loom was done in the back room at Lowell's store on Broad Street, Boston. This "machine shop" was the very frontier of American machine technology, and in the fall of 1813 it produced one of the first operating power looms in America. The cost of the model was $534.69. This loom was highly significant, because American experience with cotton technology had been confined to the preparation and spinning of the fiber into cotton yarn. Machine weaving, which transformed yarn into cloth, was still England's monopoly, and without power-loom weaving the American textile industry would remain incomplete and unable to compete with its English prototype.

The Waltham system of labor, a second innovation credited to Francis Cabot Lowell, was equally significant, and it seems to have been more nearly his solitary achievement. Before the Waltham mills, American textile entrepreneurs had copied the so-called Rhode Island system of labor, the labor system introduced by Samuel Slater in the last decade of the 18th century. Slater hired families, rather than individuals, so that men, women, and children worked in the spinning mills together. The families were generally sheltered in company housing and sometimes were a captive market for the company store. Like Slater's carding machines and spinning frames, this labor system was copied from an English model, so it roused all the nativist American fears about factory life. For the worst feature of the Rhode Island system was its natural tendency to generate a permanent class of factory workers, a class easy to collect but impossible to dissolve. This was the trap Francis Cabot Lowell set out to avoid. He proposed to hire single women primarily, young women between the ages of 15

As the prime mover behind the Boston Manufacturing Company at Waltham, Francis Cabot Lowell (1775-1817) deserves the credit for the system of industrialization in textiles that developed in the corporation towns of New England. His perseverance led to the introduction of the power loom, and his business acumen ensured its success. Although Lowell died an untimely death, his memory endures through the reputation of the city that bears his name. This silhouette, his only known likeness, descended through the family to Harriet Ropes Cabot. Courtesy, Harriet Ropes Cabot.

and 20, and train them to operate the frames and looms of his mills. These daughters of local farmers would be a transient labor force, for they were never intended to spend their whole lives in the mills. They were expected to return to the land, marry farmers, and allow their younger sisters and cousins to take their place in the factory. No one could be dead-ended in factory life and no male laborers need be seduced from the land and self-reliance. To preserve the physical and moral well-being of these young women, Lowell proposed housing them in dormitory-like buildings, supervised by trustworthy matrons who would give them three wholesome meals a day and police their behavior. Whatever objections might be found against this Waltham system, it was distinctly American.

A third innovation by the Boston Manufacturing Company, one less often celebrated, was the size of its financial base. The BMC was chartered by the Massachusetts General Court with a capitalization of $400,000, far more than any previous textile manufactory. Lowell determined to raise only one quarter of that amount, divided into 100 equal shares, $1,000 at par. To help him in this was Patrick Tracy Jackson, a lifelong friend and former partner in the Indies trade. In fact, the Jackson-Lowell saga is a useful diversion in recollecting the ways of American power.

The tale begins by the Merrimack at Newburyport in the previous generation. Jonathan Jackson and John Lowell—fathers of the future textile magnates—were classmates together at Harvard College, and their chance meeting created a friendship that altered John Lowell's future and the lives of his considerable clan. Jackson was the scion of a prominent merchant family at Newburyport, and Lowell the son of the first minister of the town's first church. When both had returned to their native town, and John Lowell had begun his law practice, it was Jonathan Jackson who introduced him to the leaders of Newburyport society and so, of course, to the pick of legal clients. In due time they shared in the construction of a double house, as was then the fashion on High Street, the town's choicest avenue. They raised their sons and daughters with the expectation that marriage would unite their families.

Jonathan Jackson married once, and well, to Hannah, the daughter of Patrick Tracy, who was the wealthiest of Newburyport's merchants at the time of the War of Independence. John Lowell married three times, and each time to the daughter of a merchant, Higginson and Cabot and Russell, though when he met Rebecca Russell she was already the widow Tyng of Dunstable. Their expectations from their children were not disappointed, as Patrick Tracy Jackson and Francis Cabot Lowell became brothers-in-law. By 1813 the Jackson-Lowell connection rested on two generations and multiple marriages, on the memory of secure alliances of affection and wealth. No enterprise like the Boston Manufacturing Company, revolutionary in so many ways, would be undertaken without some recognized tie to the past. If the departure from shipping to factory was a wrenching one for these two cronies, the wrench was soothed by the securities they took with them. Patrick Tracy Jackson bought 20 of the 100 shares in the BMC, more than any other investor and five more, in fact, than Francis Cabot Lowell.

Even as shipping declined in the face of industrial investment, fishing continued to provide livelihood and sustenance for those living in towns near the mouth of the Merrimack. A fish market on the wharf at Newburyport, photographed in about 1860, bore a sign showing a larger-scale operation dating from somewhat earlier in the century, which perhaps had occupied the same site in better days. Courtesy, Society for the Preservation of New England Antiquities.

The Lowells by 1813 had moved from church to law to trade, resuming in themselves the most respected occupations their society had known for 200 years, a trinity of gain able to snatch a pound or a dollar from the devil's own hand. With the Jacksons, they were common proprietors of a tradition of confidence, the experience of success. That tradition had carried their fathers through the political revolution and war with England, and the same tradition carried the sons, new Americans, through an economic revolution.

Jackson and Lowell sought out other investors only within their families and among the merchants of Boston they knew and trusted. Two Jackson brothers joined in the venture, as did Warren Dutton, a lawyer and a Lowell in-law. The Israel Thorndikes, father and son, each subscribed for 10 shares. Others followed with more modest amounts: Benjamin Gorham, Uriah Cotting, John Gore. Then Jackson and Lowell came to the name of Nathan Appleton, in some ways their most difficult case. Appleton was a student of

the new social science of economics, having read the works of Adam Smith, David Ricardo, John Ramsay McCulloch, and others. Still he was not attached to the values of any one particular writer. "I have always made my system conform to facts," he wrote. So he waited for facts: he was able to recognize new conditions but unwilling to make them. His pleasure and his talent lay in careful calculations and well-chosen risks. This business sense was cultivated from the experience of generations of cautious Appleton enterprise. His ancestor, Samuel, the first Appleton to settle in the New World, left England for Ipswich in Massachusetts only after demanding and getting the personal assurance of John Winthrop that there would be enough cattle to support his large family.

Nathan Appleton was well read in the science of his day, but he trusted only what he saw. Timing was the basis of sound business decisions, and for at least three years Appleton waited for the signs that cotton manufacturing was a sound investment. He had long conversations with Lowell about the subject in 1810, when it happened that both were at Edinburgh, Scotland. Appleton was interested enough to visit New Lanark, near Edinburgh, where Robert Owen had built a factory on the Clyde River so considerate of its workers that even American Virtue was not shocked at seeing it. It was proof that factories need not degrade the workers who labored in them.

Appleton monitored Lowell's progress and was duly impressed with the mechanical magic of the power loom. More appreciative of business skills, Appleton may have been even more impressed by the performance of Patrick Tracy Jackson, who came dangerously close to bankruptcy in 1811 and yet recovered his fortune. Finally, Appleton was impressed when war began with England in 1812 and the flood of English cotton imports came to an abrupt stop: domestic cotton manufacturing promised high profits for prompt investors. Still, Appleton hesitated. When Jackson and Lowell offered him 10 shares of the BMC, Appleton accepted five "until the experiment was fairly tried."

With the technology and the labor and the capital assembled at Waltham, the BMC built the first factory in any country where all the cotton processes were done by machine under one roof. This "integrated factory" was a resounding success. Even after British imports were readmitted to the American market in 1815, the Boston Manufacturing Company proved itself a type for survival. By 1817 there were two more mills at Waltham, but by 1817 all the power available from the Charles River had been used; further expansion forced the search that brought Appleton and his friends to Pawtucket Falls. Many of the individuals important to the triumph of the Boston Manufacturing had living roots in the Merrimack Valley: Lowell, Jackson, Moody, Appleton, Perkins, Dutton were all recent transplants. The move from Waltham to

Chelmsford appears then as a kind of homecoming. So it seems. But there is the career of Nathan Appleton to tell a different story. The Souhegan was his native river, and if home was the object, he twice passed up the opportunity to invest in that: the first time at New Ipswich in 1810, and the second time at Amherst in September 1821. Appleton doubted until the Boston Manufacturing Company had proved itself, and if he shared with his colleagues an instant approval of Pawtucket Falls, it was because the choice was obvious. In choosing Pawtucket Falls it was power they came to, not place.

Waterpower is measured in the ratio of volume to drop, and since Pawtucket Falls offered a drop of some 30 feet over the entire breadth of the Merrimack, it was clear that the site was a major resource. The Boston Associates, as the Waltham group came to be called, obtained a charter from the General Court in February 1822, incorporating them as the Merrimack Manufacturing Company. This corporation set out immediately to buy the land and water rights it would need at Chelmsford. Most of the land was acquired in three major blocks, the three farms of the area owned by the Fletcher, the Tyler, and the Cheever families. The rights to the power were bought from the owners of the Pawtucket Canal, who had owned them since 1792 under their legal title, the Proprietors of Locks and Canals on Merrimack River.

The Pawtucket was built as a transportation canal, merely a loop, to get river traffic around the falls when the falls were more a hazard and a nuisance in the business of commerce than a manageable source of industrial power. Now that technology had caught up to the prospect, the Merrimack Manufacturing Company intended to use the Pawtucket as a feeder canal. It would carry a volume of water maintained at the level above Pawtucket Falls, where the entrance to the canal was located, to the site of their mills so that, there, it could be dropped back into the Merrimack at a point below the falls. The water was diverted a total distance of perhaps a mile and a half on the horizontal line, and then dropped a total of 30 feet on the vertical where it reached the Merrimack Mills. The wheels were located beneath the mills, and, as was the rule, their diameter was equal to the distance of the fall. Gravity did the rest. Once the water was set loose at the top of the wheel it dropped in a direct vertical line, but the wheel translated that into a rotary motion, and it was this motion—transmitted up in a system of belts, pulleys, and shafts through the stories of the mill—that *each* machine again translated into all the motions it was designed to perform.

Like all the corporations of the Boston Associates, Merrimack Manufacturing Company followed a pattern of structure inherited from the merchant background of the principals. Its chief executive was the treasurer (Patrick Tracy Jackson), while full authority on the site was vested in an agent, Kirk Boott. Until his death in 1837, it was Boott who supervised the construction of mills and canals and the manufacturing of cloth. He was suited to the task by temperament and training. Some said he was far too suited, since his experience as a British officer had left him with the disposition of a tyrant.

Born in Boston of a British mercantile family, Anglophile Kirk Boott (1790-1837) was the resident agent of the Merrimack Manufacturing Company who had primary responsibility for planning and executing the development of Lowell. Although rigid he was respected, and this portrait by Chester Harding was commissioned by the Middlesex Mechanics Association and paid for in subscriptions democratically limited to no more than five dollars each. Begun from life, it was completed after his death. Courtesy, Pollard Memorial Library, Lowell.

Preparations were completed on schedule. The first cloth made by the Merrimack Mills came off a power loom operated by Deborah Skinner, whom Moody had brought from Waltham to train the labor force at the new mills. That was in November 1823. Only the previous May, however, the directors of Merrimack Manufacturing had met at

Chelmsford and begun the process of reorganizing its resources, retaining only the land and power needed for its own operation, and transferring all that remained of both to the Proprietors of Locks and Canals on Merrimack River. Familiarly called the Locks and Canals, this former commercial enterprise became the developer and power broker of the site, selling land to other textile corporations as these were chartered by the General Court, and leasing to them the mill powers of the Merrimack in a most exact accounting. The Locks and Canals was reconstituted in 1825, and with these financial and organizational issues resolved, the site was ready for the intense industrial activity that characterized the place for a quarter of a century.

In 1826, as if to affirm the beginning of a new era in the story of the lower Merrimack, the site of the mills at

Both neighbors and the nation were curious to see the mills that had grown up in the meadow, and several views of Lowell were made. This 1848 engraving showing the town from the Dracut shore appeared on sample folders of cloth printed by the Merrimack Manufacturing Company, and the mills depicted are (from left to right) the Massachusetts, the Boott, the Merrimack, and the Lawrence corporations. (MVTM)

Chelmsford was separated, given independent political existence, by the General Court. The new town was named in honor of Francis Cabot Lowell, who had died in 1817; it seemed fitting, at least to Appleton, to commemorate his part in the coming of age of America. Lowell was literally on the map. By coincidence, 1826 was the 50th anniversary of the Declaration of Independence. By a more arresting coincidence, it was the year that John Adams and Thomas Jefferson died, both on the Fourth of July, removing the last living tie to America's Revolution.

Textile corporations now sprang up like mushrooms. The Hamilton (1825), the Appleton (1828), the Lowell (1828), the Middlesex (1830), the Suffolk and Tremont (1832), the Lawrence (1833), the Boott (1835), and the Massachusetts (1839) were added to Merrimack Manufacturing, and these together were the Big 10 among a host of other, smaller and ancillary, operations. It was a scale that impressed contemporaries, and it's easy to see why. By 1840 these corporations controlled a capitalization of $10.5 million, while in 1813 at the same place, Fletcher and Whiting had built their cotton "manufactory" for a mere $2,500. By 1840 the Big 10 were producing over 1.1 million yards of cloth each week, most of that in cotton goods. It was also the pace that im-

MERRIMACK PRINTS

LOWELL MASS.

pressed contemporaries. In 1836 Lowell was given a city charter, only the third such charter in Massachusetts, and four years later Lowell was the second-largest city in the Commonwealth. This physical burgeoning, this explosion of population and concentration of mills, was regulated by the capacities of the engineers at the Locks and Canals to exploit every means they could devise to wring power from the Merrimack; that is where the throttle of the operation lay. Until 1845 the Locks and Canals was also the parent corporation of the Lowell Machine Shop, so that it had for those 20 years (1825-1845) a very good claim to being the most important technological firm in the nation. In addition to being a symbol of American social innovation, Lowell also was a shrine of American engineering.

To be sure, it was hydraulics, the engineering of water, that dominated at Lowell at the time. In the first decade or so it was Kirk Boott as agent of Merrimack Manufacturing, and Paul Moody as superintendent of the machine shop, who directed the design and construction of Lowell's power system. For a brief time (1834-1837), George Washington Whistler was in charge as chief engineer at the Locks and Canals. Whistler was a graduate of the military academy at West Point, which was then by far the best, and very nearly the only, school for engineers in the United States. To replace him the directors of the Locks and Canals chose his assistant, a very young man and yet another British immigrant. James B. Francis was 22 in 1837, having learned what he could of engineering from his father while in England, and from Whistler in the four years since coming to America in 1833. He followed his mentor from assignment to assignment, but at Lowell they parted. Whistler moved on, pursuing a career that took him to czarist Russia, where he died in 1849. Francis had found his career: he was chief engineer at the Locks and Canals from

George Washington Whistler (1800-1849), the son of a British soldier, became an officer in the U.S. Army and trained as an engineer at West Point. After working as a surveyor for several early railroads, Whistler became chief engineer of Lowell's Locks and Canals corporation, where from 1834-1837 he ran the machine shop and designed locomotives. His skill in civil and mechanical engineering took him to Russia, where he served as a consultant for the building of the railroad between St. Petersburg and Moscow, and where he died of cholera. Courtesy, Lowell Historical Society.

James Bicheno Francis (1815-1892), a British immigrant, succeeded Whistler as chief engineer at Locks and Canals and devoted his extraordinary talents to improving the canal system and water turbines. His book, Lowell Hydraulic Experiments, *published in 1855, made Lowell's technological advances known among engineers worldwide. (MVTM)*

1837 until his retirement in 1882.

Francis was among a handful of mathematicians and engineers—Swiss, French, and English—who developed the water turbine, a device more efficient at taking power from falling water; these began to replace the older water-wheels in the wheel pits of the Lowell mills during the later 1840s. Francis also made important improvements in the city's canal system, the system that delivered the fall of water to the turbines. In 1837 five power canals were completed at Lowell. The Hamilton (1826), the Lowell (1828), the Western (1832), and the Eastern (1835) had been added to the first power canal at Lowell, the Merrimack, completed in 1823.

However, by 1840 these "ditches" were distributing the waters of the Merrimack to 32 mills, and delivering the volume needed for this scale of things had become a strain on the capacity of the Pawtucket Canal, the only feeder bringing water into those six power canals. Moreover, in the years from 1840 to 1845 there were several seasons of drought, and that created real anxiety about the future of the mills at Lowell. Two ways were found to repair these soft points in the power system. First, Francis supervised the construction of a second feeder, the Northern Canal. The work was difficult and expensive, involving the construction of a river wall to keep the waters in the Northern separate from, and 30 feet above, the waters of the Merrimack. In conjunction with this, Francis also built the Moody Street Feeder, an underground conduit moving water directly from the Western into the Merrimack Canal. Both of these were finished in 1848, after 18 months of arduous effort and an expenditure of half a million dollars.

But marvelous as this work was, it was useless without the assurance that there would be enough water flowing down the Merrimack to maintain the canal system at capacity. And to do this the Locks and Canals took its second step to improve the system. In 1845 the corporation bought the outlets of several bays and lakes in New Hampshire and also bought the rights to control the flow of water through these outlets. In times of low water, then, the Locks and Canals was able to release the reserves in New Hampshire and so meet its contractual obligations to the textile corporations at Lowell, its legal promise to deliver a stated volume of water to their penstocks. This reserve system was regulated from Lowell on information transmitted to the city by observers reporting on rainfalls and on water levels from their locations in New Hampshire.

Impressive as these achievements were, it was his "Folly" that earned Francis the gratitude of the people of Lowell. He saw that the canal system was a physical invitation to disaster, inasmuch as it brought the waters of the Merrimack into the heart of the city. When the Merrimack reached flood stage, as it did periodically, the city would be inundated. To prevent this, Francis built a massive gate across the Pawtucket Canal shortly past the point where it leaves the river; the gate was suspended above the canal against the possibility of the rising of the Merrimack. Contemporaries were ill-advised to call it the Francis Folly, since the gate was let down once in 1852 and again in 1936 to prevent major flooding of Lowell.

In his lifetime James B. Francis wrote more than 200 papers for the learned societies of the world; in 1855 he published *The Lowell Hydraulic Experiments*. Whatever this publicity did for him, it also put the development of the lower Merrimack among the leaders of world-class engineering. Indeed, the development of human capacity to control and exploit the power of the Merrimack had been nothing short of a wonder in the half century since 1800. Then it was possible only to use the falls on the river's tributaries, and the major source of power, the Pawtucket Falls, had been an obstacle to avoid. However, in the 30 years after 1820, the falls themselves had been the site of prodigious learning, a veritable explosion of knowledge. The falls had in fact become the keystone in a vast system of power, covering hundreds of square miles of reserves in New Hampshire, and all of it focused on the need to drive the machines of textile production. Nevertheless, there was yet another step to take in this progress toward mastery of the river. After avoiding the falls in 1792, after exploiting the falls since 1820, engineers and manufacturers now moved to fabricate a falls by damming the river. That was done at the New City on the Merrimack, now Lawrence, Massachusetts, in the years from 1845 to 1848.

The site was Bodwell's Falls, a drop of some four feet that lay in the Merrimack nearly 11 miles below Lowell, at a spot where a bridge connected Andover on the southern side with Methuen on the northern. The idea for a dam on this site originated among some local entrepreneurs, notably Daniel Saunders, a man who had been involved one way or another in the manufacture of woolens since deciding, in 1817, that farming held no future for him. Local manufacturers, however, did not have the capital resources to finish anything like a project of this magnitude. So, it was again the Boston Associates, this time incorporated as the Essex Company in 1845, that undertook to finance the development of this site. The Lawrence brothers, Abbott and Amos, were most directly involved. Since organizing the Middlesex Mills at Lowell in 1830, these two late joiners had worked themselves into full membership in the Associates, and like most of these industrialists they had made their original fortune in commerce. The Essex Company included a machine shop in the plans for their New City, and though that firm never prospered financially, the building that housed it remains today perhaps the finest example of industrial architecture from that era still standing in the Valley of the lower Merrimack.

Of course, the Essex Campany also built a canal, which it located on the northern side of the Merrimack. Compared to the complex of canals at Lowell, distributed as these were and operating at two levels, the Northern Canal at Lawrence was a tame affair, finely designed but basically a straightforward trench describing a power island between itself and the river. The Great Stone Dam, however, was an epic construction. It ran the breadth of the Merrimack for more than 900 feet and rose from the bedrock of the river to a height of 36 feet. And it was built with no example in the world to follow. It was invented at the site.

Charles Storrow was the engineer in charge of construction, and it takes nothing from his task and his achievement to note that he was able to find a group of men distinguished for their talent and experience to assist and advise him. He had the services of Joseph Bennett to survey the site and locate the dam. The noted Uriah A. Boyden served as consulting engineer in the early stages of construction, while after 1846 Storrow's principal assistant was Charles Bigelow. A graduate of West Point (class of 1835), Bigelow had gained valuable experience while working with Colonel Sylvanus Thayer in building fortifications in Boston Harbor. Storrow also benefited from the advice of James B. Francis, though to what extent it is difficult to tell. But many of those experiments reported by Francis in *The Lowell Hydraulic Experiments* were done during the designing and construction of the Great Stone Dam. There were other, lesser lights who left the Locks and Canals to join Storrow in his magnificent project. There is the individual known only as Mr. Folsom, master stonecutter. And there was George Russy, who described himself as a self-trained engineer, having worked at various sites in New York State and as a draftsman for the corporation at Lowell.

Storrow himself had the benefit of opportunities that together made him one of the best-educated engineers in the country. While still an undergraduate at Harvard during the later 1820s, he had access to the books collected by the Loammi Baldwins, senior and junior, when theirs was the best engineering library in the United States outside West Point. Afterward Storrow studied at the French National School of Bridges and Roads at Paris, and made an extended tour of France and England to see for himself the engineering achievements of Europe. When he returned to America in 1833, he served as assistant to Loammi Baldwin, Jr., in building the Lowell-Boston railroad, which, as it happened, was often laid out on a line following the Middlesex Canal that Loammi Baldwin, Sr., had engineered some 40 years before. Storrow stayed with the Lowell and Boston line as general manager for 10 years after its completion in 1835. In undertaking the construction of the Great Stone Dam at Lawrence, Storrow drew on the resources of generations of experience, collected from his own study

Lawrence is shown while still under construction in the spring of 1848 in this lithograph by A. Conant of Providence. Much of Essex Street (center left) is lined with temporary wooden buildings, but the brick Mechanics Block (center right) stands completed in its square. Only the Machine Shop (left foreground) and one mill each of the Bay State and Atlantic corporations have been completed. More construction would follow until the mill island became a wall of brick. (MVTM)

and from those around him.

The dam was completed in three years to the day: the first stone was set down on September 19, 1845, and the last on September 19, 1848. The other components of the Essex Company's grand design, the North Canal and the machine shop, were also completed by 1848, so the place was made a going concern in rather a short time. Meanwhile, in 1847, the General Court of Massachusetts had set off seven square miles taken in equal portion from Andover and Methuen. Over the next decade the new town, Lawrence, saw the erection of several textile corporations designed to follow the Lowell model, each with its row of boardinghouses for the young women who were expected to labor in its mills. The Duck Mill, the impressive, nine-story Bay State Mills, the Atlantic and the Pacific, and the ill-fated Pemberton were in production before 1860. None of them, however, enjoyed the early prosperity that had marked the Lowell experience in the 1820s and 1830s. For the town of Lawrence the timing was unfortunate. The Essex Company began its project in 1845 under the sunshine of prosperity, but by the time cloth production had begun, a depression was at work in the national economy, which, then as now, seemed to operate beyond the reach of anyone's engineering.

To note that all the vast projects of power on the lower Merrimack were under the management of the Boston Associates, in its several corporate guises, is to note that a real change had come in the relations of the republic's citizens. Wealth and power were concentrated in 1860 as they had not been in 1800. Moreover, the power of the Merrimack belonged to no community on the Merrimack. It belonged rather to a new variety of community, with no particular loyalties to place and committed primarily to survival. Francis Cabot Lowell set a precedent in 1816 when he went to Washington to argue the case for a tariff to protect the new cotton industry. If there was not always a member of the Boston Associates in Congress during the succeeding years, the company was able to rely on the abilities of Daniel Webster, whose infinite appetite for money put him all too clearly in the pocket of those who provided him with "sweetners." And unlike the Federalists of the Essex Junto, the industrialists of the Boston Associates knew how to manage sectional alliances. They were called the lords of the loom, and, together with the slave-owning aristocracy of the Southern states, they were the central axis of the national Whig Party. But that party could not indefinitely contain the rising sentiment against slavery; that issue finally destroyed the Whigs as it divided the Union.

The revolution begun at Pawtucket Falls in November 1821 is so majestic in its scope that we are tempted from our vantage to see the hand of destiny at work, moving with a secret purpose to force the discovery. But that is not the story as Nathan Appleton tells it. This is what he says:

> I was at Waltham one day, when I was informed that Mr. Moody had lately been at Salisbury, when Mr. Ezra Worthen, his former partner, said to him, "I hear Messrs. Jackson and Appleton are looking out for water-power; why don't they buy up the Pawtucket Canal? That would give them the whole power of the Merrimack with a fall of over thirty feet."

His language skips along like a stone on the surface of the water, leaving behind a trail of widening circles until finally the circles touch and form a chain. This is how Appleton gets across to us, by adding segment to segment, each with the name of a person or a place and each with a verb to carry the name to the next connection. In his sentences, information comes at us in the making, the way events do. That is the reason it strikes us true: like Worthen and Moody and Appleton, we live in a network where information becomes event and event becomes information.

The process is constant and nearly invisible, as when we are at a gas station where we have been countless times before, and we meet an acquaintance who tells us his cousin is in town and his cousin has a friend whose father wants to sell his '54 T-bird. In fact, the car had been in his garage for 20 years, and it's at this point that it almost seems that the car has been waiting for us because that's how long we've been looking for it. So are events and information connected at an infinite number of points, and at each point of connection is a person. Most of these connec-

tions produce results that affect few people only, and only for a week or a month. At most they may last a lifetime. However, there are persons, and Appleton was among them, who operate in a different class of network when the information and events being swapped and sold and converted affect many people, whole regions of them and generations of them. These get more attention. These we drag out and call history.

Appleton is telling about events so successful at changing his world into ours that the events themselves come up like a wall when we try to see behind them. But here is the language of Appleton, with its construction of truth, to bring us the testimony of one who was there. It is experience and chance and attention, not Genius and not Fate, that move us across the surface of time.

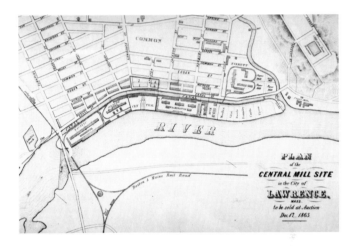

In 1863 one last mill site remained to be developed on the island along the North Canal. Sold at auction in December 1863, the central mill site became the worsted division of Pacific Mills, known as the Lower Pacific to distinguish it from the Upper Pacific located just below the dam. Because it occupied the central mill site on the island, this mill was also sometimes called the Central Pacific. The plan also shows land across the canal available for boardinghouses. (MVTM)

VI

NEW AMERICANS,
OLD DREAMS

The effective work of patriotic soldiers and sailors in the
war of the Rebellion and the war of the Revolution not only
saved the nation but made this Merrimack Valley in which we
live and labor a place where the workers of the world can
congregate in security and in peace.

— Robert Tewksbury, *Memorial Day address to a
group of schoolchildren at Lawrence,* circa 1905. Essex
Company Collection, MVTM.

In 1646 Andrew Greeley sailed up the Merrimack on a sloop that
took him as far as the head of navigation, where he was left on the sandy
banks of the river with his "store goods," farm tools, and farm supplies.
Andrew Greeley also carried leatherworking tools and presented himself
as an itinerant shoemaker. He had come some distance to the frontier of
Massachusetts, toting his goods and his skills, nursing a hope. Before him
was Haverhill, what there was of it: half a dozen log houses, each with a
clearing. Behind him, could he have seen them, were thousands like himself, tens of thousands, who reached landfall perhaps at Boston, likely at
New York, and traveled overland to the towns and cities on the

*Immigrants entered the retail trade and commercial pursuits as well as performing
factory labor. The Portugese owner and staff of Ostroff and Sousa Company's clothing
and millinery establishment on Gorham Street in Lowell pose in about 1910.
Courtesy, Lowell Historical Society.*

Two hundred years after Andrew Greeley's landing at Haverhill, the hard work of generations of immigrants had built a prosperous city. Gustavus Pfau's 1850 lithograph, taken from Silver Hill looking down Washington Street, shows a place that was home to nearly 6,000 people, a large percentage of them employed in the shoe trade. Both the railroad bridge (foreground) and the highway bridge were covered at this time. Courtesy, Boston Athenaeum.

Merrimack. For more than three centuries since 1646, now through 12 generations, a typical American has been a newcomer looking for work and ready to accept what there is of it. If one move was not enough, if conditions were not favorable or if the place became crowded—whenever success was illusive—it was possible to go elsewhere. So were the towns on the Merrimack planted, as corporate enterprises, groups of families on the move and assuming new collective names, christened by the authority of the General Court. So the Appletons, allied with others, moved from Lincolnshire to Massachusetts to New Hampshire.

A century later, when individuals were less restricted by communal control, mobility became a turbulent stream of individual ambitions. The father of Moses Hale moved his family from Newbury to Dracut, where he operated a fulling mill on Beaver Brook. In the next generation, Moses moved across the Merrimack to Chelmsford to locate his textile operation, and brother Ezekiel moved down the Merrimack to Haverhill to locate his. So, too, Oliver Whipple walked from his native Vermont to Southboro, Massachusetts, in 1815, and there he earned a capital of some several hundred dollars, which he then invested in a powder mill on the Concord at Chelmsford. Americans were made on the move and bred with the conviction that there would always be another chance. In the American experience the reality of Eden lay in the future, once a road to it was cleared. Black Africans, brought here by force to

labor for someone else, were excluded from this American dream, but the mass of arrivals, even the indentured servants of the 17th century, hoped that labor would earn them a "sufficiency," economic independence. In labor was freedom. It was a dream worth moving for.

From the time of settlement in the 1630s to the rise of Lowell two centuries later, farming dominated the economy of the Valley, and while this was true the family was the prevalent unit of labor. When nearly everything had to be done on site, it needed all the waking hours of a large family to make the farm a successful enterprise. Self-reliance was not a part-time job, nor for that matter did it ever rely exclusively on self. Driven by the Yankee virtues of thrift and industry and allowed only the enforced leisure of Sabbath, family labor was not regulated by any clock but by the rising and setting of the sun, moving within the longer rhythms of the seasons. From November to March, when New England winters put an end to nearly all work on the land, the family retreated indoors, to kitchens and barns, and filled many dreary snowbound hours making products for market. These "domestic industries" provided a significant portion of a family's support and would often mark the difference between bare survival and the addition of a small surplus, the family's profit at the end of a year's work. Normally, domestic industries centered on a product of everyday use, something of clothing or dress for instance. Considered ideal for domestic manufacture was some product, then, that had a mass market but did not require farm families to make a large investment in tools or large investments of time in learning skills they would not otherwise need in their daily and seasonal farm chores. And it helped if it was small and light enough for a child's hands, for none was left idle in the domestic labor force.

Though this tradition of manufacture can be traced nearly to the origins of Massachusetts Bay, it was in that first generation after Independence, from 1790 to 1820, that it

Farm chores didn't change with the coming of the factory, but markets for farm products expanded to include the new factory towns. This wooden pantry box for holding butter or other food protected Farmer Gray's product on its way to the point of sale or in the pantry. Similar in design to Shaker boxes, it measures eight and three-quarters inches in diameter and four inches high. Courtesy, North Andover Historical Society.

Recreational activities occupied the young of the 19th century just as they do today, although sports equipment was more primitive. Ice skates fashioned from wood with iron runners were attached to the skater's leg with leather straps. Iron spikes held the shoe firmly in place, but must have made new heels a frequent necessity. Courtesy, North Andover Historical Society.

Newburyport's Market Square, shown here about 1870, was the scene of economic transactions throughout the 19th century. Local farmers brought produce to the market building (at right, with white awning), which also housed town offices and fire engines. (MVTM)

reached its zenith. The towns on the lower Merrimack lie at the northern end of Middlesex and Essex counties, and in both counties the domestic industries of farm families were tied to the butcheries and tanneries concentrated at the southern end. A census of "American Manufactures," taken in 1810, reveals the importance of leather in the domestic manufactures on the lower Merrimack. Products and their dollar value were tabulated by county, and this makes it difficult to know the level of production attained in regions such as the Valley. Still, domestic industry produced about 2.2 million shoes in Massachusetts that year, and 86.11 percent of them were made by the households of Essex and Middlesex. Essex County alone accounted for more than 1.5 million shoes, and shoe production in Essex was in fact the only enterprise in the entire Commonwealth in 1810 with a product value of more than a million dollars.

In a textbook example of the vigor and ingenuity of Yankee economy, the census of 1810 also counted some 105,000 combs made in Essex County, carved from the horns of the same animals whose hides were stiched into shoes—or gloves. Domestic manufacture of combs of every description and quality survived in the Newburys down to the second and third decade of this century, but it was shoemaking that occupied by far the largest number of individuals and families in the towns of the lower Merrimack. In 1810 Haverhill and Bradford were already established as centers of shoemaking. The leadership of Haverhill as a shoe city in the 20th century rested securely on a knowing labor force created during the era of domestic manufacture.

Isaac Watts Merrill (1803-1878) kept a diary for nearly 50 years in which he recorded the activities of his life as a shoemaker, farmer, and ordinary citizen. His Haverhill home, built in 1828 of locally made bricks, was photographed in 1878, the year Merrill died. The men at the left are probably his nephews James and Moses Merrill, who inherited the place, and the women may be their wives or sisters. Courtesy, Trustees of the Haverhill Public Library.

Three cordwainers work at their benches in a typical shoemaker's shop. A town meeting notice is on the right wall. Known for their active political participation and often radical views, shoemakers elected a strong socialist government in Haverhill in the 1890s. (MVTM)

Economics was by no means the only dimension of family relations, no more in 1782 than in 1982, but in that dimension family had the structure of a labor exchange where there was very little cash, if there was any at all, and where the books were kept in terms of service. It was service, too, that knit scattered farmsteads into a neighborhood, for each family depended from time to time on the like economy of its neighbors so that each accepted the conditions that made cooperation necessary. Scarcity of labor made cooperation the virtue of place. Each one day would likely help a neighbor dig a well or raise a well crotch because he was certain on the next day, or the one after that, to need help himself, and this regular exchange of time and energy—not cash—made the character of their relations obvious. This may indeed be part of what Thoreau meant in his *Week on the Concord and Merrimack Rivers* when he praised labor as "carrying into practice certain essential information." It was certainly part of what Emerson acknowledged in December 1838 when he began a lecture by declaring, "a household is the school of power."

Emerson was in the lecture business, and he knew his audience would understand and accept that sort of overture because the larger part of the populations at Concord or Haverhill was still living in a mixed economy, one in which cash transactions were only a portion of the larger process of production and consumption. No doubt gain was the object and ambition a force. There are enough recorded insults given and taken, enough lawsuits over property, to keep us from idealizing these Valley residents and their economic relations. Emerson did not try to tell them that a household was the school of the feckless. The point remains that during the 1820s and 1830s, even through the 1840s, the American economy was within the comprehension of the average citizen and so put the average citizen within the possibility of effective control over some portion of it. Until the eve of the Civil War, a significant part of the Valley's population lived in an economy that offered multiple relations in getting and spending, and a series of dealings that made many persons participants in the transactions deciding their economic well-being.

There is the case of Isaac Merrill. He was born at Haverhill in 1803 and died there in 1878, making him a contemporary of Emerson, who died some four years later in 1882. Effectively, they were witness to the same America. Merrill traveled a fair amount in his long life but never very far and not for long, and he always returned to Haverhill. For his amusement Merrill kept a diary from 1828 until shortly before his death, and fortunately for us it recently was brought back to light. He was a shoemaker all his life and worked at his home, located very literally within a stone's throw of the sovereign state of New Hampshire. He earned a good living at his work, but his diary shows him spending a considerable amount of time caring for his

The shoe trade brought prosperity to Haverhill, but it suffered from the ups and downs caused by overproduction and competition, as did the textile industry. This view of Water Street, looking east from White's Corner in about 1868, shows a commercial center of some liveliness despite the snow. Many of the sleighs were probably made in and around Amesbury, famous for its carriage-building trade. Courtesy, Trustees of the Haverhill Public Library.

crops and livestock, and sometimes helping his father and occasionally a neighbor in caring for theirs. In April 1859, Merrill notes having "settled with father," that after 14 years of open account the total cash value of his indebtedness was $192.91. A part at least of his gainful employ happened outside the cash connection. By contrast, his brother Gyles, who was visiting in April 1859 was a superintendent of the Vermont Central Railway at a yearly salary of $3,000.

On the shoemaking side of Merrill's economy, he operated in a situation that allowed some choice of the dealer he would sell his shoes to and on what terms. Like all "shoemakers" Merrill did not market his own product, leaving that to the "manufacturers" who collected shoes from several makers and packed them off to markets in Philadelphia and Baltimore. In March 1832 there were 28 shoe "manufacturers" at Haverhill, and of these, 16 were also dealers in "English and West Indies Goods." It is easy to see how the dealers of shoes would often pay the makers of shoes in goods as well as cash; cash was generally at this period a small part of the price paid for making shoes. The

coming of the railroad to Haverhill in 1841 began the process of consolidating the business of marketing shoes, so that shoe "manufacturers" began to see the advantage of consolidating the business of making shoes—under their control. By April 1859 shoemakers of the Merrill type were numbering their days, poised at the beginning of a frightening decade when the market economy would turn the character of their labor inside out. An editorial published in the (Haverhill) *Gazette*, June 26, 1858, explains how reasonable the change was:

A bolt label for cloth made and printed by the Merrimack Manufacturing Company in Lowell pictures women weaving at their looms and a man adjusting a cylinder printing machine. Cloth labels marked piece lot and yardage consigned to the selling agent. Interior views of factories from this period (1840-1850) are rare, and it is unusual for a label to show the process of goods being made. Lowell was an object of nearly universal curiosity, however, which this marketing device was designed to satisfy. (MVTM)

We recently had a conversation with one of our largest and most enterprising shoe manufacturers, in which he urged the necessity of holding out inducements to shoemakers in New Hampshire and the various towns in this state, who are engaged in the business to remove into town, where they can get more pay and be more sure of work than those who live at a distance, etc., etc. Manufacturers would pay 20% more and the expense of transport would be saved &c. If manufacturers would present this subject to their workmen showing them the advantages of being located here, and pay them a little extra for their labor, when they remove we should soon have a desirable change in this respect.

For 20 percent more in cash, shoemakers would be persuaded to become shoeworkers: instead of a product to sell for a price, they would have labor to sell for wage. For 20 percent more in cash, they would entrust their economic well-being exclusively to one manufacturer's ability to follow a market of a million shoes, with no real assurance that this person had 10 times more capacity to do this than any one smaller manufacturer had used in following a market of 100,000 shoes. For cash he was asked to eliminate competition among shoe manufacturers, when that competition was the field of option where his choice was accepted as a value. So, at the time of the Civil War (1861) the shoemakers of the Merrimack Valley were about to notice what the textile workers had noticed 20 or 30 years before: labor had become an activity done for cash, and one that offered no hope of ever reaching the point of control. The control belonged to the person who bought the labor. The textile workers at Lowell were among the first Americans to make that observation, because they were among the first to be given the prospect to see it. The female mill operatives assembled on the Merrimack during the 1820s and 1830s were at the vanguard where labor in America began its transformation into American Labor, the point where the story of American working classes begins.

The technology perfected at Lowell had a long history of development, but the Lowell mill girls were almost without precedent, and by their numbers and example they were something entirely new. Before Lowell, textile mills in the Valley were small and so drew their laborers from the immediate vicinity. The physical setting of these early mills, neither country nor city, has been described as a middle landscape, and this was also an early image of Lowell advertised by friendly critics. As places of labor these mills were, again, a middle way. Much of the relations among workers and mill owners during this early period from 1790 to 1820 remains obscure, and it will take more research before the picture is clarified. However, there is no doubt that it was an intermediary stage in the evolution of the American workingman and -woman, and the introduction of the power loom was vital in ending that stage. As long as weaving was done on hand looms (until the century's second decade for cottons and the 1820s for woolens), it was necessary for mill owners to hire hand-weavers, men and women, who practiced an ancient trade, one with virtually no ceiling on the level of skill it could provoke. Machine-spun yarn was often "put out" to local weavers, and weaving done this way was a part of domestic manufactures. Otherwise, handweavers might be set up in a room or attic of a mill in a sort of shop. Wherever they were put, they were a bottleneck in the production of cloth, for no handweaver could hope to keep up with the supply of yarn spun by machine.

Paul Moody, trained first in handweaving by James Scholfield and trained later by Jacob Perkins as a machinist, was able to enjoy the practice of his abilities in both. But there were few so fortunate. The power loom eliminated the bottleneck in cloth production, and it also eliminated a degree of skill in the weaver. The skill in weaving was now shared by the skill of the machinist in making the loom, and the weaver became to some degree a machine tender. Managers and overseers were happy with this mechanization of clothmaking because it served their purpose of rationalizing the work process and brought them that much closer to total domination of the workplace. All the labor of making cloth was recast to fit the mold of their system, in which productivity and profit were the only recognized objectives and management the supreme skill.

So, in 1837, Abbott Lawrence was delighted to find William Crompton, yet another immigrant English machinist, who said he could find a way to quick-change the pattern program of a power loom. Without such a device American manufacturers could not compete in the fashion market of fancy woolens against the high quality of English imports. The power loom worked well enough with sturdy cotton yarns in 1813, and it had been improved since then to make satinet, which mixed a cotton warp with a woolen weft, and plain woolens. But the weaving of fancy woolens remained in the preserve of handweavers and constituted one of the last pockets of personal skill holding forth amid the machine technology of textiles. By 1840, Crompton delivered his invention, and the improved looms were installed in the Middlesex Mills, owned by Abbott Lawrence and his brothers. The fancy woolens made at Lowell were not quite so fine as the English product, still made by hand, but they were cheaper and that made them

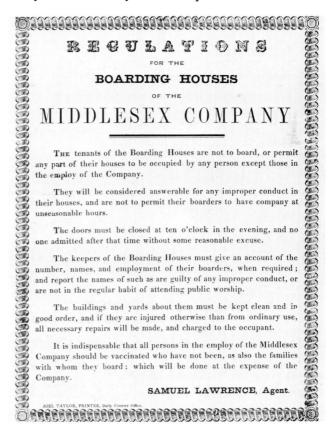

Corporation housing provided a convenient means of controlling the morality of the working population. The boardinghouse matron, acting "in loco parentis," made sure that the young women in her charge followed the regulations of curfew, good conduct, and church attendance. (MVTM)

preferable to the growing appetite of American consumers. The market economy had worked its magic, and another cluster of skilled laborers evaporated under its wand.

The loss and transfer of skills in the making of cloth was a long process and of course it was part of another process, the technological revolution. And from a beginning, say in 1790, to an end, say in 1840, the workingmen and working-women of the Valley lived between two economic systems. On the one hand was the failing economy of domestic manufactures, where products were made by households as part of the economy of family labor. On the other hand, there was the emerging economy centered on the fiscal structure of the corporation, bent on shaping and kneading a labor force to its image and likeness. In the half-century of adjustment the workers of the Valley were given a choice between them, like the Pennacooks who had preferred to bivouac where ecotonal zones offered alternate food chains on which to prey. Many men and women chose the new economy, they chose the Lowell system. However, by the decade of the 1840s it became clear to an increasing number of Lowell workers that the market economy made demands

The boardinghouse system of factory labor, as introduced at Lowell, was continued at Lawrence. It employed large numbers of single women housed together under the supervision of a resident matron who acted on behalf of the corporation. This stereograph of Lawrence in the mid-1870s affords a fine view of the Atlantic Cotton Mills at the right, and across the canal, the double rows of corporation boardinghouses along Canal and Methuen streets. The Moseley truss bridge in the center of the picture still spans the North Canal, but only a section of the mill building and one boardinghouse remain standing. (MVTM)

of them that they were not willing to meet. They rebelled and they fled, but they failed to make the voice of labor an integral part of the directorate now taking command of production at the industrial centers of the Valley.

Of all the stories told about the Merrimack Valley, none is more famous than the story of the Lowell mill girls. Poets sang about them and dignitaries came from Europe and from the far corners of America to see for themselves whether it was true that people could work in factories and still be contented and moral. The French economist Michel Chevalier, on an official visit of inspection for his government in June 1834, compared Lowell's mill girls to nuns in the neatness and femininity of their work habits. Others have preferred to compare them to students, together for a time in dormitory-like boardinghouses, laboring toward similar futures and leaving after three or four years to take with them a host of sweet and dear memories. And there was more than one minister to invoke the discipline of labor—the rod of the ancient Puritan God—to explain that Lowell was in fact both a church and a school.

But for the mill girls themselves, living through the Lowell experiment was work, long hours of it at a stretch, before they could take the time to comprehend what else it might be. In November 1823, when the Merrimack Manufacturing Company began cloth production, and for a decade after, Lowell kept the promises it made, those it needed to make, to attract farm women to labor in its mills. They were housed and fed reasonably according to the standards of the time, and the long hours of their work were no longer than they would have faced at home, on the land. Their wages were generous when compared to the alternatives open to women in the 1820s. They were paid from $2.25 to $3.50 for a 60-hour week, from which they paid their own board of one dollar a week. These figures are appalling to us, but they were then quite attractive to a girl in the farming towns of New Hampshire and Vermont. Even at 14 or 15 years of age, such a girl was quite aware what her future would be like if she rejected the opportunity of work at Lowell. She might stay at Nelson or Claremont or Woodstock and marry a farmer like her father. She might even be lucky enough to rouse the attention of a man whose land was sufficient to support a household. In any case, it would be days and seasons of work and no more freedom than her father had allowed her.

She could choose instead, or have it chosen for her, to migrate to the West. Thousands of farm families did leave New Hampshire and Vermont after 1810, happy to exchange the difficult soil of upcountry farms for the larger, flatter, and stone-free soil of the Ohio Valley. There were other thousands, however, who interpreted the American tradition of moving-on to counsel another course. These migrated to Lowell and other industrial cities then growing on the banks of the Merrimack and elsewhere. So in addition to the pull of Lowell there was the push of the land, which offered a difficult life for all in the best of economies and made it pointless for many, since the Embargo of 1807 separated them from the lucrative markets of Europe.

Lowell promised freedom from these doubts and pressures as it promised work and an income, so that arriving at Lowell must have been part relief and part exhilaration. After this came the slow discovery, delivered through a network of kin and friend, that Lowell was not only a new town but also a haven of the young where a girl might find thousands like herself to share interests common to young women through the years from 1820 to 1840: clothes, marriage, books of devotion and fiction, sound preaching from a good minister and, under it all, "self-improvement." Their motives for work were less altruistic, less centered on family, than they once were thought to have been. Still, there was more than one Lowell girl who gave part of her wages to help with a father's mortgage or a brother's education. Ties to family were not severed when it was at all possible to keep them, and this fact was significant in making Lowell's labor force a transient one. Mill girls would work for two or three years, than leave Lowell to return home, perhaps simply for the change of it but more likely for a rest from the pace and confinement of mill work. Though these women were used to long hours of labor, they were not accustomed to working with machines that set the pace of work and demanded that human partners keep up. And like their menfolk the farm women were not used to the clatter of the textile mill, and the heat and moisture needed to make carding and spinning feasible.

The Lowell mills were to these women a place to join or leave as circumstance or decision might say, but never a place to find lifelong employment. Even as late as 1845 the average length of stay at Lowell was four and a half years. Those who were tied permanently to mill work by necessity were the object of concern and pity by their sisters, and too often the object of their own curse. The Lowell experience was helpful to a majority of its workers during that first decade, but soon enough there was trouble in this paradise of labor.

The first "turnout" (strike) in the Valley occurred in 1834, when the corporations lowered wages by 12 to 25 percent. There was another turnout in 1836 when the amount withheld for room and board was increased to $1.37½ a week, an increase of $.12½. But these strikes, and others, were not effective against the textile corporations. Workers could refuse to work, but the solidarity needed to make the refusal effective was sabotaged by the fact that the strikers were also boarders in corporate housing, and by the fact as well that so many of them had no means of support during the strike. Some left the city. Yet if a woman

Working hours in mill towns were regulated by the factory bells, and corporations in Lowell resisted installation of church and city bells in order to control even the time of day. Hours were staggered to make best use of available light, but winter evening work required the use of oil and, later, gas lamps. The Saturdays closest to March 20th and September 20th were celebrated (respectively) with "Blowing Out" and "Lighting Up" balls. (MVTM)

thought she might need or want to work at a textile mill the future, she was well advised to be quiet about anything she disliked or found unjust in the Lowell system. A troublemaker was blacklisted and the list was circulated to other mill towns from Dover, New Hampshire, to Chicopee, Massachusetts, where the mills often were owned by the same men who owned the mills at Lowell.

There was no surer way to blacklisting and dismissal than for a woman to attempt to organize her fellow operatives, but the Lowell women organized nevertheless. There was a short-lived Factory Girls' Association formed during the turnout of 1836. The more durable Lowell Female Labor Reform Association was founded in January 1845 by 15 women, including the tireless Sarah Bagley. Lowell women also joined with others, male and female, to participate in the New England Workingmen's Association, which held a convention at Lowell in March 1845. The sense that workers were able to get of their situation was expressed by Josephine Baker, who signed herself J.L.B. when she wrote for the *Lowell Offering* (April 1845):

> There is a class, of whom I would speak, that work in the mills, and will while they continue in operation. Namely, the many who have no home, and who come here to seek, in this busy, bustling "City of Spindles," a competency that shall enable them in after life, to live without being a burden to society,—the many who toil on, without a murmur, for the support of an aged mother or orphaned brother and sister. For the sake of them, we earnestly hope labor may be reformed; that the miserable, selfish spirit of competition, now in our midst, may be thrust from us and consigned to eternal oblivion.

The thrust is obviously set against the argument used by the Lowell corporations when faced with worker demands, that conditions of the marketplace forced them to compete with other like corporations and that productivity had to be increased or the company would fail, and the workers would lose their income. So when weavers were "stretched out"—asked to tend three looms instead of two, or four instead of three—they were given to understand that it was necessary for their own self-interest. The same reasoning explained the "speed-up," when machines were made to run faster, or the "bonus system," which rewarded overseers for their skill at managing workers to produce at a piece rate. And indeed productivity did rise. According to figures "compilled from authentic sources"—from the corporations, that is—Lowell's 10 large corporations together produced 125 yards per worker per week in 1836, while in 1860 they produced 188 yards per worker per week. Yet, somehow, that rise of productivity never appeared in the laborers' pay envelopes. The average wage in 1860 was exactly the average in 1836: $2 a week clear of board for females and 80 cents a day clear of board for males.

There is no need to seek the hidden hand of God or the perverse will of any devil for what followed. With the best wills in the world, corporate directors were overwhelmed by the demands of leadership, which, nevertheless, they insisted was theirs alone. Panics and recessions appeared and vanished at will, and the appeal to the Natural Laws of economics made by Abbott Lawrence during the crisis of 1837 had no effect whatever except to calm his nerves. The truth is that corporate leaders were puzzled by the forces of the market and so were powerless to control them. Naturally, they lay hands on what they could control, the productive system, provided only that the productive system could be shaped to give the handles they thought should be there.

Prophecies have a way of becoming self-fulfilling, and the directors of corporate industry on the Merrimack prophesied that the end of production is profit.

Some of the women who protested the system of labor at Lowell spoke of themselves as the "daughters of freemen" and saw their struggle against the power of money as a continuation of their grandfathers' struggle against the English crown. They pleaded, threatened, explained, testified without outcome. Nothing they said or did had any consequence on the terms of their labor. It's fitting perhaps that the grave of Sarah Bagley is unknown, invisible as well as mute to us, if only because it forces us finally to hear her words published in the *Voice of Industry* as the true monument to so many lives like her own. By 1850 the same network of kin and friend that had praised labor at Lowell in the past now carried the message that despite marvels of engineering and feats of productivity, Lowell as

Sarah G. Bagley, a New Hampshire-born weaver, also worked in the warp dressing room. She may have been a drawing-in girl, like the one pictured here, drawing warp ends through the reed in preparation for setting up the loom to weave. No known likeness exists of Bagley, an articulate writer and speaker on behalf of labor reform. Founder and first president of the Female Labor Reform Association of Lowell, she worked in the mills for more than a decade between 1837-1849. (MVTM)

Winslow Homer's New England Factory Life—Bell Time, *engraved for* Harper's Weekly, *portrays the rush hour of 1868, when crowds of working people left the mills to walk home along the tree-lined canals. Carrying their lunch pails, old and young, Yankee and immigrant, they swelled the ranks of every town in the Valley after the Civil War. This scene illustrates the Washington Mills at Lawrence, where Homer's brother worked. (MVTM)*

an experiment in labor had failed. Thousands left the city and there was one, at least, who moved on and pursued elsewhere the American dream of free labor that had eluded her at Lowell.

Mary Paul had come to Lowell in November 1845, at the age of 15, and worked there, off and on, for about four years. When she left in 1849, she returned to live for a time with her father, described as a shoemaker at Claremont, New Hampshire. In the early 1850s she worked as a seamstress at Brattleboro, Vermont, but in May 1854 she arrived at the North American Phalanx (Redbank, New Jersey). It seems a strange career but it was not uncommon of its generation, sharing as that generation did the migrating habits of American workers, and wedded to a mission all its own to fabricate a better community out of self-improvement and labor reform.

There were many such communities in the 1840s and later, from Brook Farm to Salt Lake, some of them claiming descent from Christ and some of them not. The community chosen by Mary Paul followed the teachings of Charles Fourier, whose blueprint for the Phalanx promised to integrate individual ambition with the common wealth of all. Mary Paul stayed a full year at the North American Phalanx, and its failure in the summer of 1855 did not dim the vision she had found in it. For her the failure was neither conclusive nor permanent. After all, she told her father in her letters, because the Phalanx was "but an

experiment of itself there must be many failures, since man is not perfect." The community, she explained, was a joint stock corporation with the workers holding the stock and exercising authority together. There was only one member, a man, who was too poor to own even the smallest share of the venture, but she doubted that even he was denied the right to vote, "for although he is poor he is very useful & probably that balances his deficiency in *money.*" Her conclusion after one year's observation was that "imperfect as it is I have already seen enough to convince me that Association is the true life."

The daughter of a shoemaker from Claremont, "common schooled" in a farming village like most of the women who worked in the mills at Lowell, was able enough to judge for herself the character of republics as she joined and left. She did not need James Madison to tell her that man is not perfect, or that society must take notice of that. Nor did she need Emerson to tell her that, "political economy is as good a book wherein to read the life of man and the ascendency of laws over all private and hostile influences, as any Bible, which has come down to us." However, it was very different with the workers who came to replace the dispersed female workers native to New England and its traditions. By 1850 fully half of the labor force at Lowell was Irish and immigrant, and these were only the first of many Europeans who arrived, wave on wave, until the second decade of the 20th century. They arrived when the American dream of free labor already had been seriously compromised in the textile cities on the lower Merrimack. And they shared no community except the future, where independence meant having a job and economic freedom meant the opportunity to compete with other families to insure that their children would have a better one. In only one generation, the corporate ethic of competition had contradicted precisely Emerson's sense that a household is the school of power.

A number of immigrant groups that came to the Valley carried with them the memories of violence suffered for religion's sake, or persecutions that threatened the extinction of ethnic minorities by more powerful ruling castes. Such were the Jews who had lived under the German, the Austrian, or the Russian state, the three dynastic empires that divided among them the rule of eastern and central Europe at that time. Similarly, the Lebanese and Armenians had suffered for their Christian faith under the rule of the Turkish sultan at Constantinople, if the rule is the right word for such a brutal system. For these, and perhaps to a lesser degree for the Italians and Greeks, reaching the cities on the Merrimack promised the freedom to pursue unmolested their own course to God and community. They were well educated to understand Milton's counsel that "our country is where we can live as we ought," and primed to expect that its tradition of tolerance would make

Right: *Skilled workers formed an important component of the Valley's industrial work force. These women weavers and the two male loom fixers of the Merrimack Mill in Dracut posed proudly in their best clothes protected by aprons and coveralls at the turn of the century. Each worker was armed with his or her tools, wrenches or shuttles, scissors, and reed hooks. (MVTM)*

Below: *As principal landowner and developer of Lawrence, the Essex Company maintained control over land use and sales. This ''descriptive plan of shanties,'' prepared in 1857 when lots were being divided and sold, shows the location of Irish families in temporary dwellings in South Lawrence. Company housing was not provided for Irish construction workers, only for Yankee factory hands. (MVTM)*

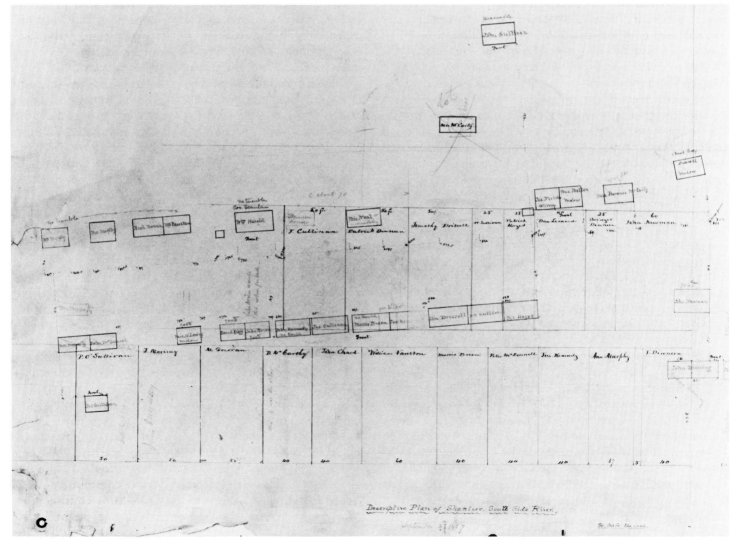

Also, of course, all the immigrant groups of the period between the Civil War (1861) and the First World War (1914) were driven by the same economic needs that had pushed and pulled the original millworkers from the farms of New England. The Irish, the French-Canadians, the Greeks, the Germans and Poles, Lithuanians and Russians, the Portugese, Italians, and Lebanese came from agricultural economies no longer able to support their explosive populations. If the immigrants to the Merrimack Valley had to adjust to a new system of laws and social convention, if they had to learn a new language, this was still not the end of the adjustments they faced. For the bulk of them, a move to the Merrimack was also a move from farm to city.

The percentage of Massachusetts people living on the lower Merrimack remained virtually unchanged between 1865 (8.51 percent) and 1915 (8.39 percent), but the concentration of those populations into cities already begun before the Civil War continued at an accelerated pace in the 50 years after it. The population of the entire lower Valley in 1865 was counted at 107,966, the population of Lowell alone was exactly one dozen persons more than that (107,978) in 1915. Two percentage values, the first from the high end and the second from the low end of the spectrum, may express most clearly this concentration of the Valley's people. The first tells us that its three largest cities (Lowell, Lawrence, Haverhill), which held 58.71 percent of the lower Valley's population in 1865, had mushroomed to contain 79.84 percent 50 years later. The second reveals that

there were six Valley towns of fewer than 2,000 persons in 1865 and that they counted 8.22 percent of the population, while in 1915 there were four such towns with a like value of 1.87 percent. It will help to focus this demographic picture to add that the four towns of less than 2,000 in 1915 were at either end of the Valley, with Tyngsborough and its population of 967 on the state boundary with New Hampshire, and Newbury (1,590), West Newbury (1,529), and Salisbury (1,717) at the seacoast end. Finally, the numbers that tell about concentration of people also give the reverse image of physical space, or the lack of it. Tyngsborough in 1915 held 57.2 persons per square mile and Dracut 192.9, while Lowell, in between, held 8,058 persons per square mile. And at Lawrence a fearsome 13,381 persons were jammed into 1,491 habitations on each of its 6.7 square miles.

Though the people of the Valley were unevenly distributed among its cities and towns, only Amesbury, Newburyport, and the four smallest towns reported less than a quarter of their populations as foreign born. The others counted from a quarter (Chelmsford, 25.80 percent) to a third (North Andover, 33.36 percent) to nearly a half (Tewksbury, 46.98 percent) of their residents in that classification. The state census of 1915 does not relate "gainful occupations" of these foreign groups by town, but the statewide tabulation makes it understood that most males of foreign birth were employed as semiskilled workers in the "manufacturing and mechanical industries." Nevertheless, there was a surprising number working as farm laborers, blacksmiths, glaziers and painters,

South Lawrence was slower to develop than the commercial center north of the river. Amidst the neat frame residences, this shanty on Kingston Street survived until the 1890s when it was recorded by Richard Hale for the Essex Company. No longer used as a dwelling, it did serve as a reminder of the difficult conditions faced by the first residents, when Lawrence was the "New City" on the Merrimack. (MVTM)

To provide a good "head" for waterpower, flashboards held the river water above the dam. Maintaining the flashboards was a regular job of the Essex Company workmen in Lawrence, pictured here in 1898. The privy allowed the crew to remain on the barge all day without offending passers-by on the nearby Broadway bridge. (MVTM)

"Professor Bill Artist Bootblack" was William R. Mobley, second from right in this circa 1900 photo of his Haverhill shop. Born in Kentucky in the 1870s, Professor Bill came to Haverhill in the late 1880s and established himself as a bootblack, tailor, and dry cleaner in 1893. One of the Valley's few black businessmen, Professor Bill was a friend and confidant of politicians and sportsmen before his death in 1948. Charles Diggs, his son-in-law, still operates the business on Merrimack Street. Courtesy, Trustees of the Haverhill Public Library.

Cotton-spinning operatives of northern European descent were photographed in December 1913 and January 1914 as part of a series of pictures made for the Pacific Mills depicting all aspects of that large corporation's activities. (MVTM)

Surrounded by their stock of furniture, the sales force of C.C. Morse and Son in Haverhill awaits the arrival of customers in the late-19th century. Traditional retail businesses flourished with the influx of population to the Valley's industrial cities. Courtesy, Trustees of the Haverhill Public Library.

plumbers and steamfitters. And there was a substantial number, particularly among the Northern Europeans, who entered the more skilled crafts as machinists, millwrights, and toolmakers. The females of all groups, for the most part, went into "domestic and personal service," when they did not work along with their children in the mills of the larger cities.

The state census of 1915 shows that, taken as a whole, fully a third of the people living on the lower Merrimack were foreign born, and in all the communities of the region their numbers became an enormous reality in the minds of the American born. There were only 203 foreign born counted at Tyngsborough that year, yet even those few made an impression when there were only 764 native-born residents in town to mingle among. The result was culture shock for both the residents established in the place and for the newcomers. Both withdrew from encounter, and for a generation or two unofficial ethnic boundaries of language and culture were at least as real as the authorized political boundaries established by the General Court. However, the native and foreign born could not avoid each other at the workplace, and labor was the steadiest contact each had with the other. Labor is the base of all community, but division was found here and even encouraged nevertheless.

Alien workers were unsure about their nationality and the workplace exposed these feelings of insecurity to exploitation and manipulation, for any protest over hours or wages or conditions of work was likely to brand them as un-American.

Like native New England farm girls half a century before who were told that protest was not ladylike, foreign-born workers had their own feelings held hostage against them. Rather than argue the demands of workers on the grounds of economic need or social justice, employers were willing and sometimes able to make a political issue of the conflict and so enlist the support of native-born voters anxious to have their votes make a positive statement, at least about themselves. And so, besides undermining with doubt the determination of the immigrant workers, the tactic had the added advantage of separating the native workers from the actual issue at hand. With so large a labor force to command, labeling all resistance as un-American was too convenient, too potent a lever of control, to let lie unused. The issue helped enliven politics at Haverhill in the last years of the past century.

Shortly after the Haverhill municipal elections of 1894 had shown that the entrenched Republican party was losing its hold on the voters of the city, the shoe manufacturers initiated a bitter controversy with their workers by requiring that part of each week's pay be left with them until $50 had accumulated on deposit. This was to insure, they said, that workers not leave their jobs without notice, but workers also suspected that the money—another hostage—would be confiscated in the event of a strike. Fifty dollars was in the neighborhood of seven percent of the average shoeworker's yearly earnings, and the hardship this deduction brought was compounded by a wage reduction earlier in the year. Also, the manufacturers had imposed production quotas on the workers in the form of mandatory contracts. When the workers struck against these exactions in December (1894), the manufacturers retaliated with a lockout: they would not give up even the appearance of control. They did not give up the substance either. When the strikers returned to their work in the spring (1895), none of the issues had been resolved in their favor. Yet despite its failure, the strike began a curious evolution in the politics of the city.

In the winter of 1895, when some strikers had been brought into police court on charges of assault, the judge in making his decision lectured the defendants, warning that their leaders were Socialists, by which he meant "men who hate the flag." As often happens with name-calling, especially when it originates in learned places like the bench, the name was accepted as a banner of truth. James Carey and John C. Chase, among some others who had been involved with a populist coalition in the first half of the 1890s, took the initiative and formed a local branch of the Socialist Labor Party. Their purpose was to run candidates for municipal office. After some impressive but failed attempts, James Carey was elected to the Haverhill city council in November 1897, which made him the first municipal official in the nation elected as a Socialist. The odd thing is that the victory upset Carey's own party more than any of his opponents. The leader of the Socialist Labor Party, Daniel DeLeon, was more than disappointed; he was scandalized by Carey's lack of fidelity to doctrine. By making allies of labor unions, by addressing local issues and worker opinion, by trying reform, in other words, when DeLeon wanted revolution, Carey had fallen away from the purity of Socialist dogma. So while the new councilman was praised by the *Gazette*, the Republican party newspaper published at Haverhill, he was denounced in the pages of *People*, the Socialist Labor organ published at New York. Carey concerned himself with unguarded railroad crossings and clothes for children who would otherwise be un-

able to go to school: this was not the stuff of revolution. "Weeping James" he was called by his party, stung by what they took to be his betrayal. Carey and Chase in February 1898 returned the charter that bound them to DeLeon's party and allied with the less dogmatic Eugene Debs and his Social Democracy Party. The elections that fall showed that party labels counted for nothing when up against leadership. In November 1898 Carey and Louis Scates were elected to the Massachusetts General Court, while in a separate election some weeks later, John C. Chase became the first Socialist elected mayor of an American city.

Haverhill elections were drawing national attention, and the elections of 1899 provided political lessons fit for the audience. The *Gazette* thought those elections "the most memorable within the recollection of the oldest inhabitants." To meet the electoral challenge of the Socialists, the local leaders of the Republican and Democratic parties combined to make up what they called the Citizens ticket headed by Mellen Pingree, a corporation lawyer, as candidate for mayor. The Citizens candidates ignored the referendums, also on the upcoming ballot, for an eight-hour day for municipal workers and for the elimination of unguarded railroad crossings, still an issue. Instead, Pingree warned the voters of Haverhill that Socialists met on Sundays and that they favored free love, and so were a threat to the traditions of New England. Socialism in fact was not American, but "imported from foreign countries" where kings ruled. This electoral strategy by Pingree and other Citizens candidates failed to excite terror or revulsion in the voters of Haverhill. Socialism at Haverhill was manifestly not what Pingree said it was. Honesty may have been the solitary joy of Weeping James, but the making of his political career was that voters could tell he was honest and they could tell because he addressed issues within their vision and grasp. To these voters the Socialist Carey in 1899 was the same person as the Populist Carey who in 1893 had demanded a "money system of the people, by the people, and for the people." Besides, who at Haverhill could confuse anything foreign with the name Chase? Anyone familiar with the place was familiar with the name, at least with the history of Haverhill published 30 years before by George Wingate Chase. In the election of 1899, John C. Chase as candidate for mayor gained 1,200 votes on his winning plurality in the previous year. Three councilmen and three aldermen also were elected on the Social Democracy ticket.

In the confused currents of Haverhill politics that crossed party lines and even made fellow Citizens of Democrats and Republicans, the followers of DeLeon managed to pick up the tactics of their ideological opponents. In the course of reporting on the elections of 1898, one of them remarked that Carey's followers were not true Socialists but rather "some few New England 'Yanks,' more anarchist Jews . . .

Socialist politician James F. Carey of Haverhill, called "Weeping James" by his party, was elected to the city council and the state legislature. His attention to local issues and gradual reform offended the more militant branch of the Socialist Labor Party. After 1898, Carey and John Chase allied Haverhill's socialists with the less dogmatic Eugene V. Debs and his Social Democracy Party. Courtesy, Trustees of the Haverhill Public Library.

John C. Chase, active in the formation of Haverhill's socialist parties, served as the city's mayor from 1899 to 1900. He was the first socialist to be elected mayor of an American city, and three councilmen and three aldermen were elected with him on the Social Democracy ticket. This portrait of Chase, based on a photograph, hangs in City Hall. Courtesy, City of Haverhill.

and still more French Canadians." But the tactic was no more effective for DeLeon than for Pingree. The workers at Haverhill were able to assimilate the issue of being un-American by their happy coincidence of a populist tradition alive with honest leadership of local constituents. At Lawrence in 1912 the currents were so large, so concentrated, that they nearly made for the revolution DeLeon had wished for at Haverhill.

The strike at Lawrence in 1912 became a world event, and that has made it hard for us to see it as the local story that it is. Also, it has suffered from familiarity. The actions of the strikers have been recited so well, as they are still by the few witnesses who remain, and they have been celebrated so often by radicals from London to Los Angeles, that now they have become outsized. So the events of the

strike come to us like the report of a foreign place called history where saints and heroes discuss fate in a white supernatural light. The story is rooted in the region nevertheless. It tells how workers new to Lawrence, immigrants from Eastern and Northern Europe, were able to combine against the corporate will of the Valley's largest textile manufacturer. Strangers to the place, the workers were also strangers to one another, but they found in the conditions of their labor the common bond between them.

The issue was wages. The legislature of Massachusetts had mandated a reduction in the number of hours worked in the textile factories of the Commonwealth. This was done over the objections of the manufacturers, who predicted that it would harm their ability to compete with the manufacturers of textiles in the nation's Southern states and with manufacturers abroad. As they were not able on this occasion to make their view prevail at the General

The Massachusetts National Guard was called up for strike duty at Lawrence. The Second Batallion of the Fifth Infantry Division was photographed in February 1912 with a panoramic "Cirkut" camera. Operated with a swinging motion, camera and film rotated independently. This camera could photograph large groups, which if posed in a semicircle appeared as a straight line in the finished picture. Buildings were not as malleable, so the Pacific Mills in the background appear distorted and curved. (MVTM)

Court, the manufacturers felt justified in cutting the wages of the workers to match the cut in hours. That would protect the fiscal health of the corporations and that, they said, was the bedrock of industry on the Merrimack. Without that, where would the workers be? The workers for their part could not afford to speculate in probable futures. It may say all there is to say about the strike of 1912 to add that this haggle over money amounted to a reduction of 30 cents a week for the average laborer at Lawrence; in the tenement districts of the city, 30 cents a week was the difference between the acceptance of a difficult life and the point of desperate resistance.

That movement of resistance began on Wednesday, January 10, with a meeting of the Italian branch of the Industrial Workers of the World, Local 20. The meeting was timed to precede the first payday of the new rates on the 11th, and the decision of the branch was that all Italian workers should refuse to work. The Lawrence Local also appealed to its parent body, asking Joseph Ettor, a professional organizer, to come and help the strikers. But the initiative had been taken at Lawrence, and on Friday the 12th workers at the Wood Worsted Mill abandoned their machines and moved through that enormous structure damaging machines, cutting drive belts, and making threats, some in Italian, to those workers who refused to join them. The next day, Saturday, was quiet on the streets of Lawrence. But Ettor had arrived and was indoors, beginning to organize the workers. Addressing the Italians of Local 20, he focused on their feelings about the owners of the mills. The owners, he said, accepted the Italians as long as they lived quietly, "next door to a dog and work for $4.20 a week. But when they want a little more...they are foreigners, then Socialists and anarchists." Ettor

saw, however, that he could not expect to organize a successful strike while ignoring the other ethnic communities at Lawrence.

Besides the Italian branch, the IWW had, before the strike, a Polish and a Franco-Belgian branch in the city. And indeed it was these three local branches that provided the core of leadership for the strike over the next eight

Serious overcrowding in the central district of Lawrence prompted a survey published in 1911. Unlike the Sanitary Survey of 1850, which found a model town, the 20th-century investigation disclosed the wretched living conditions of Lawrence's immigrant population. It was said that occupants hung their pots and pans on the outside walls of adjacent buildings and reached them through the windows. (MVTM)

weeks. Yet there were scores of other immigrant minorities at Lawrence, and the strike committee, which ruled the strikers for its duration, put together the efforts of representatives from all of them wishing to be included. The presence of such well-known agitators as Ettor and Bill Haywood, the activities of Socialist poet Arturo Giovannitti and the "red flame" Elizabeth Gurley Flynn, gave the strike at Lawrence the image of being a major front on the worldwide struggle of labor against capital. Owners of the mills at Lawrence pointed out that the workers were being used by the dark will of international communism, and that it was dangerous to bring such a godless force into the city. (Leaving us to infer that the only "safe" outside force at Lawrence was the money carted in from the banks of Boston and New York and which mortgaged the city's future production to the nameless face of American capital.) It is true that Ettor used the temper of workers at Lawrence in 1912 to recruit more members for the IWW and so push his organization ahead of its rival union, the American Federation of Labor. Yet the effort and the victory was a local event.

State militia as well as the National Guard patrolled the streets of Lawrence during the strike of 1912. Horsemen of Battery A of the state militia ride along Canal Street in front of the Washington Mills boardinghouses. In an attempt to keep the peace, the city government allowed only English-speaking people on the streets near the mills. (MVTM)

Mill Work in Lawrence

In 1913-1914, just a year after the strike, a series of almost 1,000 photographs were made of the Pacific Mills in Lawrence that recorded the numerous steps in the manufacture of printed cotton cloth and worsteds. Produced as albums for management and as stereographs with an accompanying booklet for use in the schools, these photographs document the work of thousands of individuals who labored at the Pacific. Differences in jobs and status of the workers according to nationality can also be discerned from these pictures.

Right: *Child labor was employed, if the children were over 14 and had certificates proving school attendance and literacy. Both parents and overseers bent or ignored the rules, however; many children entered the mills at 11 or 12 to help support their families. This girl empties the bins of full cops of spun yarn. (MVTM)*

Below: *The operatives working at the cotton drawing frames appear to be southern European. Lower-paying, dirtier jobs were held by the most recently arrived immigrants who shoveled coal in the yard gangs or breathed lint in the fiber preparation rooms. (MVTM)*

In the scene of the measuring and folding room for cotton cloth, one gains a sense of the production capacity of such a large operation. Pacific percales and lawns, shirting and serges, poured from the mills at the rate of more than a million yards per day. Mills at Dover, New Hampshire, and later in the South, lured the Pacific's capital investment away from Lawrence. Absorbed by Burlington Industries, the Pacific Mills ceased operation in Lawrence in the mid-1950's, just one hundred years after they began. (MVTM)

The strike at Lawrence in 1912 is a milestone of American industrial history and the only major victory that labor was able to organize against the textile manufacturers of the Merrimack Valley. The success was grounded on the cohesion of the workers around their ethnic communities, and on the ability of some of these communities to collaborate on an issue affecting them all. Not only was the wage reduction canceled, but the manufacturers now agreed to raise wages, some by as much as 20 percent. Textile manufacturers in other cities of New England felt compelled to follow the example and raised the wages of their workers. For these workers, for a while, Lawrence became the emblem of labor's emancipation.

After such a struggle, even victory is traumatic. Though there had been surprisingly little violence, given the size of

NOTICE.

The Mule Spinners of Lowell having combined together with a foreign association to coerce their employers to raise their wages, and having made a peremptory demand therefor, and to carry out their purpose having voted to "bring out the Lawrence and Massachusetts Corporations on a strike." and those of them employed by these Companies having given notice that they should quit work on the 12th instant,

NOTICE

Is hereby given that if said Spinners shall execute their threat by quitting work accordingly, the services of the Mule Spinners in the employment of this Company will not be required on and after the 14th instant.

MERRIMACK MANUFACTURING Co.,

J. S. LUDLUM, Sup't.

LOWELL, Mass., April 5th, 1875.

In 1875 the Mule Spinners Association of the United States ordered a test strike at Lowell. The mill owners responded with a lock out, a tactic often used in Lowell, and then substituted ring spinning frames for mules. In this way they reduced the level of skill involved in the spinning operation and exchanged less skilled, more tractable labor for the troublesome mule spinners. This notice records the managers' reaction to the threatened strike. (MVTM)

Lowell's "Mile of Mills" along the Merrimack employed about 17,000 people, who earned only 10 cents an hour on the average for a 62-hour week in 1900. Problems such as low water and high inventories closed the mills for several weeks each year, and no unemployment benefits were available. (MVTM)

the crowds and the presence of thousands of armed police and militiamen, the strike pursued the memories of everyone involved, whatever role they had played, whichever side they had favored. However, the reaction of Laurentians to the strike was part of the story of their cultural life in the Valley, distinct from the economic center of the strike itself.

The principal opponent to the victory of the strikers was William Wood, and that puts yet another face on the experience of immigrant labor in the Valley, and on the strike of 1912, because William Wood was born on Martha's Vineyard in 1858 to the wife of a Portuguese seaman. There were very many thousands of Portuguese immigrants at work in the textile mills of Massachusetts, especially at New Bedford and Fall River, and he had his experience of that. But Billy found his way to the fast lane in American society, where he accepted as fact that he could not change the rules but only play by them. He had a will of iron, forged, it seems, in a determination not to divide it. He bent his education to learn the skills that American society rewarded. He learned to manage men and money. He learned how to sell textiles. He learned, before they were written, the words of the Massachusetts Labor Census (1894): "Indeed, it is essential to the success of industrial operations, as at present conducted, that

Lowell Daily Courier.

FINANCIAL NEWS — ON PAGE SEVEN.

12 Pages. | 4 O'Clock.

ESTABLISHED 1845.   LOWELL, MASS., SATURDAY, MARCH 28, 1903.   PRICE ONE CENT.

FIGURES OF LOWELL FACTORIES

	Male.	Female.	Spindles.	Present Payroll.
Appleton	448	526	52,088	$ 8,300
Boott	750	800	148,000	11,000
Hamilton	900	1200	109,816	17,500
Lawrence	1200	2100	75,000	26,000
Massachusetts	680	1550	123,088	18,000
Merrimack	1900	1130	144,144	25,000
Tremont and Suffolk	1200	3000	186,000	23,000
	7078	10,306	838,136	$128,800

Total employes, 17,334 including minors and part-time workers.

The above figures as to employes, except those of the Boott mills, are as given in 1901. The payrolls are estimated in round numbers at the present day.

The average wage, figured from the above, including the minors and helpers who make comparatively small pay, is something like $7.50 per week for every employe per week.

THIEVES.

Eight Lined Up in the Police Court.

SEVEN PLEADED GUILTY.

Sentences and Fines Doled Out to the Offenders—An Old Soldier in the Hands of Thieves.

STRIKE RIOT.

Twenty-eight Persons Killed in Russian Town.

IRON WORKERS OUT.

Place Famous for the Manufacture of Damasked Scimitars and Similar Cutlery.

MAY WIN MATCH.

Americans Still Have a Fair Chance in Chess Contest.

EXPECT A CROWD.

Arranging for Quarters for Visitors to St. Louis.

GOING TO ALABAMA.

ON WOODEN HORSES.

Barn Warming Dinner Will Not Be Served on Prancing Steeds.

TO BE REMOVED.

Mayor Grant Serves Notice on License Commission.

ACTION EXPECTED.

Charges Against the Members of the Lawrence Board Will be Heard Monday.

MILL GATES SHUT

Closed at Noon for Indefinite Time.

NOTICE GIVEN AT MILLS

Employes Notified That It Is Impossible to Run During Strike, as Intended.

MASSACHUSETTS COTTON MILLS.

MERRIMACK MFG. CO.

---

capital should be massed, controlled, and directed in few hands." His work was directed to insure that his hands would be among the few in control.

The American Woolen Company, which he organized in 1899, became in time the largest manufacturer of woolen and worsted cloth in the world. He based that corporation at Lawrence, partly because he was already treasurer of the Washington Mills there, and partly because Lawrence had the reputation of having a nonmilitant labor force. There's no doubt that his effort began the spectacular growth of the city that doubled the number of workers in little more than a decade. The speed of that change was no doubt one factor that unsettled the people and labor relations at Lawrence. The independent giants in the city, the Pacific Mills and the Arlington Mills, were enlarged, and a new Everett Mill (1909) was constructed. To these were added the two large

In 1903 Lowell experienced its first city-wide strike, called by the skilled workers of the Lowell Textile Council. The strikers demanded a wage increase. Foiled by several months without work or income and the strike-breaking activities of unskilled workers, the skilled craft unions lost not only the strike but also their positions and cohesive strength. In 1912 following events in Lawrence, Lowell workers struck again and gained the wage increases granted industry-wide as a result of collective action and IWW support. Courtesy, Lowell Historical Society.

mills of Wood's American Woolen Company: the Wood Mill (1906) and the Ayer Mill (1909), each built on the southern bank of the Merrimack and powered by its own steam-generating plant. There is some measure of the drive of William Wood in the fact that the mill that bore his name, providing 68 acres of space in two parallel struc-

tures, was built and put in production between August 1905 and April 1906. Yet, in another sense, there is no measure of his ambition, because William Wood, American, refused to see the future close. There were never enough mills, never enough profits. Eventually, the American Woolen Company operated 60 mills throughout New England, in New York, and in Tennessee.

The meeting of William Wood and the strike in 1912 present such a telling circumstance that we are inclined to put a drama at the center of it. "Immigrant labors to distance himself" might fit the marquee. But it is a drama only he might have given us, and it is well that we respect his silence. In the face of that silence, no amount of evidence seems able to resolve the conflict over his memory. There are those who see in Billy Wood the typical American industrialist of his age, grasping and ambitious in his purpose, ruthless in his methods. There are those, on the other hand, who read in his career the great American success story. Even for the thousands who failed he is proof that

Above: *Masons erect a wall for the new Pacific worsted mill on Hampshire Street, Lawrence, in 1910. In the decade preceding World War I, production capacity among New England woolen and worsted mills enlarged enormously. Lawrence experienced a great building boom, the Wood and Ayer mills of American Woolen Company were constructed, and significant additions to the Arlington, Everett, and Pacific mills appeared. (MVTM)*

Facing page: *In the 1915 city directory, the Chamber of Commerce advertised Lawrence's prosperity, which reached an all-time high during the World War I period. Uniform cloth and blankets rolled off the production line to meet the high wartime demand. Despite 20th-century modifications such as coal-powered steam and electricity, this ad pointed to the waters of the Merrimack—"the river that turns more spindles than any stream on earth." (MVTM)*

E

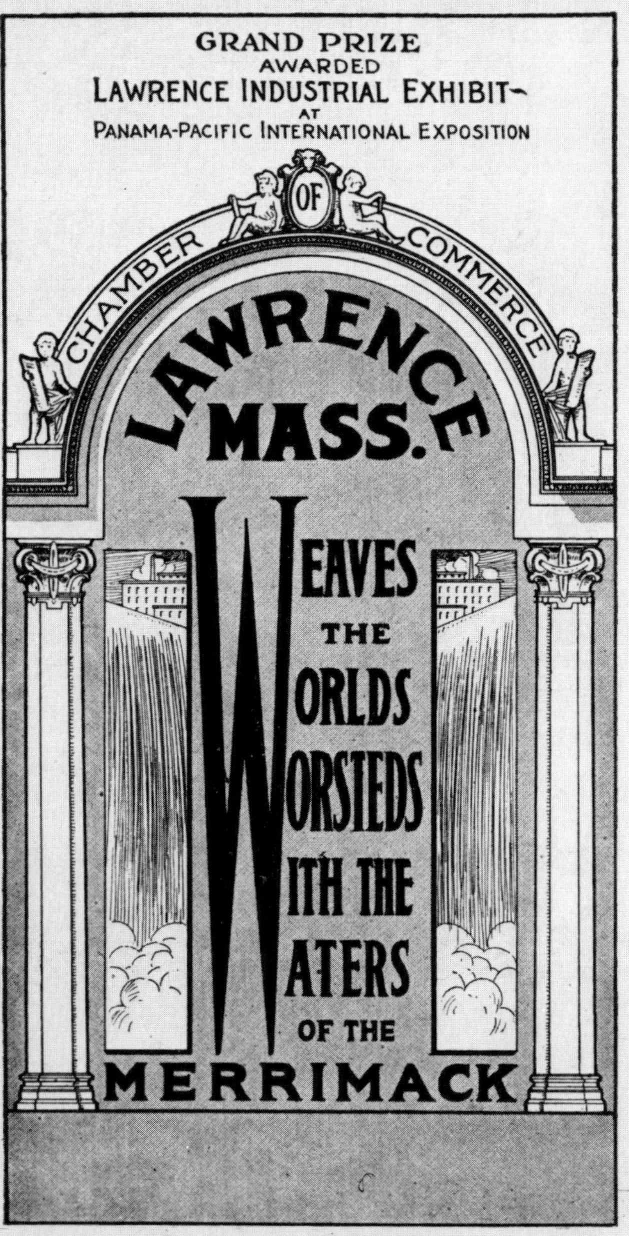

GRAND PRIZE
AWARDED
LAWRENCE INDUSTRIAL EXHIBIT
AT
PANAMA-PACIFIC INTERNATIONAL EXPOSITION

CHAMBER OF COMMERCE

LAWRENCE MASS.

WEAVES THE WORLDS WORSTEDS WITH THE WATERS OF THE MERRIMACK

LAWRENCF, MASSACHUSETTS, U. S. A.

It has a population including its suburbs of about 125,000.

It is a manufacturing centre, by reason of its location on the Merrimack River—the River that turns more spindles than any stream on earth.

It is here that is located the largest Cotton Print works and the largest Woolen mill in the United States.

It has an annual Pay Roll of over 15 millions of dollars distributed to over 40,000 operatives.

It has 11 Banks and Trust Companies with resources of $32,000,000.

It has 40 Schools, training 14,000 pupils. It has 52 Churches. A Public Library.

It has 76 Societies and Clubs, including a Y. M. C. A., a Y. W. C. A., a C. Y. M. A., a Y. M. H. A., a Country Club and Canoe Club, also 213 Fraternal and Charitable Societies.

It is governed by a Commission Form of Government.

Right: *William Madison Wood (1858-1926), son of Portuguese immigrants who settled on Martha's Vineyard, rose by his wits and abilities to become wealthy and powerful. He created the American Woolen Company, which included about 50 woolen and worsted mills in New England and New York and became the largest producer of woolen cloth in the world. Despite his success as an agressive entrepreneur, Wood's world crumbled after the death of his favorite son in 1922, and he took his own life in 1926. (MVTM)*

Below: *"Brick Shawsheen" and "White Shawsheen" housed two levels of American Woolen Company management. The more prestigious brick homes were separated by village shops and the office building from middle management's white frame dwellings. Individual garages were not constructed for either sector, however. Wood insisted on large common garages in the center to keep the feeling of a small town where executives walked to work. In this way he hoped to foster an interchange of ideas and a community spirit to benefit the corporation. (MVTM)*

they were not wrong to attempt the American dream, here, on the Merrimack.

Nor did the strike deflate his ambition. Between 1912 and 1926, when he took his own life, William Wood directed the creation of Shawsheen Village. It is located just south of the Lawrence city line in a part of Andover formerly called Frye Village. There he built an impressive structure of concrete and red brick as the headquarters of his American Woolen Company. Recently, the office building has been converted to a condominium, with the workmanship of its paneling to recommend it to its market. What is remarkable about Shawsheen Village is the attempt to give the place a totally American appearance, or at least the appearance of

residents of Shawsheen. Besides its even tone of ersatz colonial Americana, the other feature of the Village was its segregation of labor. There was a woolen mill built at Shawsheen, but unlike the manufacturers in the 1820s Wood provided no housing for the workers. What he gave was a streetcar line to take them back to Lawrence when their day's labor was done. Instead of housing for the workers, Wood directed the erection of "Red Shawsheen," brick homes for those in upper management, and "White Shawsheen," frame clapboard houses for the middle-level managers. By preferring a style of architecture that was make-believe, by shunting off most of its workers and separating the others into a hierarchy, above all in its over-

what Wood fancied as American. What we have is a homogenized rendition of preindustrial American buildings. The Village is colonial revival in its persuasion; the 19th and 20th centuries—where Wood was living his life—are pushed into the background and camouflaged. Wood did not allow the houses at Shawsheen to have garages for the residents' cars. Cars were garaged in common and residents were advised to enjoy the weather whatever it might be as they walked to or walked from.

There is the story of how William Wood, on seeing the fieldstone headquarters of Washington at Valley Forge, barked over his shoulder to one of his entourage, "Get that!" It was got and reproduced as the polling place for the

The bustle of "bell time" 20th-century style is reflected in this drawing of Lowell workers in about 1905. They came from every corner in the Old World to contribute their labor and customs in forming the New World. They found work and exploitation, kindness and prejudice, prosperity and poverty in unequal measure. (MVTM)

bearing concern with appearance, Shawsheen reflects the textile corporation of the Merrimack Valley as it entered its second century. It is a place where management becomes contrivance. Whatever else we cannot say about William Wood, we can say that he knew to which America he had come home.

VII

CULTURE, HIGH AND LOW

I heard the merry grasshopper then sing,
The black clad Cricket, bear a second part,
They kept one tune, and plaid on the same string,
Seeming to glory in their little Art.
Shall Creatures abject, thus their voices raise?
And in their kind resound their makers praise:
Whilst I as mute, can warble forth no higher layes.
— Anne Bradstreet, *Contemplations*
(Number 9), circa 1640.

How could it be that you lived, for as long as you did, so
near to this living water and not have been overcome with
words aching to be written welling up within you?
— Andrew D. Gray, *To Robert Frost,*
*Laurentian,*1981.

Anthropologists, who say they know about these things, often
measure the level of culture by the distance a people have put between
themselves and nature. According to this standard, the Pennacooks are

Members of a Newburyport bicycle club pose with their vehicles on June 29, 1891. In
the 1880s and 1890s, cycling became popular in the Valley. Bicycle clubs appeared
everywhere, and cycling women and men toured the countryside, taking picnics and
enjoying the scenery. Photo by Osgood & Foss. Courtesy, Historical Society of Old
Newbury.

called primitive because they developed neither metals nor sources of energy to alter significantly their natural environment, and so they could not see a very clear difference between themselves and the place. They had no idols, because idols demand a certain level of craft. The Puritan English, on the other hand, were intensely anxious to "rise above" nature, and their observance of the work ethic was very much a part of their need to see, before them, the farms and the industries of the Valley towns as proof of success. The towns themselves might be called their material culture, made of the labor of their bodies. The Puritans also produced a culture of the mind; indeed, there have been few communities more intent on that. However, in this as in everything, the Puritan mind was deep from want of being broad so that the stamp of the culture was its

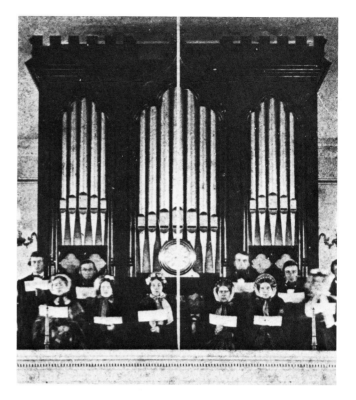

Despite the Puritan culture's disapproval of pageantry and secular music, some sacred music survived. By the 18th century hymns were part of the church service, and by the 19th century community members participated actively in church choirs. The choir of the First Parish in Newbury sings in December 1861, as the impressive organ towers as evidence that this congregation took its music seriously. Courtesy, Society for the Preservation of New England Antiquities.

Harriet West (1798-1889) is seated in this 1870s photo before a portrait of her grandfather, a physician who introduced small-pox innoculation to Haverhill and to whom she bears a strong resemblance. Courtesy, Trustees of the Haverhill Public Library.

utter concentration on the word, written and spoken, and the neglect of picture making, of sculpture and theater—the neglect, in fact, of nearly all other ways of capturing and expressing thought. This may be why, for lack of a better explanation, language and narrative have had a larger place than the plastic and performing arts in the towns on the lower Merrimack.

In the first and second generations of European settlement in the Valley, perhaps even to the eve of the War of Independence (1775), it was the preacher who bore the major part of this culture of words. At the meetinghouses from Salisbury to Dunstable it was the spoken word that went among its public, each Sabbath. Even the printed word at this time was likely as not a sermon or a collection of sermons rather than some other form into which words are cast. Few of these would reward any attention we know how to give. The purpose, the images and devices, the vocabulary of these sermons are lost on us, and except for the passion that obviously motivated their quest for meaning, there is little in them to convince us that anyone could take this sort of expression seriously. Yet the townsfolk on the Merrimack not only accepted them seriously, they also sought them out earnestly.

It is somewhat easier for us to read the secular verse of the age, just barely, and it is true that the first book of verse published by an American was written by Anne Bradstreet, who for a time was resident at Andover, "by Cochiche-wick." However, it is also true that her early verse was written before 1644 when she left Ipswich with her husband and settled close to the river. Some reservation, then, must be made in claiming Mistress Bradstreet as genetrix of writing in the Valley, though the reservation is no greater than is needed to make an American of any English Puritan born, as she was, in 1612. Besides, we have the poems, and they tell us that she was very much part of her generation in this place. Her work constantly returns to questions that her community defined as vital: the history of the world, which is to say the story of God's wonder-working Providence, themes of filial piety and obedience, the struggle to accept herself as a creature, and a constant need to keep a watch on herself, to alert herself, and warn herself of evil tendencies. Her mental life was a constant round of scrutiny, judgment, and resolution. She wrote a short story of her life, to instruct her children, typically, and there is enough of that left to give us a glimpse of how this poet was made:

> In my young years about 6 or 7, as I take it, I began to make conscience of my wayes, and what I new was sinfull, as lying, disobedience to Parents, etc., I avoided it. If at any time I was overtaken with the like evils, it was a great Trouble. I could not be at rest 'till by prayer I had confest it unto God. . . . also found much comfort in reading the Scriptures, especially those places I thought most concerned my Condition, and as I grew to have more understanding, so the more solace I took in them.

The "Condition" she speaks of was her illness, frequent companion of her youth, so that she spent much time confined to bed. It makes a touching picture of so young a girl looking to find herself in the words of aged men, wondering whether so long an affliction of her body might bespeak a corruption of the soul. Finding her own voice in a din of Hebraic proverbs and Greek philosophy was an act of valor, so true and patient was her womanly heart. Victories, then as now, were few and fleeting, but one of her *Contemplations,* written sometime between 1666 and her death six years later, shows her by the river in a brief clearing of freedom:

> Under the cooling shadow of the stately Elm
> Close sate I by a goodly Rivers side,

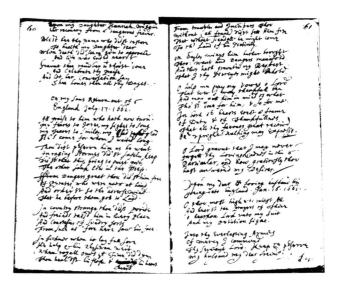

Anne Bradstreet (1612-1672), born in Lincolnshire, England, came to America with her husband Simon in 1630 in the company of Governor Winthrop and other prominent colonists. The Bradstreets lived at Salem, Cambridge, and Ipswich before joining the first band of Andover settlers in the 1640s. Often ill, Mistress Bradstreet recorded her trials in poems, where she also related the joys of her life: "Upon my Daughter Hannah Wiggin her recovery from a dangerous fever" and "On my sons Return out of England, July 17, 1662." One volume in her own hand survives. Courtesy, Trustees of the Stevens Memorial Library, North Andover, Massachusetts.

> Where gliding streams the Rocks did overwhelm;
> A lonely place, with pleasures dignifi'd.
> I once that lov'd the shady woods so well,
> Now thought the rivers did the trees excel,
> And if the sun would ever shine, there would I dwell.

Even when the religious tone had been left behind, language was used still as a tool to hone down the edges of character. Only now the command to name the evil Self and call it out became a cult of "self-improvement," which was so evident in the life of New England down to the middle of the last century. On the Merrimack, the most conspicuous example of that was undoubtedly in the much publicized cultural activity of the Lowell Girls. There is evidence to show that a number of these women went to

Lowell principally because it gave them a choice of religious congregations, just as the diary of Isaac Merrill shows him willing to travel to Atkinson, New Hampshire, and to the churches of Andover to hear a good preacher. Even Sarah Bagley, who was no friend of the Lowell system of labor, counted in its favor that the city gave her the Good News well spoken. By the 1820s, however, the spoken word was becoming secular, and there was in the Lowell Lyceum a more worldly congregation where Emerson and other famous lecturers came to talk about society and politics, about geology and minerals.

The audience of workers at Lowell also pursued the printed word. The famous *Lowell Offering* published a range of literature for and by the city's female labor force, and it was their most distinguished badge of breeding and gentility at this time when other women made a display of both exactly to distinguish themselves from the factory girls. The textile mills on the Merrimack were making a class of factory workers and that was something entirely new in the American experience, but both the women who

Operatives in top hats and hoop skirts play cribbage outside one of the factory houses at Stevens Mill, North Andover, in about 1865. Working people in the Valley's mill towns and factory villages experienced the new discipline of work regulated by the clock while still recalling the preindustrial rhythm of seasonal tasks. Some pleasures, however, did develop from the companionship found in the boardinghouse and work place. (MVTM)

were in that labor force and those who were not used language to deny what was happening. The *Offering* was first printed in October 1840, but it originated earlier that year at the so-called Improvement Circle at Lowell, where young women met after their hours of work in the mills to read aloud to one another from their own writings or from those of others that they fancied.

The notion to print these works instead of speaking them was intended to "improve" a larger circle. In a sense the magazine attempted to make the cultural community open to the entire laboring community, because for two centuries that had been the purpose of culture in the towns on the lower Merrimack. On everyone's part, the *Offering* was an attempt to deny that the mills had changed anything in this generation of New England's children. Those workers who were alarmed at the divisions and strife that factory labor brought to their communities were naturally repulsed by what they took to be a charade to hide the truth. *The Voice of Industry* was published in the later 1840s and was one attempt to use language to expose the shenanigans of the *Offering*. By its nature, however, the *Voice* and other publications like it were critical and negative, and the larger reading public tended to reject what they had to say as un-American. After all, there were the mills, and these were the production figures to show that progress was real and right.

Nostalgia for what they had left behind was a theme often expressed by the women of the *Offering*. In 1841 the magazine published "A Weaver's Reverie: No Fiction," which was signed by Ella, one of the pseudonyms used by Harriet Farley, a frequent contributor to the *Offering* and also one of its editors. She thinks on nature, Ella said, as famine victims think of food: it was the lack of it that gave her the need to seek a place to be alone. "I should love to be *alone*. Alone! where *could* I be alone?" With the hours at the mill and the slapping of belts against pulleys or the throwing of shuttles in the loom, with the activity of the boardinghouse and the hours at this meeting or that, where *indeed* could she be alone? And so, at the end of her Reverie, this weaver stands by a window of the weaveroom, having left her work to admire the blue sky. Suddenly the charm is broken: "'Your looms are going without filling,' said a loud voice at my elbow; so I ran as fast as possible, and changed my shuttles."

Farley's "Reverie" was followed by something called "A New Society," and that neglects the past to turn toward the future. It was written by Betsey Chamberlin, who followed the affectation of her peers and used a pen name, Tabitha. She recounts that once while reading quietly in her room a boy entered and handed her a newspaper. Then the boy left, never speaking a word. Her eye fell at once to an article headed "Annual Meeting of the Society for the promotion of Industry, Virtue and Knowledge." She read on. The

Society had enacted several "resolves," all of them unanimously. Some of these demand equality between the sexes in the "advantages" of education and in wages. Another resolve changes focus somewhat and puts all workers together to define a right common to all. It states that "as the laborer is worthy of his hire the price for labor shall be sufficient to enable the working-people to pay a proper attention to scientific and literary pursuits." It demands an eight-hour workday that will leave all the members of the Society with the time and energy to read and to write. Yet, if each is given the chance to use language for self-expression, none is allowed to do that only. For Tabitha reads, the Society resolves that they "will not patronize the writings of any person who does not spend at least three hours in each day, when health will permit, either in manual labor, or in some employment which will be a public benefit, and shall not appertain to literary pursuits." This New Society has her full approval, because work in the mills at Lowell has put her in a position to see the improvement in what it resolves to do. Still this news left her with a puzzle: sitting in a room reading, she knew it to be 1841, but the newspaper was dated April 1, 1860. The puzzle was quickly solved for her when, on her way up the stairs to tell the other girls, she "stumbled, and awoke."

Putting these two articles back to back may have been the inspiration of a good editor or it may have been the inspiration of chance. Whichever it was still leaves us now with the delight of finding them nestled against each other, one head dreaming of the past and the other dreaming of the future, while both are dreaming *out* of Lowell in 1841. Both writers do with words what dreams do with waking reality, and that seems appropriate; language and dreams are a precious yoke, since both are subversive and break through the denial of social change that the *Offering* was peddling to the "waking" populations of the Valley. Miss Chamberlin introduced her New Society with a verse that makes the point.

Dreams are but interludes which fancy makes;
When monarch reason sleeps, this mimic wakes;
Compounds a medley of disjointed things,
A court of cobblers, a mob of kings.

Lowell was the subject of much national interest, and international visitors added their comments to our written picture of its development. Novels, stories, and plays depicted its daily events. The women workers, known for their magazines and their militancy, created a market for cultural events, lectures, and recitals. A play conceived in 1849, "A new local drama. . . written for this Theatre," the Mill Girls of Lowell *included local scenery, mechanical effects, and a moralistic ending: "Virtue and Industry Rewarded; The Mill Girls of Lowell Triumphant." Courtesy, Lowell Historical Society.*

The pace of life at Lowell, the stepped-up pitch of labor regulated by the mechanical works of the clock and the loom, the noise of the city and the close isolation of living within sight of thousands of strangers, all of these were new to nearly everyone who came to the factory towns on the Merrimack. Like Harriet Farley and Betsey Chamberlin, all of them owned the living memory of a previous life, and for them it was a struggle to find ways of expressing the shock of the city. Language, then, exploded with breathy reports of what they found, as though a prudent and careful observer of country livestock fairs had suddenly been called on to write home about these beasts called camels and giraffes. Novels came pouring out of the presses, each with a stock description of what a factory girl, hybrid creature, might be.

There was the breathy sentiment of *The Factory Girls: or, Gardez la Coeur* by A.I. Cummings, MD, published at Lowell in 1847, a novel that tells the story of the trials and triumphs of Calliste Barton. Some dozen years later there was the heavier breathing of *Flora Montgomerie, The Factory Girl: Tale of the Lowell Factories* in which "kisses and caresses were submitted to by females, and enjoyed by males." The author of this novel called himself Charles Paul de Kock for some clearly commercial reason and used the transparent device of putting his heroine naked in front

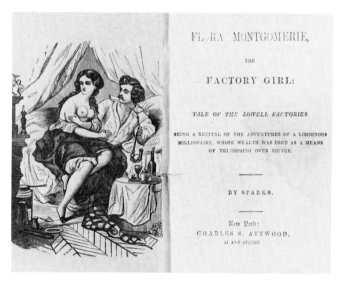

Factory fiction described life in the factory as imagined by novelists who had never worked there, yet it appealed to the audience of working women who no doubt enjoyed the fantasy of figuring as heroines of these tales. Some novels were more lurid than others; Flora Montgomerie shows a hookah being introduced to a topless, hapless, operative. Very little of the plot and action actually concerned the making of cloth, but the mills served as a convenient setting to reach the market of factory girls and to warn young women against the potential dangers of strange men and city ways. (MVTM)

of a mirror so that she could describe herself to herself. Meanwhile, the reader is modestly kept outside, watching, "but not with LUSTFUL eyes." Heaven forbid! Private is private after all, and so we get the visible ***** to displace the invisible sexual gymnastics in these gilded sinks of iniquity. Sex is presented as a reasonably elaborate if somewhat clumsy fan dance: now it's there, now it's not. On the other hand, one murder and one case of embezzlement are given in full frontal view.

These pulp novels not only described factory life on the Merrimack, they also were a thing gone out into the nation, a commodity like the other commodities pouring out of the factories of America. The story was often a coarse package perhaps, but good enough to satisfy the growing habit of thoughtless consumption. Yet all the fiction using the milltown for a setting was neither sentimental nor so erotic. For instance, *Merrimack: or, Life at the Loom* (1854) is moderate in expression and thoughtful in content. Written by Day Kellogg Lee, this novel makes the attempt to describe characters of complete human dimension, using the model of the immensely popular Dickens.

While much of a certain brand of fiction was written by hacks and published out of back rooms in New York, some observers living on the lower Merrimack were trying to fashion something better than gossip from their culture of words. They made the most exact demands on their craft and shared an immediate concern with this place. Five in particular found the language that the reading public in America, at one time or another, was ready to accept as its own: Henry Thoreau and John Greenleaf Whittier in the last century; John Marquand and Jack Kerouac to match them in the 20th and Robert Frost in between. These writers among the many who have lived and worked in the Valley received the attention of a national—and international—audience.

Of the five, Thoreau was most attached to locale. His writing attempts the closest observation of the dynamics and spectacles of nature. Equally important to Thoreau, however, is the platform from which he makes those observations. For the circumference that is nature is described from the center, which can only be the mind of the individual; there is not one universe but many, as many as there are observers. Calling Thoreau a nature writer, then, is only a half-truth that has confused and misled readers since his work was first published. Late in 1849 James Russell Lowell reviewed Thoreau's *Week on the Concord and Merrimack Rivers* for the *Atlantic Monthly*. Lowell was perplexed in a generous sort of way; he complained that after accepting what he thought was an invitation to a boating party, he was sat down at the bow and preached at by the helmsman. Lowell could not accept finding long, extended digressions on religion, on friendship, on poetry, in a book he thought should be about the fishes and the

Top: *Although not a native of the Valley, Robert Frost was the son of two native Laurentians and moved to Lawrence in 1885 at the age of 12. This photo was taken when he graduated from Lawrence High School in 1892. Although Frost's life as a farmer in Derry, New Hampshire, had more influence on his poetry than his Lawrence experiences, certain poems recall his past in the Valley, such as "A Brook in the City" and "A Lone Striker." Courtesy, Jones Library, Amherst, Massachusetts.*

Above: *Andover children enjoy the sandy shore of Haggett's Pond in the 1890s. The several church services and prohibition of activity on the Puritan Sabbath gave way two centuries later to the pursuit of nature and the perfect Sunday picnic spot. Courtesy, Andover Historical Society.*

fowl. In fact, *A Week on the Concord and Merrimack Rivers* reports a voyage Thoreau made with his brother John during the last week of August and the first week of September, that time when high summer is about to turn and give a show of choice even when we know there is none. That was in 1839, but Thoreau did not write his *Week* until that famous retreat he took at Walden Pond from 1845 to 1847. In those years when the Essex Company was building its Great Stone Dam across the river, Thoreau, alone for a good part of his days and nights, was busy calibrating a different sort of energy from the Merrimack. The mills on the river were then a powerful symbol of a new society, an open society in which individuals were free to compete for distinction and wealth. The American way promised that persons would earn, not inherit, what they got. Nearly always out of step with the business of his time, Thoreau gave in his *Week* his own definition of the self-made man. It is solitary confrontation with nature, not culture, that generates the full stature of personality. We are all self-made men, he seems to be saying, only some of us pay attention.

It's significant that Thoreau was nearly totally free of our national obsession with time, free that is from the need to find what history "means." The Great Seal of the Republic proclaimed "a new order of the ages" (*novus ordo seclorum*) and after 1800, as if on cue, there appeared an endless number of schemes to make the "new order" materialize in this promised land. Between the time of his birth in 1817 and his death in 1862, Thoreau's America was alive with an enormous variety of social experiments and movements of reform, all with the purpose of self-improvement and some hoping to assist in the birth of the Millennium, that thousand years of peace and justice that Scripture promises will follow the second coming of Christ. In this cultural fever, some writers used language very much as the Puritan preacher had, very much, that is, like the pharmacist uses chemistry to formulate nostrums and cures that reach well beyond chemistry. In moments of power or bravura, they also claimed to be the doctor.

One of these was William Lloyd Garrison, born at Newburyport in 1805. At 13, Garrison began a seven-year apprenticeship with Ephraim W. Allen, editor of the Newburyport *Herald*, and during these years, young Garrison used his skills at the printing press to make war on drink, Sabbath-breaking, and a number of other vices. But it was not until he heard the Quaker abolitionist Benjamin Lundy speak against the slavery of blacks that Garrison knew he had found the cause worthy of his editorials. He became an influential journalist, founder and editor of the *Liberator* in 1830. This combination of journalism, poetry, and reform typified the culture of words in antebellum America. It marked the career of another Newburyporter, George Lunt (1803-1885), and of John Greenleaf Whittier, born at haverhill in 1807. We remember Whittier now as a

John Greenleaf Whittier's poem, "The Barefoot Boy," evoked his own boyhood on the family farm in Haverhill and symbolized the typical American rural experience at that time. The Whittier homestead, painted by Thomas Hill in 1868, came to represent this way of life to many, and the painting was reproduced as a chromolithograph that was hung in thousands of parlors around the country. Courtesy, Trustees of the Haverhill Public Library.

talented poet, some of whose works are genuine masterpieces of regional poetry. "The Barefoot Boy" retains some of the charm of his early years and the moments of freedom stolen from the hours of labor on the family farm. Yet, in his own day, Whittier was known as well for his prose writing; he was editor of newspapers at Boston, Hartford, Philadelphia, and Lowell. Whittier published his first poem in Garrison's *Free Press* in 1826, and the two men were associated in one way or another until Garrison's death in 1879. Yet the moral tone Whittier brought to his work was more restrained and in a sense wider. Whittier protested the slavery of blacks, but on one occasion he also joined the protest of factory labor, here on the lower Merrimack. In 1852 he took the side of the workers against management during a strike at the Amesbury/Salisbury woolen mills. Whittier was born in the Valley before industry made its startling transformations of the place, and in the end he was not convinced that Lowell—or any other factory town on the river—was the birthplace of the "Millennium of Mechanism." When he was a young man, the factory system on the Merrimack promised to free Humanity from toil, to lift Mankind into a radically improved way of life, but as both Whittier and the system matured he noticed that it did not

end toil so much as make a new distribution of labor among the populations of the textile cities. It was not machines that would disclose the meaning of the American experience of freedom.

Writers in this century have been less obvious about awaiting or abetting the opening of the American millennium. Yet both John Marquand and Jack Kerouac, who had not very much in common, set out to explain America; both were inspired by John Galsworthy's *Forsythe Saga* to produce a family chronicle in fiction as a symbol of the American story in fact. John P. Marquand spent half a century at Curzon's Mill in West Newbury, and he was a sort of Merrimack industry in himself, earning about $10 million as a wordsmith in just under 40 years. Some of that was found in the Hollywood market by the popular stories of the instructable Mr. Moto. Many of his other novels, however, show us a character in the process of discovering that the American success story—money and the "women of the upper brackets" who come with it—is at heart a tragedy, for the futility of the prize is hidden until the game is played out. The novels are, on reflection, the story of Marquand's own life, cautionary tales that perhaps indicate the traps of culture without indicating an escape.

Kerouac's story, although beginning so differently from Marquand's, nevertheless finds a similar end. Like the older writer, Kerouac knew the influence of Galsworthy, but being of the generation next after Marquand's he also knew the work of Thomas Wolfe, closer to home. Both Kerouac's parents were children of French-speaking Canadians and Jack's first look at America was from the inside of the working class in a textile city past its prime. Despite that, and because of it as well, he was devoted to the power of words,

Descended from French-Canadian mill workers, Jack Kerouac graduated from Lowell High School in 1939, when this photo was taken. While attending Columbia University on a football scholarship, an injury interrupted his career, and he turned to writing adventures with himself as the central character. His 1957 novel, On the Road, *caught the imagination of the Beat generation and inspired the flower children of the 1960s, but Kerouac also wrote five novels about Lowell that are less famous. Courtesy, University of Lowell Collection.*

using language to dramatize himself in stories of mythic proportions, epics of spiritual emancipation and beatitude. He was born at Lowell in 1922 and left the city in 1939, and he later wrote five novels set in that locale. However, those novels have never commanded the kind of response given to *On the Road*, published in 1957. All his work is autobiographical but it was in this book that America recognized itself. So, the saga of the town on the river goes unread while Kerouac, "King of the Beats," still races time across the whole of the American continent, a trajectory without a center, as one of his cronies said of him. In the right place at the right time, Kerouac helped the next generation accept speed as the latest commodity in our national cycles of discovery and consumption.

Any attempt at reading the culture of a people and of a generation in the career and work of one individual is risky at best. Given the entire range of the performance and presence of these writers, however, it is difficult to ignore the lack of care and grace that Americans have shown for this place in their anxiety to discover the secrets of the future.

The word "culture"—so the dictionary tells us—derives from the same root and stem as the word "cult"; both originate in the Latin verb *colere*, meaning to attend to, to

respect. The sense of experience behind that is flexible enough to describe mental things—respect for Apollo, attending to the oracle at Delphi—and to describe as well some very earthbound things like the culture of tulips or pinto beans or maize. But nowadays the word nearly always has the sense given to it here, the sense of human culture that comprises the ways and forms of expression we use to attend to ourselves, to reflect on what we do and find what there is to respect in that. There has been human culture on the lower Merrimack for several thousands of years but it has been for less than two centuries that culture has reflected so many human forms and images that no one has been able to attend to them all. The Pennacook sense of respect for this Strong Place was eradicated, consumed in the burning need the Puritans had to tell God's Time in their beating out of the measure and cadence of Scripture. The experience of the past 200 years has multiplied the things we ought or might attend to and left us not very certain which of them to respect. We are left, now, with many cultures separated from one another by language, customs, and religious ideas and rites, as well as by education and income, so that while we are here at the same time we do not share really the same place.

One sign of that is our material culture, for instance in the separation of the workplace from the living place. That was begun by tying production to a machine and the machine to a central source of power, and it was completed when the automobile made so many of us independently mobile. Or, again, the styles of domestic architecture also bespeak cultural fragmentation and hint at cultural conflict. Until the 1820s there was a remarkable degree of simplicity and uniformity in the style of dwelling of the residents on the lower Merrimack. There was cohesion, therefore, in the appearance of the towns. But between 1820 and 1860, four styles of building gave a choice to those with the means to choose how they wanted to represent themselves to their neighbors, or distinguish themselves from the common lot of those around them. Greek Revival, Gothic Revival, Italianate, and Empire all made their appearance in one generation, and it is emblematic of how material culture changed and continues to change in this region, as in the nation at large. So rapidly, in fact, that the way of life of one generation is not readily accessible, perhaps hardly plausible, to the next; the tools and the place of labor of the fathers no longer apprentice the sons to a way of life common to both. What we have now, in our architectural heritage, is a bewildering collection of heirlooms and hybrids, a built-up environment that reflects a persistent confusion about what time it is in the Valley.

The varieties in material culture fostered by the revolution in production and mobility were overlayed, and not a little camouflaged, by the arrival of spectacular cultural varieties from Europe.

Architectural Culture

One readily apparent facet of culture is architecture. In the Merrimack Valley a multiplicity of styles remains to show the affluence and taste developed by the middle and upper classes during the 19th century. Architectural studies of individual communities and the region as a whole document both surviving structures and those lost to "progress." Two books in particular are worth noting. John Mead Howell's *The Architectural Heritage of the Merrimack: Early Houses and Gardens* (1941; reprinted 1980) treats the 18th- and early 19th-century legacy, with particular attention to Newburyport. John Coolidge, in *Mill and Mansion: A Study of Architecture and Society in Lowell, Massachusetts, 1820-1865* (1942; reprinted 1967), discusses the relationship of factory buildings and housing in the evolution of the city.

Below: John Coolidge described the influential square, solid Italianate style with its inevitable tower as "rich and substantial, although varied and not stuffy." Built in 1852 the William Livingstone house, located on Thorndike Street at Chelmsford Street in Lowell, had lost some of its pairs of brackets and other details by the time Coolidge took this photo in the late 1930s, but it still displayed the overall plan of the Italianate style: a great cube with a wing, porches, and balconies, topped by bracketed eaves and a cupola. (MVTM)

Above: Built in about 1839, this house on Howard Street displays the common combination of Gothic and Classical elements. The pointed windows and decorative bargeboards are Gothic details above the doorway's Ionic columns. The flush-boarded facade and recessed doorway are Classical. (MVTM)

Above: *Near the Livingstone house, a Highland Street neighbor imitated its forms—cupola, porches, quoins—in a compressed format later in the 1850s. Bow windows replaced open porches and balconies, but the builder kept the cupola and loggia in nearly exact replication on a smaller scale. The mansard roofs of its neighbors are the most prevalent characteristic of the French Second Empire style of architecture, also frequently found in Lowell and throughout the Valley. (MVTM)*

Right: *By the 1830s the basic New England frame house had been embellished with details such as the Greek Revival pedimented portico and Ionic columns built as part of Kirk Boott's Lowell mansion in about 1825. Its pillared portico bears a strong resemblance to those of Southern plantation mansions, recalling the close link between the economic interests of the manufacturers and planters of cotton. After Boott's death in 1837, the house was moved and served as the Corporation Hospital. When later incorporated into St. Joseph's Hospital, run by the Sisters of Charity of Quebec province, it bore a sign in French: "Hôpital." (MVTM)*

In 1892 the Hale family of Lawrence enjoys an outing to a farm and Haggett's Pond in Andover's West Parish. The decorated wagon represents a Mediterranean agricultural tradition reminiscent of the Old World. Andover's West Parish contained rich farmlands along the Merrimack, and Armenian families joined the Yankee, Scottish, and English families who had settled there earlier. (MVTM)

Foreign-born laborers began arriving in numbers at the textile cities on the lower Merrimack during the 1840s— Irish immigrants looking for work and escaping the horrors of famine at home. These strangers and those who came after were taken by the native American for an ominous sign with no clear intention but with certain obscure dangers for the traditions of the Merrimack towns. The foreign born themselves reacted to the Anglo majority by closing circle, unaware as yet of the irony that put them inside the wagons while the natives whooped and hollered around them. This siege mentality drove scores of ethnic groups and made citadels of their neighborhoods, whose boundaries were defended on more than one occasion with brawn and bricks. These ethnic enclaves, small cultural republics, might be crowded and unsanitary like the tenement districts of Lowell and Lawrence, or they might be more healthy and spacious like the farms of Pleasant Valley in Methuen or those in Andover's West Parish.

Always, however, the enclave served to buffer the transition from the old country to this one, to surround the immigrant with the assurance of the familiar in dress, food, and language. In this way, and in many others, the Polish and Russian immigrant or the Italian and Greek coming to these towns behaved just like the English who founded them two centuries before. Always, the church—as a building and as a community—was the center of these ethnic groups, and worship in the traditional language was often an issue of intense feelings among new and later arrivals. The use of Lithuanian in Lithuanian Catholic churches, the

use of French among the French-speaking Canadians, was a matter charged not only with the conditions that immigrants found on the Merrimack, but also by the conditions in the country of origin, where language was often a badge of solidarity with the past. Schools were only slightly less important than the church to these ethnic groups, and often they were tied to the parish in funding, administration, and curriculum.

Aside from providing psychological security, the ethnic communities also gave some measure of social insurance, a real fiscal safety net to individuals and to families. In those years before the first term of Franklin Roosevelt when the New Deal owned up to the economic and social costs of a market economy, charitable organizations and mutual-assistance societies were the last resort for the jobless or the destitute, or for anyone who seemed stranded in a bleak and hopeless present. Each club or society was organized to serve one particular ethnic group, and in the decades that began this century there were hundreds of them in the cities and towns on the lower Merrimack. They paid for food and shelter, for drugs and health care, and for burial in consecrated ground. The sense of community included the dead.

Observing these ethnic communities from the outside and seldom with a friendly eye, native Americans failed to notice the points of similarity among them as they almost willfully neglected the points of similarity between themselves and the newcomers in the Valley. Because these newcomers were ignorant of the English language, they were too often counted illiterate when in fact language, spoken and written, was highly prized as a pledge of survival, a vessel in transit from past to future. It was in the nature of the place and the process that this regard for language was most often put to liturgical uses. The *Librarie Biron*, for example, doing business in the heart of Lowell's Little Canada, was a kind of literary arsenal, selling and circulating books printed in Quebec and Montreal as so many arms in the ongoing experience of struggle and survival. At Lawrence, on the other hand, the Lebanese community printed a book of grammar codifying the rules of that language and making it more accessible to more people. The book found a market outside the Valley. Lawrence, in fact, was something of a center of foreign-language press in the nation, turning out books in Lithuanian, Polish, Italian, German, French, and other "native tongues." Finally, the towns and cities on the lower Merrimack were active centers of foreign-language journalism. Dailies and weeklies brought news from the Old Country and news of what was happening within the readers' own ethnic community. Also, these newspapers were often the only alternative to the priest or rabbi for information about the wider world outside the Valley and its many communities. This was often important, though it led to tugs of war between priest

Not all of the supporters of the 1912 strike were radical anarchists. The strikers did have a just cause, vindicated by their victory and the national support shown at Congressional hearings and in reports by progressive journalists. In order to commemorate the strike without the tinge of anarchy, Pleasant Valley Citizens Club, a German social organization, records its solidarity with the positive aspect of reform: "For the struggle of the Strike of 1912." Courtesy, Immigrant City Archives.

and editor for leadership of this or that group.

The barrier of language was real. Sometimes the misunderstanding was not intended, sometimes it was humorous. The French-speaking Canadians at Lowell tended to pronounce Moody Street as though they were saying "Maudit" Street, that is, Cursed or Damned Street. So subtle is the alchemy of language in the relation of word to its context, that mere sound can transform the name of a respected mechanic into a cuss word. However, the humor in the trick depended on a knowledge of two languages and a certain distance from both, in the same way that visual depth is perceived. Other misunderstandings were not so innocent and involved bitter contest over the meaning of English words, words "translated" from one group's experience by another group's memory of it.

In September 1912 a public meeting was held at Lawrence by some of the strikers of the previous winter; they called themselves Anarchists and displayed banners advocating "No God, No Country." And as they *were* anarchists and they *were* immigrants, those banners proclaimed their conviction that this place fit the description of things they had learned to recognize before seeing them put before them in the Valley. Those at the meeting in September meant that both God and Country had become the idols

of another clan, that they were names used by their corporate employers only to cover with decency the indecent fragmentation brought into the lives of workers by what employers liked to call the "organization" of production. Those words—God and Country—struck their souls with the same chilling effect as the water from the hoses turned on their bodies during the demonstrations of the previous winter. Each side in this war of words was so sure of its own rendition of the facts that the other side's view of it was put down to bad faith rather than bad vision. The workers themselves were divided on the question and large segments of them had kept away from strike activity, partly at least because so much of the propaganda of the strikers was red and communist and godless. So, when Father O'Reilly of St. Mary's church organized a parade "For God and Country" on Columbus Day (1912), there were 32,000 marchers behind him to give witness that God and Country were well wedded at Lawrence. Most of these marchers were workers, of course, and some of them no doubt had been among the strikers who demonstrated in the earlier months of the year for what they had called "bread and roses."

There can only be one public language of course, and it was inevitable and necessary that the public language of these cities and towns should be English. Teaching the English language to the foreign born was one motive that prompted some women of the upper classes from the Lawrence area to found the International Institute of that city in 1913. This was one response to the strike of the previous year, resting on the faith that all conflict is the result of ignorance and misunderstanding. The institute continues

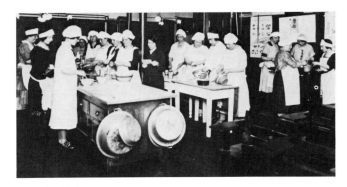

Americanization as an institutionalized process developed wherever the native-born population felt threatened or overwhelmed by the customs, language, and numbers of immigrants. Throughout the Merrimack Valley, classes in English language and American citizenship competed with ethnic clubs and churches. Instruction for women included domestic duties, nutrition, health, and child care. A cooking class for immigrant women at Lowell's girls' vocational school on Lee Street follows the directions read by instructor Miss Soroka, circa 1920. Courtesy, Lowell Historical Society.

Education in the Valley

The culture of the word on the lower Merrimack was manifest in the concern the founders of its towns showed for educating the young and the dependent. Paramount in this early concern was to teach "children and apprentices so much learning as may enable them perfectly to read the English tongue." The effort at public education in the Valley began in 1639 when the town of Newbury voted 10 acres of land to Anthony Somerby, "for his encouragement to keep schoole for one year." Gradually, improving conditions of security and economy allowed for common schools at Bradford in 1701 and at Andover the year before, at Methuen in 1735 and at Dunstable not until 1748.

Private academies were also founded. The first of these was the Dummer school at South Byfield (Newbury), established in March 1763 following the will and bequest of the late Lieutenant Governor William Dummer. Still flourishing as Dummer Academy, it was the first independent boarding school in the Commonwealth. Somewhat later, Samuel Phillips of Andover, with the help of uncles John and William, founded the academy that still bears their name. Phillips Academy began offering courses of instruction in 1778, but it was not until Octo-

ber 1780 that it was legally incorporated by the General Court "for the purpose of instructing youth, not only in english & latin grammar, writing, arithmetic, and those Sciences wherein they are commonly taught, but more especially to learn them the *great end and real business of living.*"

A similar institution in the town's North Parish was the first incorporated academy in the Commonwealth to admit girls; named the Franklin Academy, it survived until the middle of the past century. Another educational institution for young women founded in 1803 survives to this day as Bradford College, though it is now coeducational. Yet another, Abbot Academy, founded in 1828 at Andover, has in recent years been merged with Phillips.

Andover was also the site of a theological seminary opened in 1808 to combat what some took to be a growing laxity in the teaching of Calvinism at Harvard College. Although located at Andover, the seminary was begun with the support, spiritual and financial, of William Bartlett and Moses Brown, both wealthy merchants of Newburyport. The seminary was a regional effort at recalling the true purpose and real business of the communities on the lower Merrimack. In 1908 it was moved to Cambridge by special agreement with the Harvard Divinity School. Similar sentiments led the Augustinian Fathers to found Merrimack College in 1947, so that Catholic households in the area of greater Lawrence might have a place of higher education to send their children. The region is served also by the Northern Essex Community College at Haverhill and by the University of Lowell, organized recently by combining the Lowell State Teachers College and the former Lowell Textile Institute, which traced its origins to 1893.

Andover—a name synonomous with education—was home to the Theological Seminary, Phillips Academy, and Abbot Academy when this lithograph was published by local businessman W.F. Draper in 1857. The three portions of town, known in jest as the Mill, the Till, and the Hill, appear from left to right. The academy and seminary buildings occupy the lofty heights of the hill at right center. (MVTM)

Above: *The Haverhill High School class of 1935 included four sets of twins. Haverhill's first high school building was built in 1873 on the site of the first town schoolhouse. In the spirit of the 19th-century commitment to free public education, the advancement of learning was an early goal of Valley settlers, fulfilled by dame schools and private academies. Courtesy, Trustees of the Haverhill Public Library.*

Left: *Isaac Roberts became the first black graduate of Haverhill High School in 1895 and embarked upon an interesting career. Born in Liberia, he was brought to the United States as a boy. His father, a Baptist minister, served at Calvary Baptist Church in Haverhill as well as in Brooklyn, New York, and Connecticut churches. Always interested in science, Roberts studied soil chemistry and took the knowledge back to Africa, where he successfully owned and managed plantations. He served his country as a politician, ran a trading and exporting company, and was knighted by Liberia's President King. Courtesy, Trustees of the Haverhill Public Library.*

Phillip Coombs made a stereograph of people and carriages at the "Great Gathering," at sandy Salisbury Beach on September 17, 1861. (Private Collection)

to this day to help immigrant women and men adapt to the primary culture of the Valley, to find and to use the opportunities it holds for them.

One way to register and to calibrate the changes of culture, the innovations and crosscurrents of the past, is to look at our material culture, to learn to read our physical man-made environment as closely as archaeologists may learn to read the artifacts of cultures no longer living. And the beach at Salisbury is one place more convenient than most in the Valley to do this. The uses we have made of the seashore and the ways used to develop its commercial potential—certainly the design and purpose of the buildings erected there—all combine to reveal the transformation of our cultural values.

Up to the time of the Civil War, the seafront at Salisbury was very much as the wind and sea had shaped it in the centuries before the Europeans arrived on the Merrimack. Salisbury was incorporated in 1640, and for two centuries after that it was not different from most of the other towns on the river. Its economy was mainly agricultural, but with a district called The Mills at its western end where the waters of the Powow were put to textile production in the 1820s. The seafront end of the town, then, must have been very like what we see today at the wildlife reservation on

Plum Island, some few miles to the south. It is worth the mention that these seafront parcels were the very last pieces of Valley land to go from the estates of the descendants of the original proprietors. The Newbury lands on Plum Island were not finally divided until 1823, and the shares that held the beachfront at Salisbury were not sold by the common proprietors until 1911.

The diary of Isaac Merrill shows him on occasional excursions to Plum Island as early as the 1820s. Sometimes this was done by large parties in a festive mood, sometimes in more intimate groups suited to finding contemplation or to placing a confidence. In any case, it seems safe to say that his generation—born soon after 1800—was less restrained in its enjoyment of nature, less determined to maintain a strict frontier between the natural environment and human culture. We even find Merrill reaching for the word "transcendental" to describe the beauty he found in this place, a term very much in vogue in the higher circles of New England culture, the heady sphere inhabitated by Thoreau and Emerson and their Concord friends.

We can suppose, then that the Beach at Salisbury was also a place of visitation even before the tradition of Tenting on the Beach that Whittier wrote about later in the century. Also, there were Great Gatherings, so called, held in late summer during the middle years of the century and mixing an abundance of food with a garnish of oratory such as once was provided by Caleb Cushing. There were no residents on the Beach until the first cottage was built in

*Just as the river steamer became outmoded, the automobile re-
placed the trolley car as the primary means of transportation to
Salisbury Beach. Reflecting America's love affair with the auto,
the Dodg'em car ride was developed as an amusement at the
beach. First introduced in 1921, the car was manufactured in
Lawrence out of sheet metal provided by J.F. Bingham Company. Established in 1888 and still in business, the metal company has turned from making tea kettles and Dodg'em panels
to parts for computers and electronics equipment. (Private Collection)*

1864, but the growth of the place must have been very
rapid, for the first plank road giving access to the Beach was
laid down only two years later, in 1866. These dates mark
the beginning of Salisbury as a resort, and for a half a century afterwards the story of that is more or less the story of
the rise and fall of Edward Payson Shaw.

Shaw was born at Newburyport in 1841, a boy from a
middling sort of family whose interest in the development
of the Beach came in good measure from his venture in the
manufacture of trolley cars and the operation of local transit lines. The fact that in one week in 1871, 1,158 carriages
rode over the plank road bearing nature-hungry visitors to
the Beach no doubt helped Shaw to see the potential of the
entertainment market in the residents on the lower Merrimack. Before he was through, Shaw owned the larger part
of the action to be had in freighting people to the Beach and
housing and feeding them once they got there. His most
romantic enterprise perhaps, one that still is fondly
recollected by some of the Valley's oldest residents, was the
river steamer *Merrimac*. She was built in the shipyard of
Lemuel Marquand at Ring's Island in 1892, and until 1915
she rode the waters of the river during season, carrying
tourists from Haverhill or other ports along the way, to the
Black Rocks at Salisbury. There, the passengers disem-
barked and found that Shaw's trolley cars were waiting to
carry them to the resort center. The *Merrimac* carried its
passengers from Haverhill to the Beach and back again for
25 cents, and that included a bowl of Colby's much-
esteemed chowder.

In addition, Shaw owned and operated the Cushing
Hotel at the Beach. Built in the manner of those large
wooden-frame structures of the late 19th century, the
Cushing served a class clientele and not the dailies who

Top: *Employees of the Brightwood Mills, North Andover, and their children enjoy an outing to Salisbury Beach in 1912. Despite the elaborate network of trolley lines, which brought workers from as far away as Lowell to the beach, this group traveled together in an early vehicle in the fleet of the Trombly Bus Company. (MVTM)*

Above: *Continuing the march of modernity, the streamlined design of the 1930s came to Salisbury Beach. The New Ocean Echo, revamped as the Frolics in a more modern style, became a nightclub offering dancing, big bands, and popular singing stars. By the 1950s fried clams, french fries, and pizza replaced the shore dinner of an earlier era. (Private Collection)*

made up the larger part of the passengers in the supply side of Shaw's operation. All of this came to a rather rude end for him in 1911, when heavy investment losses forced Shaw to sell his Beach properties to a group calling itself the Salisbury Beach Associates. Local residents resented this intrusion of developers who were based at Lawrence, and those common proprietors who still retained control over their shares of the Beach took legal action to prevent it. They failed, however, and their failure signaled the beginning of another era in the story of this resort on the Atlantic.

The break from the past is rather clean, marked clearly in September 1913 by a great fire that destroyed the Cushing Hotel and other structures at the Beach center. It also consumed some 100 cottages built along the oceanfront to the south of that. Instead of rebuilding the Cushing or another hotel like it, the Salisbury Beach Associates created a different sort of resort, offering faster-paced and more-transient entertainment. The physical center was now the Ocean Echo, a dance hall large enough to hold hundreds of spooning couples, who more and more often would arrive by auto rather than trolley. When this building was destroyed by fire in January 1920, a New Ocean Echo took its place. Several hotels were built during those years just before and just after the First World War, but none of them ever achieved the status or the success of the Cushing.

After 1913 the character of the Beach changed, and that was unmistakably apparent not only in the dance hall but also in the fun house, arcades, and rides, in the vending of food on the Beach, and in the live performers to entertain visitors. Salisbury Beach had lost the face of a somewhat genteel, if not thoroughly top-drawer, resort. During the Roaring Twenties, the Beach reflected instead the rather short-term expectation of flappers and their beaus. One novelty was the "Dodgem" which offered controlled mayhem and safe aggression. The Dodgem was developed and manufactured at Lawrence and introduced to the world during the 1921 season at Salisbury. A roller coaster was built also. Noise, speed, and crowds became the accepted ingredients of fun and entertainment. As an alternative to labor, it seemed badly designed to bring balance and refreshment to the environment of the textile workers who went there. Also, it was only after the fire of 1913 that buildings were put on the Beach itself. This of course created a street parallel to the shoreline, and the buildings along this street turned their backs to the Atlantic; they faced those happy throngs of paying tourists. The street is still called Oceanfront in flat denial of where it is and what it is.

It was during the period between the First World War and the Second World War that the southern end of the Beach was built up into ethnic neighborhoods, designed by imitation of the mill towns upriver and reflecting the cultural divisions of their labor force. This was yet another face put on the Beach, more quiet, less hectic, and oriented to the needs and pace of family vacations and outings. In 1936 this southern end was razed to make room for a public state reservation. Still there and still very popular, the reservation has in late years become a haven for recreational vehicles and the devotees of a seminomadic subculture.

Through the 1930s the Great Depression brought a scaled-down mix of entertainment to the beach. The New Ocean Echo was the site of more than one dance marathon and of Beano games only slightly less compulsive. Salisbury became so notorious for rum running that the local lifesaving station was transformed into a Coast Guard Station with a staff of some 30 persons. On the eve of the Second World War, the dance hall, the New Ocean Echo was transformed into something called the Frolics, which was a dinner club attracting customers with its reputation for tasty lobster and big-name entertainment. Getting there was as simple as owning a car and knowing the roads. The enterprise was a success through to the late 1950s, presenting star attractions of the time like Patti Page, Liberace, and the McGuire Sisters. Eventually, however, other and more highly capitalized places such as Las Vegas and Miami Beach could afford such staggering weekly engagement fees to these entertainers that Salisbury was forced out of the high end of the business. A decade ago the roller coaster and the Dodgem and the carousel were removed, and what Salisbury Beach has now are high-tech rides designed and made in France, and new arcades stocked with videogames designed and made in Japan.

The Beach has been called the industrial park of Salisbury in what may be an attempt to upgrade the image it has among its Merrimack neighbors, which once had world-reputed capacities for production. The shopping mall, however, is a better analogy, because the Beach is an environment saturated by the culture of consumption. Concessions and arcades and rides are now owned by local families—Irish, Lebanese, Jewish—who are in the second and third generation of enterprise at Salisbury. From that viewpoint, it remains local and native to the region of the lower Merrimack. But to its thousands of visitors during any one day of the summer months, it might as well be the Methuen Mall stocked with a constant flow of enticements designed, it seems, to prevent one moment from following another. Visitors at Salisbury, however, take away no product; what they consume is time.

VIII

FINDING THE FUTURE

Critical acumen is exerted in vain to uncover the past; the *past* cannot be *presented*; we cannot know what we are not. But one veil hangs over past, present, and future, and it is the province of the historian to find out, not what was, but what is.
—Henry David Thoreau, *A Week on the Concord and Merrimack Rivers*, 1849.

Could we, indeed, say what we want, could we give a description of the child that is lost, he would be found.
–Margaret Fuller, *The Dial*, July 1840

Wilkes Allen, in his history of the town, betrayed no doubts in the advice he gave the townsmen of Chelmsford, very likely because, in 1820, he saw no reason to question how the world is made. He reported one altar, one town, one community, deployed for a single purpose and all set at play in "the" planetary system. When Isaac Newton disclosed the clockwork of the planets in 1687, he confirmed the only piece of science uniformly anticipated by every Christian, namely that the one living God

Despite the Depression, Valley residents managed to find enjoyment at little or no cost, such as swimming. This group cools off in Haverhill's Lake Saltonstall during the summer of 1935. Courtesy, Trustees of the Haverhill Public Library.

Haverhill's river front, shown in the early 20th century before construction of the Basilier Bridge in 1924-1925, was an important commercial and manufacturing district. The stern-wheeler at the wharf carried passengers to Newburyport and Salisbury Beach. Courtesy, Trustees of the Haverhill Public Library.

created only one universe, a harmony of magnitudes glorifying one motive. So, "the" planetary system he described looked familiar even when it was brand spanking new. It was a description of the universe both elementary and compelling; its mathematical formulas appealed to intellectuals, while the clockwork metaphor put it within the understanding of even the illiterate. Also, it was a description of the universe that expected and half invited the mechanics of industrial production. Newton's picture of how things are put together and how they work is clear, direct, certain. In 1820 it was evident to all the readers of *The History of Chelmsford*. Simply by reminding them of where they were—reminding them of their place in the system—Allen was asking the citizens of Chelmsford to find the future in their own convictions.

The Reverend Mr. Allen appealed for unity and harmony. The fabric of town life, he said, is made of its social and spiritual ends as well as the economic and political. All the ends of human life should come together as in the cloth, and they should work together as in the pattern. He wanted

A West Newbury farmhouse in winter forms a scene of stark but timeless beauty. Photo by Bill Lane.

human culture to imitate the design of Nature, and it is evident from his book that he expected Chelmsford—the town itself, the town together—would continue to be the most accessible and responsive tool in shaping culture. It was a hope natural enough for a minister of the Lord in this Valley where town had replaced church as the primary community. After all, in 1820 the towns on the lower Merrimack were nearly two centuries old, and their 200 years of tradition included the practice of economic regulation. However, in 1820 this traditional way of getting things done was old enough to be revered, old enough to be protected by its age alone. At town meeting on May 25, 1801, the voters of Dracut unanimously resolved against a petition then before the General Court of Massachusetts to allow "the erection of a dam across Merrimack River at Pawtucket Falls." They were against it, they said, because a dam would:

> totally destroy the fish in the said river and deprive the people [of Dracut] of the important privilege which they for a long time, even from time immemorial, have enjoyed without molestation; of taking neare theire doors the most delicate food and much of the real necessaries of Life.

The voters of the Merrimack towns had replaced the "saints" with their vested right and power to find the future, even if the voters trusted the omens of economic development rather more than the opaque directions of Holy Writ. But the voters at Dracut tended to find a future that looked very much like the past, and so, in 1801, they preferred the "necessaries" of fishing to the "necessaries" of manufacturing. From a strictly economic point of view their ideas were old-fashioned, and the towns had become agents of preservation rather than invention. They stood in the ways of "progress." Then, in February 1822, the General Court of Massachusetts began erecting manufacturing corporations, and these corporations came in time to rival the towns of the Valley in deciding the future.

The Merrimack Manufacturing Company was the first of them, but many textile corporations followed that one, and all of them together engineered a major revolution in the Valley. It was easy for these corporations, compared with the towns, to make a break with the past and find a new future—easier since all their decisions were economic ones, decisions cut loose from their social and political consequences for people and place. In the early years of industry on the Merrimack, the textile manufacturers had proven their social conscience and demonstrated a real concern for the well-being of everyone involved in production. By the time of the Civil War, however, that point of view was left behind by the large manufacturers at Lowell and Lawrence, and the republican model of production was replaced by the cult of the bottom line. The center of this new corporate universe existed in books, among production figures, cost-analysis figures, and the figures of profit margins—percentages and fractions of percentages. Imagining the process of production as a system of numbers gave it a complete and secure appearance; numbers validated conclusions and intentions the way mathematics had validated Newton's system of the planets.

The Merrimack Valley Militia trained each summer at Camp Dewey in Framingham. Notice the bed linen and wash stand, as well as the reclining chairs. Courtesy, Trustees of the Haverhill Public Library.

Essex County's Eighth Regiment mobilized at Camp Thomas, Chicamauga, Georgia, on the way to Cuba in 1898. Their model sanitary record saved them from the scourge of typhoid that killed more men than the Spanish-American War. Courtesy, Trustees of the Haverhill Public Library.

Figures, then, were set out in the boardrooms of Boston, where corporate directors used them to lay down odds on how the future would go. They were weighted with unnatural gravity and able to pull in their wake all the other factors of production, so that the well-being and job security of the laborers, the economic and ecological security of the region, became satellites of the system rather than partners of it. The great textile corporataions on the lower Merrimack did in fact invent a new future after 1820, but they did this by imposing a hierarchy of value rather than disclosing an increase of harmony.

Within a century, however, and even in less than a century, the textile manufacturers began making a grim discovery. They found that the towns on the lower Merrimack were aging, were "old" in fact. By the 1920s the opinion was firmly rooted that, like textile cities and towns throughout New England, Lowell and Lawrence had antiquated plants and obsolete machinery. They were cramped and congested, making traffic an added burden to organization. Some of the factories at Lowell and Lawrence even looked like "castles," towers and all. Anyone who looked for signs of age would find them, and eventually even a lover cannot ignore what is apparent. Age of course is relative, and if the Valley towns were old they had to be old in comparison to another place. That other place was in the Southern states of the Union, principally in the Carolinas and Georgia. Textile production in the Southern states was enormously increased in the years between the 1880s and the opening decades of this century. By the 1920s the Southern mills showed a clear competitive advantage

over those of New England. One estimate made in 1923 claimed that Southern mills had a cost advantage of 14 percent, and that 85 percent of this advantage resulted from the lower wages paid to the Southern textile workers.

The Southern mills were also said to have a second advantage: the newest and most productive machinery. In the cotton industry, that technological superiority was centered on the so-called automatic loom, a loom equipped with an automatic bobbin changer that became available in 1894. That single device produced a tremendous leap in productivity and created a significant cost advantage for manufacturers using the automatic loom over those who did not. Northern manufacturers bought 104,955 of the looms in the years between 1909 and 1916, a figure comparing favorably with the 76,786 bought by Southern manufacturers during the same period. Sustained by the demands for cloth that came with the First World War, this expansion of productivity was the last undertaken by Northern textile corporations. It was in the postwar slump that manufacturers in New England judged, and judged correctly, that productivity of the industry *nationally* had outrun the market and that, other things being equal, the lower labor cost of Southern manufacturers would inevitably drive Northern products from the marketplace. Having made that determination, Northern manufacturers removed a considerable amount of machinery already installed in their mills and shipped it to locations in the South. One study made in 1934 estimated that 4.8 million spindles and 109,000 cotton looms had been transferred in this way during the previous decade. It is difficult to see in the move anything but an attempt by Northern manufacturers at fixing the odds to favor the wager they had already made on the future.

The relocation of Northern textile operations to Southern points was a complex process, involving social and political adjustments. From a fiscal point of view, textile manufacturers had no choice but to pursue survival according to the rules of the market economy. And in that they were merely following the values they had set themselves in the previous 100 years. Yet the economic and social consequences for Lowell and Lawrence—and for other Merrimack towns as well—were prolonged and severe. For those left behind in this "old" place, the transfer of operations looked more like a "runaway" than a "relocation." It seemed to them that the social costs of production, the taxes and the regulations imposed by state or local authority, were not separate from industrial manufacturing. Public authority did not invent social costs but merely added them after corporations had refused to take them into account in their anxious devotion to making the figures come out "right." Nevertheless, these social costs were far lower or totally absent in Southern locations, and that was another attraction drawing manufacturers to the South. Finally, the

By the 1930s, few clam shacks remained in Newburyport's Joppa Flats, and one had taken to cooking the clams. The ever-popular fried clam is said to have been invented on Massachusetts' North Shore. Courtesy, Historical Society of Old Newbury.

Above: *The automatic bobbin changer, developed for the cotton loom in 1894, was adapted for worsted weaving by the early 20th century. Shown here on worsted looms of the Pacific Mills, Lawrence, in 1912, the device is the cylindrical part filled with bobbins, visible at the center bottom of the photo and on each loom in the center rows. (MVTM)*

Left: *When the textile industry began to leave the Valley, houses as well as factory buildings were included on the auction block. Workers faced the double jeopardy of losing both jobs and company housing. Unemployed operatives couldn't buy their homes, and many were forced to relocate, following textile jobs south or learning a new trade, which was not easy during the Depression. (MVTM)*

A group of skiers await the Boston and Maine "snow train" in 1936. Courtesy, Trustees of the Haverhill Public Library.

abundance of waterpower that once had favored the textile cities on the lower Merrimack no longer prevailed against the cheaper, more efficient drive of steam or electricity.

In 1886 Charles T. Main, then assistant superintendent of the Lower Pacific Mills at Lawrence, calculated the cost of steam relative to waterpower and concluded that the saving per day for his firm was $27.73. That is a considerable amount counted over the life of this basic capital investment. Besides, Main said, even "were there no gain in actual money charged to running expenses, there is a great gain in having a steady power throughout the year . . . independent of the rise and fall of a river." There were unexpected benefits as well. Steady power meant steady employment, and that, according to Main, procured "the better class of operatives." Overall, he concluded:

> The many advantages which may be gained in the selection of the site, such as nearness to markets, low freights, cheap coal and favorable conditions for building, can be attained with steam as the motive power far more frequently than with water as the power.

All this was not news to the textile manufacturers on the Merrimack, not even in 1886. In the previous decade steam

had displaced water as the prime motive force in the mills at Lowell, overtaking the 10,000 horsepower generated by the Locks and Canals from Pawtucket Falls. However, the low cost and convenience of steam—and electricity—was not decisive until the other variables had been added to the equation.

Then, abruptly it seemed, in the early 1920s things began to fall apart. Labor cost, social cost, power cost were set to compete in the marketplace crowded by the overextension of productivity, and there, in that marketplace, Lowell and Lawrence no doubt gave an appearance of age. Abbott Lawrence told his constituents in March 1837 that those he called money holders "can transfer their persons and property to any given place in or out of the country, having means always about them to do so." Those with investments in the textile industries on the lower Merrimack, having always had the means, now found the reasons to withdraw their capital.

Relocation or runaway, both words contain a judgement; the choice between them is political and the choice reminds us that vocabulary is never neutral. But whatever it's called, the process was long and difficult and uneven. Cotton

Betty Shannon worked at her father's Newburyport filling station during World War II. Women filled the jobs of men away serving in the armed services. Courtesy, Historical Society of Old Newbury.

manufacturers were the first to go, and because of that Lowell was most directly affected in the early years. Where the census of 1920 counted 29,693 wage earners at Lowell, 12,590 of those jobs had disappeared *before* the Great Depression added its impact in the fall of 1929. When hard times came to the rest of the country and to other industries, the residents of Lowell had already known the worse.

By 1940 only three of the Spindle City's original corporate giants were in operation. Two of these, the Merrimack Manufacturing Company and the Boott Mills, were closed in the mid-1950s. The third, the Lawrence Company, was acquired by the Ames Worsted Company in 1926, and the two were merged in 1955 as the Ames Textile Corporation. The woolen and worsted manufacturers on the Merrimack fared better than the cotton-goods industry, at least for a time. And so, Lawrence, a worsted center of the world, lost

A Newburyport High School mechanics class prepares students for war-related work in 1942. Courtesy, Historical Society of Old Newbury.

Etta and Fannie, the Kimel sisters, owned one of Haverhill's shoe manufacturing companies in the 1920s, a rare example of female entrepreneurship. Women operatives constituted an important part of the work force in boots and shoes, but they did not often own the operations. Courtesy, Trustees of the Haverhill Public Library.

Workmen stretch hides at the Hamel Leather Company in Haverhill, circa 1935. Tanneries, in addition to wooden-heel and last manufacturers, developed to serve Haverhill's important shoe industry. By 1930, the boot and shoe industry employed nearly 80 percent of Haverhill's manufacturing work force and accounted for more than 70 percent of the value of products manufactured. Courtesy, Trustees of the Haverhill Public Library.

only one-third of its workforce during those years from 1920 to 1940, compared to an attrition rate of more than 50 percent at Lowell. Production at Lawrence actually increased during the 1940s to meet the demand of the armed services during the Second World War. Prosperity survived the war but, as in the case of Lowell, the conclusion was swift once events were set in motion. Operating at near capacity in 1947, the Lawrence mills by 1952 had released 20,000 unemployed textile workers into the city. By the middle of the decade, all the city's major employers—the Pacific Mills, the Arlington Mill, the mills of the American Woolen Company—had ceased production. Walter Winchell predicted to his national audience that grass would soon grow in the streets of Lawrence, and Edward R. Murrow focused one of his television broadcasts on the plight of its residents.

Conditions in the shoe and leather industry were hardly better. When the labor statistics for Haverhill are added to those of Lowell and Lawrence, we find that the number of wage earners in these three cities was cut by more than half between 1920 and 1940. Not all the Merrimack towns were so seriously affected, of course. In those years Amesbury and North Andover retained their textile operations, and Andover was able to add to its stock of jobs. Yet those decades brought more hardship to more residents of the Valley than any before or since. Even when they were done with, those years survived as a legacy of bad feeling about the place itself.

A cloud of failure seemed to hang over Lowell and Lawrence and Haverhill. Psychologists say that individuals who are abandoned often react with guilt; they blame themselves for their predicament, if only because it is the nature of the problem that no one else is there to share the blame. In talking now with people who were left behind to deal with the thousands of unemployed and the acres of empty buildings, it is easy to conclude that communities react in much the same way. The textile and shoe industries had been powerful forces on the lower Merrimack, and their loss restored the full measure of responsibility to the cities for their own future. But finding a way through their legacy of negativism proved as difficult a task as solving the economic problems of the region for the two generations charting the way.

George Bower is a native of Lawrence and the author of *November . . . December*, a novel that pictures what life was like in that city in 1962. It is the story of B.D. Jordan and the relationship he enjoys with his father, and, in a sense, the action turns on the fact that B.D. discovers he can trust what his father has learned and use it to shape his own future. B.D. admires the strength of his grandparents, who "locked their egos in the mills" so that he could "develop as much as he wanted." And he is grateful that "they hadn't lived into the late forties when the woolen and worsted

While stumping for local Democrats in 1952, President Harry S. Truman visited Lawrence. Margaret Truman sat on the platform and listened with a youthful John F. Kennedy (at right). (Private Collection)

companies abandoned Lawrence for cheaper labor in the South." In the end, however, it is his father whom he admires and trusts. B.D. is a freshman at Tufts University but he returns to Lawrence for the usual academic holidays, and it is there that David Jordan advises his son to leave the city because, as he puts it, "just being a man here is a fight. . . . This city, mill cities like it, are dirty and Old World. . . . The truth is no one ever became anything by staying here and doing it." Harsh words, but David Jordan is talking from the bitterness of his own sense of defeat. Educated as a lawyer and elected to the state senate, he ran for Congress and lost.

If you really want to be a good lawyer [he tells his son] or mayor or public servant of any kind you've got to be able to breathe. If you strike too hard for excellence here you'll kill yourself because there's no atmosphere for excellence, the city doesn't understand it, what it is or what it means. You'll

finally be beaten by the people because they'll try to narrow you and condense you to what they are. And they will.

It is a tale of private virtue set against public indifference. It is a moral tale familiar in Valley fiction, at least since Flora Montgomery agonized over her future. Near the end of the book, David Jordan suffers a heart attack just as he has made important revelations about himself to his son. The drama of that scene seems contrived, set as it is on the banks of the Merrimack and within sight of the Great Stone Dam. Yet the point of the action remains true enough, that for both generations at Lawrence in 1962 there was no future to be found; not for those on the upside or for those on the downside of a life-plan. David Jordan is in fact killed by his heart, dying in the ambulance while it races death through the streets of "his wretched city." Consequently, B.D. accepts a football scholarship that will take him to sunny California, young California. He plans to be there in the very next month, January of a new year.

The man who *was* mayor of Lawrence in 1962 doesn't share the views of these fictional characters. John J. Buckley stayed in the city and was a prime mover in shaping policies for nearly 20 years. He was mayor of Lawrence from 1952 to 1966 and again from 1972 to 1978. John Buckley's recollection of events is that during those very bleak years of the early fifties, the city was left entirely to its own resources. Though given the extraordinary privilege of addressing the stockholders of the American Woolen Company, Buckley could not convince them of what he saw as their corporate responsibility to their employees and to the city, and so he could not affect the company's decision to divorce itself from both. The mayor also pleaded the case of Lawrence before public authority. He went to Washington soon after the 1952 election of Dwight Eisenhower, and he had a conference with the President together with Massachusetts Governor Christian Herter, Senator Henry Cabot Lodge, and Secretary Wilbur Weeks of the Commerce Department. Eisenhower, however, failed to recognize the promise he had made on the Lawrence Common during the campaign of 1952. Eisenhower the candidate had promised federal help, but now he thought better of that, and he defined the problem of Lawrence as local. The solution, he said, would have to be found by the city.

Since that time, state and federal authorities have become

In 1925, Haverhill's Water Street, the heart of the commercial district, included numerous enterprises reflecting a variety of building styles, especially obvious in window treatments and cornices. The street is now flanked by a high-rise building on the right and a shopping mall on the left. Courtesy, Trustees of the Haverhill Public Library.

very much involved in planning the future of Merrimack communities and have provided enormous amounts of money to help carry it off. The four cities on the lower Merrimack—Newburyport, Haverhill, Lawrence, Lowell— have all participated in projects of urban renewal and preservation and in programs of environmental control and rehabilitation. Since the 1960s, for instance, nearly a billion dollars has been spent in cleaning up the river, and 75 percent of that was provided by the federal government. In the area of urban planning, Lowell and Haverhill offer instructive contrasts on how to use the funds and how to combine federal and local government with the private sector of the region's economy as an effective coalition. From the early 1960s to the mid-1970s, millions of dollars were granted by federal agencies to renew Haverhill's center city.

Yet the number of "plans" written, the number of city planners, the variety of consultants—with offices in New York, Palo Alto, or Dallas—robbed all efforts of coordinated and cumulative results. The center of Haverhill was razed and turned over to the culture of the automobile. There is a shopping mall that reflects the most advanced thinking of the 1950s, though this one was built in the 1970s. And like most malls, this one is reached over a four-lane roadway, cut through the inner city and parallel to the river. This roadway, however, connects nothing with nothing and leads to nowhere, because federal policies about its funding changed before the connection could be made. One new result of all this was to alienate a fair part of

The Renaissance of Lowell

Lowell's renaissance, the result of grass-roots deter-mination and solid organization at the local level, has benefited from federal and state support channeled through the Lowell Historic Preservation Commission. The Commission, a board composed of federal, state, and local officials, monitors the historic district and both initiates and supports programs in architectural preser-vation and rehabilitation, cutural events, and com-munity projects. The turning point that spurred Lowell's dramatic rebirth was the demolition of the Dutton Street

boardinghouses in 1966. Community response mobilized an effort that culminated in the Lowell Plan, the creation by Congress of the Lowell Historic Canal District Commission (1975), and the establishment of the Lowell Historical National Park (1978), the United States' first urban national park. A state heritage park, proposed in 1974 and mandated by the Massachusetts legislature in 1978, provides visitor services. Lowell's early years as a world-renowned industrial experiment are receiving new attention from both historians and tourists, the result of its increased visibility and variety of programs.

Left: *Built in the first half of the 19th century, these brick blocks on Dutton Street housed the operatives of Lowell's Mer-rimack Manufacturing Company. After a heated local debate that drew national attention from historians and concerned pre-servationists, the buildings were lost to the wrecking ball in 1966. (MVTM)*

Below: *Photographed immediately prior to their demolition in 1966, the Dutton Street boardinghouses sit serenely beside the Merrimack Canal, awaiting destruction. Their loss triggered a local response that ultimately led to Lowell's present commit-ment to its historic industrial past. (MVTM)*

the city's citizens from the city government. Like many clouds, however, this one has its silver lining. Enough citizens were put off by civic authorities to organize their own efforts at rehabilitating Haverhill. These local plans produced the Ward Hill industrial area and garnered a citation for Haverhill as all All-American City in 1978.

By contrast, the "Lowell Plan" included city, state, and federal participation from the time it was first put down on the back of a placemat at a local restaurant. The private business sector was included as well. Coordination came in the form of the Lowell Historic Preservation Commission, with representatives from all sectors involved in writing and executing the Lowell Plan. The commission was an agency of the Department of the Interior, which is also responsible for the operation of the Lowell National Historical Park. Lowell is the site of the first national urban park, and the park itself is an important part of the Lowell Plan. When Congress created the LHPC in 1978, it also committed 40 million federal dollars to fund its 10-year lease on life. It was, as Senator Paul Tsongas called it, a $40-million "wager," and not a "bailout."

In the last quarter of the 20th century, Western Electric and later Lucent Industries, employed thousands at its Haverhill plant. Other large corporations in the field of communications—Honeywell, Digital Equipment Corporation, and Wang Laboratories—also sited large operations in the region. Electronics, high technology, and communications were the industries which replaced the departed textile companies as the largest employers on the lower Merrimack. However, by the turn of the millennium, or soon after, these employers had moved to other locations or closed altogether. Of those large employers with a 20 or 30 year history in the region, only the Raytheon Company, a defense contractor in Andover, survived. The same economic forces which took away the textile giants in the first half of the century, were active in the case of electronics and communications, at the end of the century.

There is one aspect of the high-tech and communications industries that continues to have its impact. For, aside from the economics of the matter, those industries generate a new language in a radical sense. They generate new forms of picturing and understanding human activity, whether individual or social. This "language" shapes how we think of what we do, and so it shapes what provisions we make for the future we think we see. Surely, as mathematics replaced the Holy Word as the prism of focus, communications technology withholds yet another form of humanity for future revelation. This picture will be so clear and distinct that all previous peoples on the lower Merrimack look like strangers to the places, much as the certitudes of the Reverend Wilkes Allen prepared the ready acceptance of the industrial age.

Twenty years ago the signs of the renaissance on the lower

Symbolic of Lawrence's new look, the Water Tower on Tower Hill recently underwent renovation with federal funds under the direction of Joseph P. Markey, alderman and director of engineering. The Water Tower is listed on the National Register of Historic Places. Photo by Gayton Osgood.

Above: *Collections and programs of the Lowell Museum record the past of every ethnic group and business enterprise, private citizen and municipal organization. This photo of the International Night competitors of 1925 is an example of the museum's rich documentary collection. Courtesy, Lowell Museum*

Left: *In the 1980s Newburyport's fisherman continue their work, mending nets and going out to sea. Photo by Bill Lane*

Concerned students and veterans protest against the Vietnam War in 1972. The energy of the 1960s generation pushed against traditional society in many ways. Courtesy, Trustees of the Haverhill Public Library.

Merrimack were unmistakable. Theater, music, and poetry flourished in the Merrimack Valley Regional Theatre (Lowell) and the Merrimack Valley Philharmonic (Lawrence). Poets, such as those responsible for the publication of *Looms* at Lowell, discovered again that the river is a unit of life and that the Valley is a locale. Also, Valley residents began to recollect the region's industrial heritage with pride rather than embarrassment. State Heritage Parks at Lowell and Lawrence and the National Historical Park at Lowell drew attention to the accomplishments of the past. Moreover, these establishments attracted tourists, and tourism is a major consideration in the region's economy.

Finding the future calls for attention to the present, a concentration and a focus not many of us can spare from the attention and concentration it takes just to accomplish our daily, routine tasks. "Getting and spending," as the poet said, we misplace our native ability to take a longer view. Still, it is worth the effort. Context rules and chronology is context. As individuals and as peoples our vision of the future will be real and compelling only where we find ourselves at home in the long rhythms of the past.

The socially conscious spirit of the 1960s is evident in the concerned faces of these students at a peace rally in 1972. That spirit appeared to have been shorn along with hair and beards by the 1980s, but a resurgence shows that social responsibility is appearing once again in the Clamshell Alliance and other antinuclear organizations proliferating in the Valley. Courtesy, Trustees of the Haverhill Public Library.

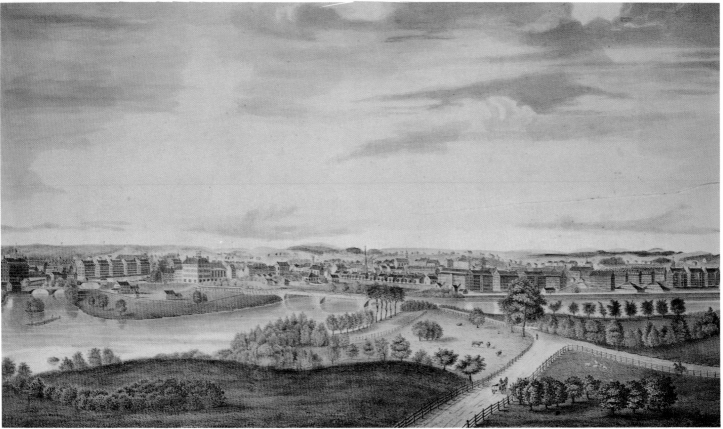

Top: *Painted by an anonymous artist,* The Howard
Farmhouse in 1830. Pond Hills, Amesbury *shows a
prosperous Valley farm. The hay wagon at the right may
be loaded with hay from nearby salt marshes or from the farm's
own hay meadow. Courtesy, Historical Society of Old Newbury.*

Above: *Lowell was not yet fully grown when this view by
E.A. Farrar was lithographed in 1834, but the row of brick
mills already formed an impressive sight. At this date neither
the Boott nor the Massachusetts mills had been started, so there
is a clear view straight into the heart of the city. (MVTM)*

View on the Merrimack *from the Store House by Charles Hubbard shows the crude early bridge at the Pawtucket Falls and the village of Pawtucket in about 1833. Pawtucket, at first a part of Dracut, was annexed by Lowell in the 1870s. (Private Collection)*

Pennacook Indians in West Newbury mixed local deer hair and porcupine quills on hide with European trade goods, such as glass beads, to fashion this embroidered quill pouch, made about 1650-1675. Courtesy, Peabody Museum of Salem.

Painted by an unidentified artist in about 1845, this canvas portrays the Middlesex Company Woolen Mills of Lowell, the largest woolen mill in the country at that time. Women enter the mill to work at left, walking between rows of blue woolen cloth stretched on tenterhooks to dry. The Middlesex was famous for this fabric, which was used for uniforms and known as "police coatings." (MVTM)

Ballardvale, a section of Andover that drew waterpower from the Shawsheen River, had a fulling mill by the late-17th century. Woolen and worsted mills persisted there until the mid-20th century. Charles Sheeler (1883-1965) painted this dramatic view of a Ballardvale mill in 1946 following his tenure as artist-in-residence at Phillips Academy in Andover. Courtesy, Addison Gallery of American Art, Phillips Academy, Andover, Massachusetts.

New York artist Ralph Fasanella came to Lawrence in the mid-1970s, where he painted for several years. His Lawrence canvases portray the vitality of mill work and the legacy of labor struggles made famous by the 1912 strike. This 1977 canvas, Mill Workers—Lower Pacific Mills, *represents the mill as it might have appeared when occupied by the company's worsted division. The plant is now tenanted with nontextile industries. Courtesy, Ralph Fasanella.*

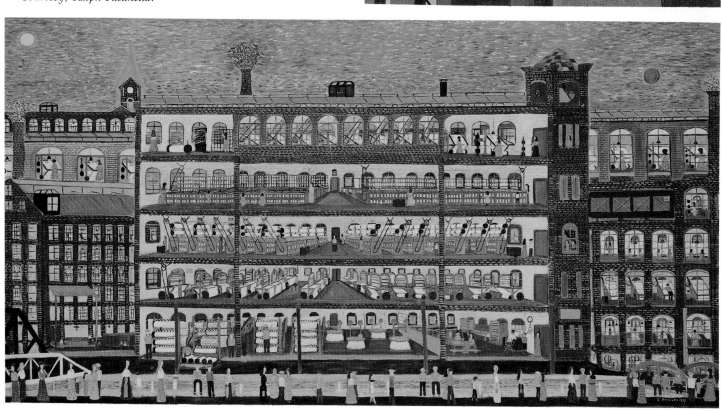

Art in public places is part of the new spirit in Lowell. This
Worthen Street mural shows Lowell's pride in its industrial
past and the laborers who built the city, canals, and mills.
Photo by JoAnne B. Weisman.

John Phillips Marquand achieved great success as a novelist, writing both serious, ironic fiction about American society and popular mysteries featuring Mr. Moto the detective. Marquand lived at Curzon's Mill, West Newbury, for much of his life. Portrait by Alexander James, 1944. Courtesy, Custom House Maritime Museum, Newburyport.

Salt-marsh hay grown as a cash crop on the marshes of Newbury and Salisbury was once a thriving and profitable industry. William Sherburne "Sherb" Eaton (1900-1982), the last of a line of Salisbury salt-marsh hay farmers, holds examples of three types of the hay: black grass, goose grass, and thatch grass. Photo by Betsy Woodman.

Facing page: Bert Fafard's painting, The Course of the Merrimack, provides an historical overview of the Valley's culture from 18th-century Newburyport, at bottom, to 20th-century Lowell, at center. Twenty famous persons born in the Valley are depicted at the top. John Greenleaf Whittier of Haverhill figures most prominently in the center, flanked by Bette Davis and James Abbott McNeil Whistler, both born in Lowell. Fafard's huge canvas hangs at Northern Essex Community College in Haverhill. Photo by Cliff Lawrence.

Above: *Opened and dedicated on January 27, 1998, the Tsongas Arena Park bears the name of the late Senator Paul E. Tsongas, a Lowell native. The arena is home to the Lowell Lock Monsters, the American Hockey League affiliate of the Carolina Hurricanes, and the NCAA Division I UMass-Lowell River Hawks hockey team. Courtesy, James Higgins.*

A reenactment at Minute Man National Historical Park in Concord, Massachusetts. This is the site of the first forcible Colonial action on April 19, 1775 which marked "the shot heard 'round the world." Courtesy, Merrimack Valley Convention and Visitors Bureau.

The Jack Kerouac Commemorative contains excerpts from the work of Lowell's own champion of the American language. There is symbolic language in the design of the commerorative which combines the cross of Christianity and a mandala—the icon of infinite variety that is native to the thinking of Hindus and Buddhists. This reflects Kerouac's own spiritual journey and reflects the current mix of religious beliefs among Lowell residents. Dedicated in 1988, the Jack Kerouac Commemorative is located in Eastern Canal Park. Courtesy, James Higgins.

Facing page: *Located in three towns, the Lowell-Dracut-Tyngsboro State Forest contains 1,200 acres including 180 acres of ponds, swamps, and wetlands. Courtesy, James Higgins.*

Above: *A beaver dam in the Lowell-Dracut-Tyngsboro State Forest, circa 2003. Courtesy, James Higgins.*

Above: *Rocks Village in the easternmost part of Haverhill is an historic district of great unspoiled charm. The Ingersoll-Johnson House, built in about 1740 at the corner of Wharf Lane, sits directly on the Merrimack River. Photo by Peter Randall.*

Right: *Children everywhere love to clown for the camera, and these youngsters at Methuen's Tenney Street Playground are no exception. Photo by Denise Goudreault.*

Facing page
Top: *Built in 1784, the mansion of North Andover's Doctor Thomas Kittredge is one of the high-style residences that were built even in the smaller Valley communities. Photo by Gayton Osgood.*

Bottom: *Historic homes line the training field in West Newbury, where militia men have trained since the 1730s. Photo by Peter Randall.*

Above: *Newburyport's warm, red brick and blue water provide the perfect backdrop for white sails, which evoke the merchant ships of yesterday amid the fishing and pleasure craft of today. Photo by Peter Randall.*

Right: *Shown here is the dam at the head of Pawtucket Falls, built to enhance the drop of over 30 feet that occurs naturally in the riverbed's descent. In the foreground to the left, the corner of the gatehouse can be seen, which controls the flow of water into the Northern Canal. The construction of the "Northern" was a major element in the improvements of Lowell's power system undertaken by the Proprietors of Locks and Canals between 1845 and 1848. Courtesy, James Higgins.*

Above: *The Merrimack River trail winds through huge white pines and broad meadows filled with wildflowers. It is a popular trail for local runners and mountain bikers. Courtesy, James Higgins.*

Right: *The Southeast Asian Water Festival is an annual celebration of the cultural and environmental importance of water to the large communities of Cambodians and Laotians who have relocated to the area. Boat racing is a big part of this event, which takes place at the end of August on the Merrimack River. Courtesy, James Higgins.*

The Lowell-Dracut-Tyngsboro State Forest, circa 2003. The forest has six miles of trails offering hiking, bicycling, horseback riding, cross-country skiing, and snowmobiling. Courtesy, James Higgins.

IX

THE PEOPLE OF THE THIRD SETTLEMENT

The face of the water, in time, became a wonderful book...And it was not a book to be read once and thrown aside, for it had a new story to tell every day.
Mark Twain, *Life on the Mississippi*, 1883.

Driving east out of Rocks Village toward Amesbury, or driving out of Lowell through Dracut and Methuen, we have the river in sight but not always parallel to the road we're on. It will run parallel for a stretch, a few hundred yards to the right, then it will veer off and disappear 'round a bend, go out of sight. From a number of points along the way, we see the river close-off at both ends, so it looks like a pond, an isolated patch of water rather than a continuous stream; and there are even places where the river and the road are at right angles, or nearly, so that the river appears to cut across our path. The river, in fact, seems to go to pieces. It comes into view segment by segment. The effect is obvious in winter, when trees are bare and sightlines are open. Rivers have always played in the mind as a metaphor of time, and the visual segmentation of the Merrimack is a useful reminder of that as we open a prospect on the last 20 years.

Writing history as chapters, segmenting time, was a natural habit of mind for the people of the second settlement. Europeans—the people who arrived from the east—settled in the Merrimack Valley in the 1630s, con-

The full moon over the Ayer Mill Clock Tower in Lawrence, Massachusetts. Photo by Lisa Goss, courtesy Family Service, Inc.

vinced they were adding to a story already ancient and venerable. That was the story of the Hebrew patriarchs. The Puritans we call them, "the godly" they called themselves, failed to build Zion on the Merrimack, and yet we who live in the towns they founded persist in the habit of adding new chapters to an old story. Like them, we derive a kind of security by giving titles to those chapters, building a big picture, framing an all-inclusive time map. That map tells us where we are in the story in the way that road maps show location, suggest a direction.

The people of the first settlement, who did not write history—who wrote nothing at all—had a different attitude to time and the river. Their time map was bound by the memory of living generations, and they never moved their story, one place to another, on the surface of the planet. The people of the first settlement lived in the valley of the Merrimack for several thousand years and never got beyond counting the cycle of seasons. It never occured to them that decades or centuries were realities, markers to navigate their lives by. We humans experience time as no other species does, and one way or another all peoples must transact their own passage. As individuals, all of us will go for a stretch of time, even years, where the scenery around us doesn't change; where everyone we know stays in place and events keep to familiar patterns. But then something snags our attention, holds it there, in the present, and suddenly we notice how far we've moved along. At these points of recollection, as individuals, we play catch-up. Autobiography or history, it's all done the same, only in a different voice. Here we review the past two decades of doings on the lower Merrimack. History is the process that measures how far we've come by taking a look at where we are. Or, as Thoreau put it, we find out what is.

The most obvious innovation on the landscape of the region is the same one that has spread over the rest of the planet since the mid-1980s. The World Wide Web is a global phenomenon. It lives up to the name. During the last decades of the last century, "www" became the symbol of a prodigy that somehow bridges the gap between artifact and life form. "The web" is an artificial, man-made thing while also being its own thing, a network of networks involved in discovering a native logic. Communications technology is not all that novel in this region. It made an appearance in the previous chapter on the Lower Merrimack, particularly in the spectacular development of Wang Laboratories, one of the early success stories in the manufacture of computing hardware. Unfortunately, the spectacular rise was followed by an equally spectacular "flame-out" in the late '80s and early '90s. Informants attribute this reversal of fortune to the inability of Wang's leadership to adapt to market realities, specifically its failure to recognize the coming market in personal computers. This case, like the more recent case of Lucent Technologies in North Andover, demonstrates the vital role played by corporate leaders in the well-being of the region, a distinct arena of leadership forecast by the advent of the Merrimack Manufacturing Company in February 1822.

Back then, local leadership operated in a mental landscape called "political-economy" where politics and economics were not yet fully separated spheres of activity. That is the mental location occupied by Wilkes Allen in his *History of Chelmsford* (1820). In that text (see the epigraph in Chapter V), Allen is reminding the townsmen of Chelmsford that the town's "increasing prosperity" depends on their corporate leadership. Because in 1820, in the public mind, corporation was a word identified with the word "town." In 1820 corporations stood close to the original legal definition of "bodies politic." But Allen's history was published at the end of two centuries of that tradition. The *History of Chelmsford* is a valedictory to that entire segment of the valley's past. Corporations, as they're now familiar, began to evolve in the legal systems of the New Republic after 1789; and the corporate giants built at "the Neck" in Chelmsford during the 1820s and 1830s, were a triumph of this new way of organizing production. Described in the language of evolution, they were a "successful type. The marvels of innovation in machine technology and power technology held the attention of the people of Chelmsford when they watched the new factories go up by the river, and the same marvels now hold the attention of visitors from all over the nation who come take the tours of the Lowell National Historical Park.

But none of that is *the* story here. The story on the lower Merrimack since the '80s, the story of this chapter, is in the NGOs.

Non-governmental organizations (NGOs) perform public tasks and functions, acting as agents of government without being part of government. They could be defined as the not-for-profit arena of privatization. NGO's are hardly a new concept, they have been a worldwide phenomenon for half a century. During that time, however, NGOs were known mainly in the Third World where they were used as implements to support newly created nation-states. What is novel here is their regional orientation, and the success they've had in the recent past in making use of communication technologies. There are 200-odd Merrimack Valley entries listed on Google.

All the sites share a concern for the social and economic well-being of the region. All of them, to some extent, in one way or another, actively promote long-term, regional analysis and planning. Every city and town on the lower Merrimack is now also sited on the World Wide Web. Anyone online, anywhere on the planet, is able to access these community sites—all of which give geographic location and often provide a thumbnail sketch of its history. Also, of course, the sites serve to inform residents about current and upcoming events on the social or political calendar. Some towns, Amesbury is a prime example, are including the town's

People come to enjoy concerts under the stars at Boarding House Park during the months of July, August, and early September as part of the Lowell Summer Music Series. Photo by Jim Higgins (Higgins and Ross), courtesy Merrimack Valley Convention and Visitors Bureau.

A reenactment of the Road to Revolution, on the five-mile Battle Road Trail, at Minute Man National Historic Park located in Lexington, Massachusetts. Courtesy, Merrimack Valley Convention and Visitors Bureau.

website in the process of writing a master plan, highlighting links "to get to more detailed information about the plan and its development process." Planning at Amesbury began in February 2003, and looked to set goals and programs for the coming 20 years. Besides the official site of the region's 16 communities, new communications technologies over the past 20 years have added a whole other aspect to the traditional role played by local libraries.

The libraries at Lowell, Haverhill, Andover, and Newburyport have undergone extensive renovations in the past decade. Some of the work was undertaken to restore and rehabilitate buildings, or expand them. Coincidentally, the renovations presented the opportunity to install multiple terminals where citizens are given free access to "the net." Plans are now being made for similar transformation of the library at West Newbury.

The 16 communities on the Lower Merrimack also participate in The Merrimack Valley Library Consortium (MVLC), a network of public libraries serving 35 communities throughout the northeast region of Massachusetts. Nearly 3 million items are available through MVLC. Anyone online can access the catalog of any of the participating libraries and make an electronic request for any one of those items—books, magazines, or sound and video recordings. The MVLC

Left: *The Newburyport Public Library, 2004. A corner of the original structure, built in 1771 as the home of Nathaniel Tracy who was an important financier of the War for Independence, is seen in the foreground. In the background is the addition that was built in 2001. The Newburyport Public Library serves more than 270,000 people a year. Courtesy, Newburyport Public Library.*

Middle and bottom: *The Tsongas Industrial History Center offers a dozen school programs for children grades three through 12 and college groups. More than 60,000 students come for a unique learning experience during any given school year. Older children experience the development of water power technology first hand (above) and young children study the changing landscape at the site of Spindle City by the placement of tokens that represent structures–wigwams to factories (right). Courtesy, Tsongas Industrial History Center.*

homepage offers a community information database with a keyword menu including language, agency name, contact person, affiliation, area served, or meeting room. Also available at the homepage is the OCLC, the Online Union Catalog, and the Massachusetts Special Collections Directory.

Communications technologies have also transformed public schools; and as is the case with the libraries, however, change and adaptation has been uneven. By one measure—percentage of classrooms connected to the internet—we find Haverhill (57 percent) at one end of the distribution and Dracut, North Andover, and Newburyport (100 percent) at the other. The two largest cities in the region, Lowell (99 percent) and Lawrence (91 percent), achieve a near perfect score. Amesbury (76 percent), Chelmsford (88 percent), and Tyngsborough (71 percent) on the other hand, performed to a lesser degree than residents expected (according to figures reported in October 2000). "Percentage of classrooms connected" is only one indicator of how schools have used revolutionary technologies to achieve their public mission. However, it would take a chapter of its own, about budgets, about equipment and personnel changes, and curriculum expansion, to give an adequate account of that.

Ironically, it is federal and state funding that maintains many of the regional NGOs. The Reagan administrations, in the '80s, brought a restatement of federalism, a stricter reading of the constitution of 1787 that gave more latitude to states' rights. In keeping with that outlook, the decision was made to distribute federal funding through block-grants

People from all over the country come to experience a 90-minute tour of the Pawtucket Canal through Guard Locks and onto the Merrimack River. Photo by Jim Higgins (Higgins and Ross), courtesy Merrimack Valley Convention and Visitors Bureau.

awarded to the states. Grants, though federally funded, were now awarded at the state level. Partly as a response to this stimulus and partly growing out of pressures internal to Massachusetts, the Commonwealth during the '80s was divided into seven planning and development regions (Northeast, Greater Boston, Southeast, Cape and the Islands, Central, Pioneer Valley, Berkshire.). The result of this convergence of federal and state policies has been a network of boards, agencies, committees, and commissions—a network that is sometimes impressive, sometimes bewildering. Consider that in May 2003 the Merrimack Valley Planning Commission (MVPC) published a Comprehensive Economic Development Strategy (CEDS), a document mandated by the terms of funding granted by the U. S. Economic Development Administration (EDA).

Consider also that this document includes a summary description of no fewer than eight statewide agencies including the Economic Research and Analysis Service of the Massachusetts Department of Employment & Training; the Massachusetts Office of Business Development; the Department of Housing and Community Development; the Massachusetts Office of International Trade; the Massachusetts State Office of Minority and Women Business Assistance; the Massachusetts Technology Development Corporation; the Massachusetts Development Finance Agency; and the Massachusetts Alliance for Economic Development. Taken all together, the changes since the mid-'80s, in policies and agencies at both the state and federal levels, restructure the channels of enterprise; they are an attempt to ease the flow that leads from vision through research and development to production. This is clearly enunciated in the analysis, vision statement, and action plan of the CEDS. The development strategy combines long-term social goals with purely economic ones, aiming to achieve balance in development and environmental issues and to generate routes of advancement for low income populations. All this while creating a "diversified and sustained regional economy."

The MV Planning Commission singles out the Merrimack River as "the region's most precious natural economic resource." As often happens, appreciation of its value was brought home, so to speak, when the resource was threatened. In the early '80s the metropolitan water district of Boston began looking to the Merrimack as a source for its projected future needs. That was enough to unite the populations on the Lower Merrimack in opposition to the idea, which was ultimately abandoned. Until the middle of the 20th century industrial waste and household effluent gave the river a nasty odor, and made it unsafe for swimming and unattractive for boating. The clean-up undertaken during the '60s and '70s has erased that from the region's collective memory. The planning commission concludes in its report of May 2003 that "while the monetary value associated with the river's rebirth has never been quantified, it is no doubt enormous." Increased riparian land values is certainly apparent in the single-family dwellings that have mushroomed along the river in Amesbury, Merrimack, and West Newbury since the '80s.

Other environmental concerns now hold attention in the region. Perhaps the most pressing of these, and one with high long-term negativity, is the release of air-borne pollutants—mercury in particular. There are nine facilities statewide for municipal solid waste combustion (MSWC), and three of them are located along the Merrimack in close proximity—in the cities of Haverhill and Lawrence, and in the town of North Andover in between. Environmental groups from each of these communities have banded together to form the Merrimack Valley Environmental Coalition. The MVEC maintains a website where it keeps people posted on air quality (health alert and toxic alert), and tries to motivate community action (information alert and political action alert). Those efforts have had some success. Two other MSWC plants in the region have been closed. The three plants remaining still produce, on average, 1.9 million tons of airborne mercury a year, based on stack test data from 1991-1994. As the MVPC's comprehensive strategy points out, "this represents 62 percent of the total mercury emission for the state as a whole."

Related concerns for habitat loss and degradation, for the preservation of open space, for proper disposal of hazardous waste and groundwater protection have also been the focus of political and legal action. In 1997 the MVPC supervised an opinion poll in the region to measure citizen attitude toward population growth and economic development. Seventy-six percent of respondents said they would support increased taxation to protect drinking water. Since 1997 the planning commission has assumed an active role, providing detailed computer-generated maps of water resources and other help so the towns and cities of the region can make informed decisions on water management.

In an effort to drive more people to the World Wide Web, this billboard, sponsored by the Economic Development Council, was displayed along Interstate 495 in Lawrence. Courtesy, Merrimack Valley Economic Development Council.

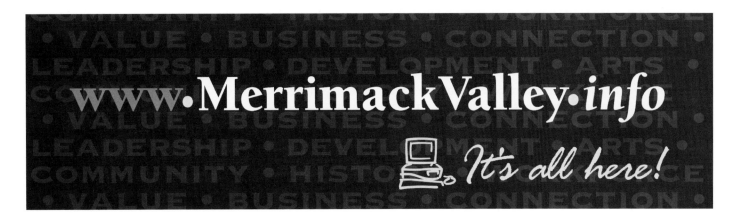

Also in 1997 the MV Planning Commission created a not-for-profit subsidiary, the Merrimack Valley Economic Development Corporation (MVEDC) to administer a revolving loan fund to support the growth and retention of jobs. This $1 million fund was capitalized by combining federal grant (EDA) with state money (MDHCD), with income targeted on assistance to small business start-ups in the region. In the following year, 1998, the Merrimack Valley Workforce Investment Board (MVWIB) was one of several created by the Commonwealth of Massachusetts from funding provided in the federal Workforce Investment Act. The MVWIB published a "Labor Force Blueprint" in October 2003, an in-depth analysis of the distribution of existing populations and their job skills. This was a blueprint written to institute a long-term match-up of emerging industries with regional training systems. The focus on jobs by the MVEDC and the MVWIB is timely in any case since the most recent national economic indicators are describing a jobless recovery. The Comprehensive Economic Development Strategy of May 2003 states that the labor force in the region is expected to grow by 33 percent between 1980 and 2030. That language occupies the ground somewhere between prediction and hope; and the CEDS bolsters the credibility of its hopeful predictions by under-

Above and facing page: *This parade was one event in a year-long series when Andover gave itself a 350th birthday party in 1996. The original site of settlement in 1646 now lies in the town of North Andover, which apparently lost this claim to fame in 1856 when the General Court of Massachusetts created two towns where there had been only one. Courtesy, Andover Historical Society.*

scoring that the strategy uses an "econometric model built specifically for the Merrimack Valley region." This model was designed by Regional Economic Models, Inc. (REMI) of Amherst, Massachusetts whose website states that the whole purpose of socioeconomic modeling is "to improve the quality of research-based decision making."

One other recent report deserves attention before we close this survey. That is the Merrimack Valley Industry Cluster Analysis which was released in June 2002. This research was sponsored by the MV Planning Commission, and is based on data from the years 1997 to 2000. The notion of cluster analysis is a new conceptual tool, a scientific discovery in this sense that it puts the decision makers in an objective, quantified, and measured location. A kind of surreal Merrimack Valley. After extensive statistical analyses, the report identifies five export clusters in the MV Planning Commission area including computers and communications hardware and defense; diversified industrial support and defense; healthcare technology and instruments; software and communications services; and knowledge creation. The choice of these clusters is corroborated by separate research done by the Massachusetts Technological Collaborative (MTC) and Mas-

The 35 acres on the shores of Lake Cochichewick are known as Half-Mile Hill, an area enjoyed by locals and tourists alike. Photo by Susan Lapides, courtesy, The Trust for Public Land.

sachusetts Benchmarks (MB) as constituting important export industry sectors for the commonwealth.

Changes in the practices and policies of government which fostered regional planning operated in the larger geographies of nation and state. Here on the Lower Merrimack the impact of those changes increased exponentially with the deliberate intervention of UMASS/Lowell—the University of Massachusetts at Lowell. In the mid '90s state government attempted to reorganize the structure of higher education in the Commonwealth; and in the process of that, William Hogan, the chancellor at UMASS/Lowell, opted to invest the public function of this "public university" with practical sense. As a result of his decision, Lowell is now the site of a number of research and study centers that explore one facet or another of future time—from the physical (Center for Advanced Materials) to the economic (Center for Industrial Competitiveness) and

the social (Center for Diversity and Pluralism). The chancellor's program amounted to a deliberate dismantling of the university as an ivory tower, a departure from the traditional image not welcome among all the faculties at UMASS/Lowell. The reorientation of this public university has an outreach element aimed at a number of populations in Greater Lowell. The Center for Advanced Electronics Technology directs a program for gifted high school students and an initiative called Technology Early Reach-Out. The Center for Family, Work, and Community has involved itself with Lowell's "new immigrants" in a variety of programs or events that have the common, underlying purpose of fostering leadership within these communities.

Perhaps the centerpiece in this new thinking at UMASS/Lowell, certainly its summation, is the Regional Economic and Social Development (RESD) department. Organized in 1993 the department awards degrees, including a master's degree, in a number of fields of concentration, environmental policy and the social dynamics of development among them. Found on its website, RESD currently lists 16 members with degrees in economics, law, sociology, history, and psychology. The department collaborates with the Committee on Industrial

Theory and Assessment (CITA, also at UMASS/Lowell), in organizing an annual conference. The conference of October 2000 was titled "Approaches to Sustainable Regional Development: The Role of the University in the Globalizing Economy," and this is interesting because the publication that came out of the conference is titled *Approaches to Sustainable Development: The Public University in the Regional Economy* (2001). There is a significant difference in those titles. In either case the focus is on *sustainable* growth, but the context of the university's work shifts from global in 2000 to regional in 2001. Yet there is no contradiction. Globalization and regionalism are complementary notions, the one implies the other. Global economy and regional economy are in actual fact the same economy, only looked at from opposite ends. That is how it happens that regional planning has taken hold of imaginations, and why students from all over the world have responded to the degree programs offered by RESD.

The link-up of academics and regional planning at Lowell is now 10 years along and it is an elemental piece in constructing "research-based decisions" in an emerging global environment. This link-up is unusual, though not unique. Research Triangle Park—"the largest research park in the world"—in North Carolina is affiliated with no fewer than three universities. Downriver from Lowell, at Lawrence, the city government is taking a more direct approach to fitting the local economy in the emerging global era. Lawrence is gearing up to open the South Canal International Business

Center (SCIBC). Located on the south side of the Merrimack the center will take up 80,000 square feet of a former mill building. City government worked hard—"aggressively" one informant said—to involve the Anglo-Irish Bank as a primary financial partner and the Small Business Corporation of the Republic of Korea. Local firms such as Enterprise America, Arthur J. McCabe & Associates, The Heron Group, and North West Marketing are participants in the center, and helped design its programs. It helped, too, that in 1996 and again in 1999 Lawrence received grants from the U. S. Economic Development Administration, funds which went to hiring an economic development director and the organizing of the Center for Entrepreneurship and Business Development.

The SCIBC defines itself as a private enterprise, and its brochure states that government agencies "are most useful in support roles after the private sector business objectives have been established and an appropriate entry strategy designed." This defines the public/private relationship favored by Mayor

The large population of southeast Asians in Lowell has led to the transfer of a racing tradition from the Mekong to the Merrimack. Shown her is one of the teams competing at a recent Annual Water Festival. Courtesy, Rady Mom

The Jack Kerouac Commemorative is located in Kerouac Park on Bridge Street. Dedicated in 1988, the commemorative contains excerpts from Kerouac's writings. Courtesy, James Higgins.

Michael J. Sullivan. Mayor Sullivan has a background in marketing and enjoys his function as "broker of deals," adding that it makes it easier when the players are local. Closing is quicker and cleaner when the principals are in the room. He notes, on the public side, how the state came in "big time" with funding for the transportation component of two major construction projects.

The plan of the SCIBC is to provide research and marketing help as well as financial assistance to foreign investors looking for a friendly environment to site their production facilities. Creating and holding industrial jobs is a hot issue throughout the Lower Merrimack, a prime object of concern. Malden Mills is a case in point.

The complex occupies the boundary between the Arlington district of Lawrence and neighboring Methuen. Malden Mills was destroyed by fire on the evening of December 11, 1995. This became an international story when Aaron Feuerstein announced his decision to keep his employees, all 1,500 of them, on the payroll while rebuilding the plant. Feuerstein became an emblem of corporate responsibility. Nearly a decade later, he finds it will be necessary to turn-over a million square feet of his mills to a real estate developer. By renovating the space into 600 low and moderately priced rental units, Malden Mills will gain the investment it needs to keep the research and production going at the 28-acre site. This tactic—merging industrial production with other revenue streams—has been successful elsewhere and is a classic instance of inventive spirit.

The future is considered and administered in parcels. The Community Preservation Act (CPA), the website tells us, is a new tool to help communities preserve open space and historic sites and create affordable housing. Enacted in 2000 by the Massachusetts legislature, CPA has been implemented in Chelmsford, Dracut, North Andover, Newburyport, and Tyngsborough. Though well-intended, the act has led to intense conflict between long-term and short-terms views of what's to be done with the town's future. A conflict of temporal location acted out on the issue of space. The confrontation at North Andover was so intense that the moderator at a town meeting jokingly advised that "people leave their guns at the door."

Regionalism on the Lower Merrimack is real, but real only at the level of structure in the work of the NGOs. The region is not yet a space in the mind, a theater of action, to the local populations. *The Bridge Review* describes itself as "an online journal about the culture of the Greater Merrimack Valley of Massachusetts and southern New Hampshire." Its mission is to explore the interwoven concepts of place, nature, culture, and society. This is a worthwhile ambition, but the principals behind the effort, Paul Marion and Charles Nikitopoulos, recognize that the project is a challenge. And maybe that is what led them to describe the *Review*'s range as a bioregion. *The Bridge Review*—it says on the website—will publish "creative and scholarly works relevant to our bioregion." That, we've already been told, extends to southern New Hampshire. The logical end of that extension, of course, is the entire watershed of the Merrimack, as a single unit of life. But at the moment that is more vision than prospect.

The truth of the matter is that Lower Merrimack, and "bioregion" get a better response keyed into a web search than they do among the populations living here. Both are better sited on the web than on the ground. Our situation is similar to where American colonials found themselves during the crisis of the 1770s. They opted then to take hold of the tools at hand, the political institutions, and make use of them to tell their own story.

Economist Paul Krugman tells us that "to be taken seriously an idea has to be *something you can model*." But that begs the question of who does the modeling. Here is an opportunity. This region might do better than most at political invention in the contest now raging globally for a further definition of democracy. Here is the challenge. It would take a population able to model itself in place, and, more problematic, it would take a population able to tell time on its own. It will take the people of the third settlement.

The Bridge Review *is an online journal that addresses the culture of the Greater Merrimack Valley and southern New Hampshire. Courtesy,* The Bridge Review.

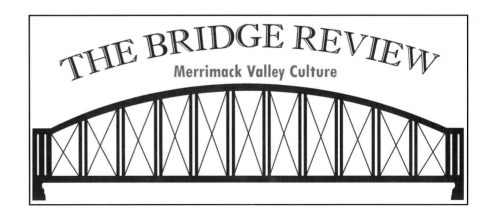

X

CHRONICLES
OF LEADERSHIP

The institutions whose histories are recounted in the following pages are not a scientific cross-section of the Merrimack Valley's corporations. Yet their variety suggests an important truth about economic activity in the area today: No longer does a single industry dominate the scene. It is also apparent that a large number of men and women whose parents or grandparents came here as employees are now employers. Yesterday's immigrants have become today's establishment, joining the Yankees who once seemed to own everything in sight.

The task of gathering these histories was a rewarding one. Interestingly enough, many of these business leaders were unwilling to attribute their success to causes more profound than pluck, luck, or father. Perhaps the most common characteristic of the leaders of the corporations treated here is their strong commitment to community service.

It is often remarked of the New England Yankee that typically he or she felt that serving the common weal was a moral responsibility. If that is true, then it seems clear that this healthy attitude has been transmitted to successive waves of immigrants of all persuasions.

Space does not permit a recitation of individual service but the record is clear: Area hospitals, schools, colleges, united fund agencies, churches, and communities have been and are today the beneficiaries of thousands of hours of volunteer service and millions of charitable dollars provided by generations of local residents. These traits continue to distinguish the Merrimack Valley's business community—employer and employee alike.

As the original watercolor design for the city seal of Lowell, this painting has strong symbolic meaning. The river, railroad, mill buildings, smokestacks, and cotton bales all represent the industrial "revolution" in manufacturing and transportation that transformed the farms of East Chelmsford into the city of Lowell. The cornucopia signifies prosperity. (Private Collection)

THE LOWELL FIVE CENT SAVINGS BANK

The Lowell Five Cent Savings Bank was founded more than a century and a half ago with a pure-and-simple purpose—to offer a savings account to everyone in its Massachusetts community. That basic mission remains intact and has helped the bank steer its way to success through the decades.

In the early 1800s the mill town of Lowell was just beginning to take shape. Many hardworking laborers found stable employment in the area's booming textile industry and were pleased to call Lowell home. The population rapidly increased, and Lowell became the second largest city in New England by the 1840s.

During that exciting time of evolution for the town, a young Harvard-educated clergyman settled in Lowell to lead the Free Chapel on Middlesex Street. Reverend Horatio Wood was in touch with his congregation and community. and he recognized a true need to help the young and working class.

In 1854 Reverend Wood gathered community leaders to discuss the situation. The young reverend proposed to

The bank's principal founder and first president, Reverend Horatio Wood.

the group, which included Judge Nathan Crosby, Mayor Sewall Mack, and Boott Mills agent Linus Childs, that they head the effort to form a new savings bank.

On April 12, 1854 The Lowell Five Cent Saving Bank was founded, and Reverend Wood was named president. He determined that the bank's focus

"should strike lower down and more extensively among the masses." The founders understood the value of filling a niche market and were determined not to cannibalize from the five existing banks—all of which required a deposit minimum of $1—and, instead, offered savings services for a five-cent minimum.

The low deposit amount made opening an interest-bearing bank account possible for many of the town's mill workers for the very first time. On opening day, in June 1854, more than 300 accounts were opened—29 with a five-cent deposit. Almost 250 depositors were under the age of 14 and two-thirds were women, many being "mill girls." In one year the bank, which was located on Central Street, held deposits of more than $200,000.

By 1871 deposits had reached $1.8 million, and The Lowell Five Cent Savings had outgrown the building it originally shared with Prescott National. So, the owners purchased the northern corner of Merrimack and John streets and construction of the new facility began in 1873.

A little more than a year later the $80,000 Italianate Gothic-style building opened, with gleaming marble and impressive architectural details befitting a strong and viable financial institution. The four-story building was not only a tribute to the city's growth, but also to the economic impact to Lowell by "the common man."

During this time period Wood stepped down from his guiding post at the bank after 31 years of service, and Seawall G. Mack was named president. Wood died six years later in May 1891.

By 1887 deposits had topped $3 million. However, in July of that year The Lowell Five Cent Savings suffered a blow. Errant rumors begin to circulate through the city that the bank was in financial trouble. The rumors gained momentum and panic set in amongst the customers, as the Federal Deposit Insurance Corportation guarantee had

The bank's 100th anniversary celebration in 1954.

not yet been established. More than $50,000 was withdrawn, but bank leaders appealed to the community and convinced their customers that the bank was in solid shape. The damage control effort was simply practice for the years to come.

The next five decades brought a series of serious challenges as well as stability to the bank. In 1889 a recession hit, leaving the bank with $100,000 in uncollected interest. The debt resulted in a freeze on accepting deposits, paying dividends, and allowing withdrawals by the state banking commissioner.

Again, the bank survived the financial crisis and found its way back to a stable course of business. By 1907 the bank had more than 16,000 accounts and almost $5 million in deposits.

Just six years later, The Lowell Five Cent battled panic again when the local Traders National Bank closed. Bank leaders again met the problem head-on by communicating directly with its clients. The result was the return of former customers who had renewed faith in the bank and new customers who were displaced from the Traders Bank closure.

By 1911 the bank had accrued more than $2 million in mortgage loans. The institution had grown stronger during World War I and was readying to relocate once again. In 1922 the bank purchased the Curley Block, located at the corner of Lee and John streets. Another stately, beautiful building was constructed. The finest materials were used, reflecting the strength and endurance of The Lowell Five Cent, and the new bank opened its ornate doors on August 1, 1923.

Growth continued, and by 1930, the bank's assets were listed at more than $10 million. However, some of the town's long-standing mills had already begun closing in the mid-1920s, as a precursor to the Great Depression.

Two of the town's savings banks were lost to the depression and The Lowell Five owned more than $1 mil-

The Lowell Five Cent Savings Bank's main office, located at 34 John Street in Lowell.

lion in foreclosed real estate by 1933. But the bank weathered the economic storm due to conservative wartime management who was led by bank president, Austin Chadwick.

The bank began, once again, to prosper and moved into the 1950s with promise. The mortgage business grew, business services increased, and new bank branches were opened. In May 1960 the depository made a strategic move and merged with Merrimack River Savings Back on Central Street. This resulted in assets of more than $32 million. Two years later, the bank acquired the City Institution for Savings located on the corner of Central and Hurd streets, bringing assets even higher—to the $53 million mark.

The technology boom of the '80s was followed by a recession that hit the

savings industry hard. However, using their historically proven track record of conservative management, the bank remained unscathed.

Today, the bank continues to celebrate more than 150 years of service and dedication to the Greater Lowell Area. Lead by President Robert Caruso, the bank holds in excess of $660 million in assets. It now has 11 branches including two in Lowell and others in the surrounding communities of Billerica, Chelmsford, Dracut, Tewksbury, Westford, Wilmington, Tyngsboro, and Pepperell. Customers can choose from savings, retirement, mortgage, commercial, and consumer financial products, while receiving the personal customer service for which Lowell Five is known.

Not far from its earnest original goal to serve the area's hardworking individuals, Lowell Five continues to offer a helping hand. Bank employees and leaders give time, talents, and funds in support of charitable and civic organizations. The bank is also active in education and youth development. In fact, children can open a school savings account today with a minimum deposit of only 25 cents.

Honoring the vision of Reverend Wood and its other founding fathers, bank leaders remain focused on working for the common good of its depositors. The Lowell Five will move into the future with the same mission that created the bank—investing in the people of its communities.

ADVANCE REPRODUCTIONS CORPORATION

Advance Reproductions Corporation has been a pioneer in the image reproduction industry for over 30 years. The family-owned company is located in North Andover, Massachusetts, just outside the Route 128 high technology belt. More than 70 employees operate out of the impressive 37,000-square-foot manufacturing plant that houses both the electronic imaging and the digital graphics divisions for which the company has become so well-known.

The company's beginnings are as humble as the man responsible for them. Charles Nigrelli started out as a photographer in the Air Force during World War II. His official position was photo lab chief and, by good fortune, his wing commander was Colonel James Stewart. Jimmy Stewart was not only a household name at the time; he was a fine officer who routinely led high-risk operations. Young Nigrelli admired the man and would often take photographs of Stewart as he returned from dangerous missions. The photos were captivating and his photography transformed from a job—to a passion.

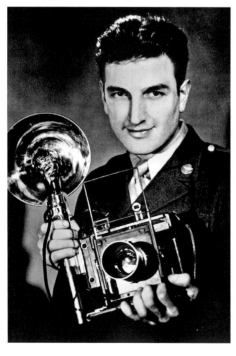

Charles Nigrelli, technical sargeant, in 1943.

Charles Photo camera store on Essex Street in Lawrence, Massachusetts, circa 1957.

Nigrelli was determined to continue his well-honed artistic ability after the war.

Freelance photography, however, did not present the opportunities that Nigrelli had hoped. Thankfully, he had saved money during his time in the service and in 1946 he had enough to purchase an old photographic studio. His business began to grow as he specialized in baby photos and family portraits. Soon, his work became known and he was asked to photograph weddings. His workload grew and at times he photographed up to 10 weddings in a single day. After a number of years of working seven days a week, he realized his profession was too demanding to continue until retirement. With his family a priority and his well-being a consideration, Nigrelli began to explore other possibilities related to his expertise and the world of photography.

Printed circuitry, using photography to aid in the electronic production process, was just beginning to make an impact in the photographic industry. Nigrelli knew he would need a special camera and equipment to have the ability to produce the types of images demanded by the electronics industry.

Again, he was prudent with his money. "I used to buy a car every two years," Nigrelli says. "That year I bought a camera instead of a new car ."

The year was 1961 and the camera was a Robertson Process Camera, a 20-foot, high-precision camera with the capability of accurately enlarging and reducing images onto film. The massive camera was cutting-edge and the necessary piece of equipment for this groundbreaking photographic process. It not only enabled Nigrelli to photograph line art and text pages, it also made it possible for him to capture electronic component and circuit artmasters which aided in mass producing electronic devices. Nigrelli's forethought paid off and his growing company became a leader in the electronic imaging industry.

Electronic imaging is made possible through the process of creating photomasks and photo tools which are utilized by the electronics industry to mass produce electronic circuits and components used for computers, radios, televisions, etc. Photomasking is the process of taking a circuit image, provided by the customer, and reproducing the image onto another piece of film or glass as many times as possible. The multi-imaged film or piece of glass is then used by the customer to mass produce their circuits or components. Because of this process, electronic imaging became Advance Reproductions' core business.

In 1963 Nigrelli faced an event that would either break him or make him stronger. His business, which was located on Essex Street in Lawrence right above a storefront, caught fire in the middle of the night. Nigrelli awoke to a phone call informing him that the building was destroyed and his business no longer existed. When he went to investigate the damage, he found what was left of his prized Robertson Camera on the charred ground floor of the store below. With no insurance and no savings to start over, Nigrelli was devastated. "I told my wife, we started with nothing and we'll just have to start all over again."

Nigrelli had always been a hard worker who was known by his clients for always delivering jobs on time. It was their financial assistance that aided him and gave him a fresh start. The respect that Nigrelli had from his customers was uncommon and their loyalty speaks for itself. With their help and an advance from his bank, Nigrelli built a new facility in Andover.

It was in that location that the business expanded into new areas and further developed existing ones. A client, Western Electric, convinced Nigrelli to expand into the printing business. He did so and purchased six printing presses to accommodate the

In 1982 the company sold its building on Route 114 and constructed a new 35,000-square-foot facility on Flagship Drive in North Andover.

amount of work offered by Western Electric and other clients. In the meantime, the graphics division was growing steadily. Because of his good fortune, Nigrelli needed to expand once again and in 1967 he sold the Andover facility and built a new 12,000-square-foot building in North Andover.

In 1976 the opportunity arose to purchase the photomasking division of Transitron, a company that manufactured transistors for the semiconductor industry. The acquisition of the division included several high-precision reduction cameras that enabled new and more sophisticated capabilities in the step-reduction process. It was then that Nigrelli decided to sell the printing division of his company and concentrate on the more lucrative business of photo graphics.

Once again Nigrelli found his manufacturing operation outgrowing his facility. So in 1981 he purchased a plot of land one mile away in North Andover's Willow Industrial Park. There he built a 35,000-square-foot facility that presently houses the company's operations.

In 1974 Charles Nigrelli's son, Tom, joined ranks in the business full-time. Tom and his brother Paul had worked summers for their father since their high school days. But in 1974 Tom was 24 and ready to become a full-fledged part of the family business. Paul was 25 when he came on board later in 1981.

Tom, now president and treasurer, oversees the financial operations of the company. Paul, corporate vice president, handles sales, marketing, and advertising. In 1995 Tom and Paul's sister, Pauline, joined the company as well. She is the purchasing agent for the company.

The three offspring of the company's founder are very proud of their father. "He's the one who set it all up," Paul Nigrelli says. "It's his intuition and decision making that made the company a success." When asked if *his* children are going to join the business, Tom Nigrelli says, "I will give them the same advice our dad gave to Pauline, Paul, and me. 'Go out and spread your wings first, then if you still want to work in the family business, you are more than welcome.'"

In 1967 the firm sold its Andover building and constructed a new 12,000-square-foot facility on Route 114 in North Andover.

ADVANCED SURFACE TECHNOLOGY (AST PRODUCTS, INC.)

Did you ever wonder how various medical devices can exist inside the human body in order to actually save lives? After all, the body typically rejects any foreign object. Or how is it that contact lenses can effectively lay atop the human eye? Dr Ih-Houng Loh and his team of researchers at Advanced Surface Technology (AST) ask questions of this type every day—and then discover how to answer them.

AST Products, Inc. was founded in 1989 to develop novel surface technologies and coatings for medical devices. Initially a research-based organization, AST now offers a line of patented and proprietary coatings for the medical device and special materials industries. It also provides specially engineered plasma reactors and analysis equipment that facilitate the application of their advanced coatings.

Dr. Ih-Houng Loh, the founder and president of AST, holds a doctorate in materials science and engineering from the prestigious Massachusetts Institute

Dr. Min-Shyan Sheu (right), a customer from Taiwan (center), and Dr. Ih-Houng Loh (left) in front of the AST offices. Dr. Sheu, vice president of research and development, has worked for the company for more than 13 years.

Dr. Loh with his expecting wife in front of AST's first office in 1989.

of Technology (M.I.T.), and it's entrepreneurial blood that flows through his veins. This is not surprising, as Dr. Loh's father was an entrepreneur himself.

When China and Taiwan became separate countries, Dr. Loh's father moved to Taiwan and developed a tool manufacturing company. Workers primarily made small hand tools, which were sold through the Sears-Roebuck Company. After graduating from Tsing-Hua University in Taiwan, Dr. Loh made his way to the United States

where he completed his education and soon set up a business himself.

Upon graduation from M.I.T., Dr. Loh had several offers from large firms, but ultimately went to work for his academic advisor who was recruiting people for his new company. From there Dr. Loh went to another organization doing semiconductor research. He was the first chemist to join that company and he found himself writing many grant proposals for new technology development. Dr. Loh sought and secured several small business innovation grants which totaled $2 million.

In the course of his work Dr. Loh saw the potential to create a new field, so he asked the president of the company for the chance to spin-off a new venture. However, the president refused. Seeing there was little opportunity for advancement and growth, 20 days later Dr. Loh left that company and started his own.

"It was a very busy and unsettled time," Dr. Loh recalls. "For one thing, we learned in the middle of this transition that my wife was pregnant" Meanwhile, back in Taiwan, Dr. Loh's father was very sick.

One month before his father's death, Dr. Loh made the trip back to be with him. "I am from a very traditional family," Dr. Loh says. "I was fortunate to be at my father's bedside before his death and to be able to ask him what I could do for him." His father confessed two hopes for his son. One, that he might one day own his own business, and two, that he might have a son to carry on the family name. Within the next nine months, Dr. Loh experienced the good fortune of realizing both of his father's wishes.

In starting the business, Dr. Loh needed a location. Fortunately, he knew a person with a building in Waltham, Massachusetts, who generously offered him 300 square feet where he could begin. The friend told Dr. Loh that when he had started out someone had assisted him with space, now he

wanted to do the same for someone else. All that he requested was that Dr. Loh would do the same for another person some day. Indeed, Dr. Loh has honored that request many times over.

In 1992 AST moved to Billerica, Massachusetts where Dr. Loh rented what is now his current building—and eventually bought it. It is comprised of 23,000 square feet and over the past 10 years, Dr. Loh has helped many other people start their businesses by offering them free space rent.

Dr. Loh immediately recognized that excellent employees would need freedom in their environment and the opportunity for growth. Though he held sole ownership of the company in the beginning, today seven others participate and hold up to 15 percent of the firm's shares. Another four or five people have spun off from AST to form new companies in which Dr. Loh also participates with varying degrees of ownership.

Surface chemistry as it applies to biomedical applications is AST's specialty area. It looks to improve the bio-compatibility of devices in the human body as the body detects the surface area of any implement and is quick to reject it. For instance, catheters need to be lubricious or else they are very painful and might puncture blood vessels. AST

AST's 23,000-square-foot office space also houses a modern laboratory.

has developed a technology to add to the surfaces of these devices to make smoother and more compatible.

In addition to medical coatings, AST develops contact angle analysis equipment which examines surfaces; and its third area of business is pharmaceuticals. Its pharmaceuticals area aims to combine drugs with medical device applications. One of the best examples of this is a metal stent which is covered with anti-restenotic coating that prevents blood vessels from re-closing after angioplasty.

Last but not least, AST is committed to new ventures. It has identified unique opportunities and has developed technologies to meet those market needs. When they do not fit into AST's business focus, they are either spun-off as separate entities or made into a joint venture. Some of AST's new ventures have included Hunter Urology which has developed the world's first antimicrobial coated catheter. Another venture is Astrogen Biosciences, Inc. which has developed a novel approach

to the manufacture of low cost, high quality, reproducible micro-array slides. As AST continues to be adept at cutting-edge technology and meeting customer's needs in surface technology, it creates new ventures to address tomorrow's problems.

Within Chinese mythology there is a story about golden eggs which says each egg contains a dream that needs to be brought to earth. These eggs quiver with notes of music not yet heard, mighty cities to be built, stars to be flung into the universe. The reader is told, "Pick up an egg and place it in your lap. What you dream here will be manifest in the cosmos." Similarly, western literature has a myth about golden eggs where the goose who lays them is prized and nurtured.

Dr. Loh says his company seeks to reflect the philosophy of the golden eggs. AST will always be committed to ensuring its employees can meet their ultimate levels of success. As such, AST works tirelessly to be a center of knowledge, always spinning off new companies that can continue to develop the future of technology.

Dr. Loh stands in front of an AST trade show booth in 1991.

ALTERNATIVE CARE PROVIDERS, INC.

Alternative Care Providers, Inc., a full-service home medical equipment supplier based in North Chelmsford, Massachusetts, has turned customer service into an art form. As its name suggests, the company takes a different approach to health services by providing a unique environment that makes shopping for the right product a positive and gratifying experience.

Catherine Schleipfer started the business in 1994 after working in the healthcare industry for many years as a hospital pharmacy technician and later as an HME customer service representative. She believed that these typically drab and dreary environments needed a more lively setting. Her vision was to sell medical supplies in an atmosphere that was both upscale and homey.

Her husband Michael, a construction engineer, assisted her in the evenings and on weekends. Alternative Care Providers continued to grow, and in 2001 he left the construction industry and devoted his full-time attention to the family business. Today, the company

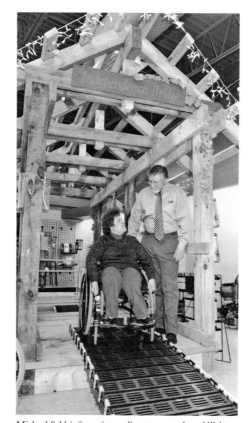

Michael Schleipfer assists a client to assess her abilities using the store's "Independence Bridge."

Nashua Mayor Bernie Streeter, with longtime company client Nanette Goodwin, cuts the ribbon at the grand opening ceremony for the Nahsua, New Hampshire store. Co-owners Michael and Catherine Schleipfer watch from the sides.

has 14 employees and serves customers in Massachusetts and southern New Hampshire. In addition to the 3,000-square-foot warehouse in Chelmsford, the company opened a retail outlet store, ACP Home Medical Products, in Nashua, New Hampshire in November 2003.

"The store is structured in such a way that when customers walk inside, the focus is taken away from their limitations and is instead placed on the opportunities available to them," says Michael Schleipfer. "We have the equipment displayed so that it doesn't have a sterile, medical appearance. The store is very friendly and accommodating, with a warm, inviting feel."

The husband and wife team combined their extensive knowledge in the healthcare and contracting industries to create a one-of-a-kind retail store that does, in fact, reinvent the image of a typical medical supplier. They also sought expert advice from an agency that designs stores for companies such as Nike and Harley-Davidson.

"Independence Bridge" is the centerpiece of the store. The covered bridge, with its arched wooden beams, houses a 16-foot ramp where customers can try out wheelchairs and select the one that is the best fit for their particular needs.

The bridge's name is symbolic of what the store offers to a customer—the opportunity for a quality life, even in the face of health needs and limitations. "Independence plays a big part in everyone's life. That's what we live for and something we take for granted," says Schleipfer. "But when a person suffers a stroke, or is paralyzed in an accident, then he or she is faced with the question of what will give them back some of that independence."

Wheelchairs, both manual and powered, are one of the primary products sold by Alternative Care Providers. The chairs are specifically fitted to individual needs with various options for leg rests, tilt and recline seating positions, and electronic control systems. Chairs are also available which operate by head movements or by chin or mouth controls. The "sip and puff" device is one such method, in which air blown into a straw-like mouthpiece propels the chair forward or turns it around.

The store is divided into sections that lend an easygoing flow with plenty of open space. There are sample bedrooms and bathrooms, which demonstrate ways to arrange medical equipment in a home setting. Folk paintings displayed on the walls of these rooms enhance the sense of a relaxing atmosphere. This soothing feel is also accented by the beige walls, brown carpet, and soft lighting. Other conversation pieces in the store are the marbleized columns and the early 1800s hand-carved sideboard which is used as a cashier's table.

What the Schleipfers take the most pride in is not the aesthetic appeal of the store, however. For them, superb customer service is the bottom line. "We want customers to be able to come to our store and ask someone with experience to advise them, to be a confidant. The first step is to become deserving of their trust, someone to whom they can convey their concerns," explains Schleipfer.

Several of the employees at Alternative Care Providers are individuals who have worked for decades in healthcare and related industries. Their intimate knowledge of the products they sell and empathy for customers is an invaluable asset to the company. "We don't set a time limit. We are simply available to answer the customer's questions and show them the possibilities," Schleipfer says. "Until we have a completely satisfied customer, we don't stop."

The Advanced Care Providers team.

Although the majority of the company's customers are privately-insured individuals, Alternative Care Providers also supplies equipment to hospitals, rehabilitation centers, and nursing homes. The company does it all—renting, selling, delivering, and servicing the equipment. Its technicians also service medical equipment that customers purchase from other suppliers.

Because Alternative Care Providers offers a comprehensive line of products in a comfortable and aesthetically pleasing environment, the company has been dubbed the "Starbucks of healthcare equipment." In addition to wheelchairs, the store sells scooters; walkers; canes; crutches; lift chairs; hospital beds; ambulatory aids; orthotics; grab bars; hand-held showers; bath seats; systems that lift a person in and out of the tub; and the Toilevator, a platform which raises the toilet for people who experience difficulty standing up.

Oxygen concentrator systems, nebulizers, and accessories are avail-

able for respiratory therapy. In the low-vision section, individuals who have macular degeneration or other eye diseases can find products such as magnifiers and reading lamps to aid their visual acuity. Other specialty products assist those with diabetic, urological, and eternal nutritional needs.

As the baby boomer generation edges closer to the golden years of life, demands for healthcare services and products are expected to reach an all-time high. Alternative Care Providers, Inc. will be there to offer the newest equipment, but the company's basic philosophy will remain unchanged. "Service, service, and more service—that's an old-fashioned value that brings success. We're here to serve, to fulfill a need that exists in the marketplace," says Schleipfer. "It all begins with earning the customer's trust—with caring about people and their needs."

BEACON INSURANCE AGENCY, INCORPORATED

Beacon Insurance Agency, located in North Chelmsford, is a full-service insurance agency proficient in both personal and commercial insurance coverage. The agency, whose logo is a flashing lighthouse signaling guidance and leading the way to safety, has been providing direction for its clients for more than 15 years. The owner and operator of the company is Deborah Grimshaw. It is through her vision that Beacon has remained a constant source of comfort for her clients.

"I see them in the good times and the bad," Grimshaw says about her clients. "They come to me when they are about to be married and they want insurance for an engagement ring. I'll also see them when they've had an accident and need help with a car insurance claim." She is invested in the circumstances of people's lives, assisting them in both positive and negative times. She regards her clients as friends, as well as patrons, and has an open-door policy encouraging them to stop by to conduct business or just to say hello. This is an approach Grimshaw learned early on when she accompanied her father as he visited his local insurance agent.

Deborah Grimshaw's first impressions of an insurance agency happened at a very early age. She remembers going to the Cooney Insurance Agency

The headquarters for Beacon Insurance.

as a little girl about six years old. Her father would sit her on the counter as he would meet with his insurance agent and discuss his policy needs for the coming year. Grimshaw has fond memories of visiting Cooney, remembering it as a warm and friendly environment with kind employees, some of whom she would work with years later.

Grimshaw attended Lowell High School where she completed the usual requirements, but she also took an elective course in business. She knew college was not something she wanted to pursue and she set her sites on an office job. The business class taught her secretarial skills such as typing, filing, and shorthand. She honed her organizational abilities, as well. These were the perfect qualifications for assisting in any office situation.

Local businesses had an agreement with Lowell High School where the school's guidance counselor would keep an eye out for qualified students to join the businesses in their areas of need. It just so happened that the year Grimshaw graduated from High School, Cooney Insurance Agency was looking for a student to come on board part-time. Grimshaw's guidance counselor thought she would make a nice fit for the company and sent Grimshaw to Cooney for an interview. Grimshaw recalled her childhood visits to the company and eagerly set out for the interview. She landed the part-time position which soon turned into a full-time job. She remained at Cooney Insurance for the next 15 years.

At age 33, Grimshaw was a licensed insurance broker at Cooney Insurance. She respected her co-workers and had a genuine concern for the well-being of her clients. Even though she was content, an opportunity for a career change was presented to her and she was obliged to consider the possibilities.

A co-worker's father, who was a self-employed businessman, encouraged Grimshaw to use her license and experience to branch out on her own. Grimshaw weighed the risks and decided to embark upon this new independent

Laura Grimshaw, customer service representative.

venture taking her co-worker, Leanne, with her. She gave notice to Cooney on her birthday. "I figured my boss wouldn't yell at me on my birthday," Grimshaw quips. In September of 1989 Grimshaw found a comfortable office space where her clients could feel at home. Then she began to set up her business.

The agency had a location, but it needed a name. When Grimshaw applied for a business license she wrote down three choices and sent them in to the state office for one to be approved. One of the names was Beacon, named for the street on which she had always lived and where she now resided with her husband and their two children. Beacon was the name that was accepted and the agency's growing legacy has been built on the strong lighthouse image ever since.

"People seem to be fond of lighthouses," says Grimshaw, who has a sign depicting a lighthouse standing in the front lawn of her home-style office building. Over the years, customers have given her various items with the image of a lighthouse. She keeps them on display in her front office. The image has become synonymous with her agency. It signifies the confident guidance she imparts to her customers.

Simonne Skoczolek, customer service representative.

The beginning months were difficult for Grimshaw in her new endeavor. Her husband, who was very supportive of her new business, was laid off from his job just three months after she opened. She had already used her monthly house payment as a down-payment for her new office location, so money was tight. It was then that Grimshaw had an idea to get the word out about Beacon. She placed an advertisement in the local newspaper with herself and her employees' photographs. Her previous clients started pouring in. Her clients from Cooney wondered where she had gone and now were very happy to find her and discover her new company.

Satisfied customers then spread the word and her business quickly grew.

The steadily growing agency now has clients in both Massachusetts and New Hampshire. Beacon has three employees, Simonne Skoczolek; Laura Grimshaw, Deborah Grimshaw's daughter; and Grimshaw herself. Skoczolek and Laura Grimshaw run the personal insurance department; Deborah Grimshaw handles the commercial end of the business. However, there is crossover between the two departments. If a customer is satisfied with his company's coverage he will approach Beacon for his personal insurance needs and vice-versa. Beacon is known for its consistency in its offerings for coverage. If one company is offered a certain rate, Beacon ensures the same rate to other companies in need of similar coverage.

Beacon Insurance has been a source of comfort for its customers in the North Chelmsford community and surrounding areas for 15 years. Deborah Grimshaw's professional expertise and personal touch are the reasons. Her focus is a strong beam of light, insuring her clients' futures.

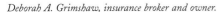

Deborah A. Grimshaw, insurance broker and owner.

BUTLER BANK

For more than a century Butler Bank has been a cornerstone for the community of Lowell, Massachusetts, priding itself on providing citizens with old-fashioned customer service. Through its commitment to builder construction loans, the company has been instrumental for many in the area who have been able to realize the dream of building their own homes. Known in the construction and building community for its support of residential real estate growth, the bank sustains business practices that keep it true to its long-held motto, "Building America One House at a Time."

The Pearson family has run Butler Bank since its founding in 1901. It was General Gardner W. Pearson who named the bank for his guardian, famous Civil War general and statesman General Benjamin Franklin Butler. Butler's numerous accomplishments as a soldier, politician, and attorney include acting as the military governor of New Orleans during the Civil War, serving for two terms in Congress, and in 1882, being elected governor of the Commonwealth of Massachusetts. A champion of the working class, Butler was also an early advocate for women's suffrage. He died in 1893.

Butler Bank was one of two businesses that General Pearson, who fought in the Spanish-American War and World War I, founded concurrently. The other is Pearson & Pearson, LLP, a law firm specializing in patents, copyrights, and trademarks. Originally both were housed in Central Block, which lies close to the confluence of the Concord and Merrimack rivers. The businesses were moved into new headquarters in 1997 at the Gateway Center at 10 George Street.

Since Butler Bank's humble beginning, the Pearson family has focused on lending money to people who plan to build single-family homes. The bank's niche is what is known as the "sweat-equity loan," catering to tradesmen such as carpenters, electricians, and plumbers who typically make up in

General Gardner Pearson, head of Butler Bank for over 50 years.

home-building and construction skills what they might lack in liquid assets. It was important to General Pearson, as it had been to General Butler, to show how deeply he cared for this community of people. Butler Bank continues to honor this commitment today, holding true to its founding principles.

General Pearson directed the bank's operations until his death in 1954, when his son, Colonel John H. Pearson, took the reins as president and chairman of the board. Colonel Pearson passed away in 1985. Today, the third generation, Colonel Pearson's son, John H. Pearson, Jr., is Butler Bank's president and CEO. He began working with the bank in his early teens. Like his father and his forefathers, he has a deep interest in people and seeing them succeed. He constantly keeps an important

lesson from his father in mind: "Always act like there could be another Depression tomorrow."

That, he says, has been one of Butler Bank's keys to success. Though the construction industry can be a risky one to loan to, the company has already weathered the Great Depression, nine recessions since World War II, and innumerable market fluctuations over the last century. Meanwhile it boasts one of the largest percentages of construction loans to total loan portfolio of any bank in New England. Pearson says this has been accomplished through being selective in who it make its loans to and by closely overseeing building projects. His bankers often know the projects they lend to as well as they know the borrower. They go out and visit construction sites in person so they can monitor progress first-hand. Some of the bank's lenders even have construction licenses of their own.

Pearson is proud of the fact that Butler Bank is one of the area's fastest-growing banks with over $118 million in assets. The organization strives to maintain a growth rate of around 20 to 25 percent per year, with little debt. It has 55 employees and growing. The bank has one of the highest approval rates for loans in the state, along with a consistently outstanding return on investment funds. Its Construction Loan Division is the largest division in the bank. Although it also offers commercial and residential mortgages, construction loans make up 90 percent of its overall loan portfolio, says Pearson.

Offerings also include, of course, typical consumer bank products such as checking, savings, and term-deposit accounts. The bank considers depositors a priority, and as such, pays them the highest possible dividends. With the slogan "The Magnet of Solutions," staff members strive to offer immediate access to decision makers and customer service personnel. Separate locations include a loan processing office in Kennebunk, Maine to service builders in Maine and southern New Hampshire. Its growing residential mortgage department recently moved to a new office located at Gateway Center II, 151 Warren Street in Lowell. Its construction lending division is moving into the second floor of Gateway Center II.

Pearson himself lives in his father's former home, five houses away from where his grandfather, General Pearson, lived. Pearson wears another hat as a registered patent attorney and owner/senior partner of the family's law firm. His wife, the Honorable Barbara Pearson, is a local judge. The family and its businesses are very active in the community, supporting a variety of nonprofit and charitable organizations. Butler Bank and its staff support over 25 foundations throughout the Merrimack Valley, New Hampshire, and Maine, contributing over $100,000 in annual donations and sponsorships. These include Cardigan Mountain Schools, the Merrimack Repertory Theater, Lowell Folk Festival, Lowell Association for the Blind, the Boston Pops,

and The Starlight Foundation of New England. A member of the board of Lowell General Hospital for 25 years, Pearson became the chairman of the board in 2004. He is also chairman of Lowell's famed American Textile Museum.

The fourth generation of Pearsons is beginning to grow into managerial roles at Butler Bank. Daughter, Ginger, leads marketing efforts in addition to working for the family law firm, and son, John H. Pearson III, though still a student at Hamilton College in Clinton, New York, was elected clerk of the corporation by the bank's board of directors in 2003.

Pearson says embracing change is of the utmost importance to the bank's future and he strives to foster an unwavering entrepreneurial spirit. He says many businesses don't understand how crucial it is to stay ahead of the

John H. Pearson, Jr. in front of a picture of John H. Pearson, Sr., present and past leaders of Butler Bank.

competition. In recent years he has seen the imperative become "grow or die."

"We firmly believe in the sales culture," says Pearson. "You have to go out and get the business. We don't believe you can sit and wait for it all to come to you." He is in constant pursuit of a larger share of the market between Portland, Maine and Boston. His vision is to grow the bank's profitability while strengthening its business focus and customer loyalty, holding true to the values that have been at its heart for the last century. As long as the Pearson family is in charge, the Butler Bank will continue its future as an independent and profitable community bank in a class of its own.

DIAMOND IRONWORKS

Founded in 1994, Diamond Ironworks is a steel fabrication company primarily catering to the commercial construction business in the New England area. Located in Lawrence, Massachusetts, the company was started by Stephen Doherty as a small concern and has grown considerably, boasting a business volume that reaches into the millions of dollars each year. Today Diamond Ironworks counts among its clientele some of the top contracting firms in the United States.

A key to the success of Diamond Ironworks is Doherty's years of experience in the steel fabrication industry. He began working in the fencing business in 1977 while he was still a high school student in his hometown of Tewksbury, Massachusetts—just a few miles south from where he now has his business. Working part-time and over the summers as a teenager, Doherty first worked for a neighbor who was in the fencing business. He then went on to a company called Glenview Iron, which had given his neighbor several contract jobs. The company fabricated and installed railings and fences for many of the area's high-end residential

The clock tower in Methuen Square was built for the town of Methuen.

properties, including large condominium projects.

Though he started out as a sweeper at Glenview, Doherty also began to gain the practical knowledge about the basics of the business. It was there that he first realized how much he enjoyed

doing that type of work. He was ambitious and took an interest in different aspects of the business, and this did not go unnoticed by his superiors. They put Doherty to work full-time during the summers until he finished high school, and then hired him as a regular employee when he graduated. It wasn't exactly what his parents had in mind as a career for their son, but they could see he enjoyed what he was doing and that counted for alot.

Doherty worked at Glenview from 1977 until 1985, working his way up through the ranks until he became one of the shop foremen. He also put his excellent math skills to good use estimating many of the company's residential projects. In 1985 a friend told Doherty that Mill City Ironworks in Lowell, Massachusetts was hiring. It was a larger company whose focus was more on the commercial end of the steel fabricating business. Doherty got an interview and was hired on the spot. He quickly rose to a senior manager position at Mill City and in less than a year, he was promoted to general manager.

Now dealing with large, commercial projects, Doherty learned at a rapid pace. After years of watching his superiors bid on projects successfully— and unsuccessfully—he took that knowledge and began to handle the estimation and bidding himself. He consistently won bids for Mill City. "You learn that you have to have a sharp pencil when you estimate and bid," Doherty says. "You can't throw extra money on a project and think you're going to get the job."

Doherty stayed at Mill City Ironworks until January 1994. Then, at the age of 33, he decided it was time to set out on his own. In just a few months he had landed a few accounts and found a 4,000-square-foot shop in an old building in Lawrence, Massachusetts."It was the right size and the right price in the right spot at the right time," Doherty says. He called his new business Diamond Ironworks.

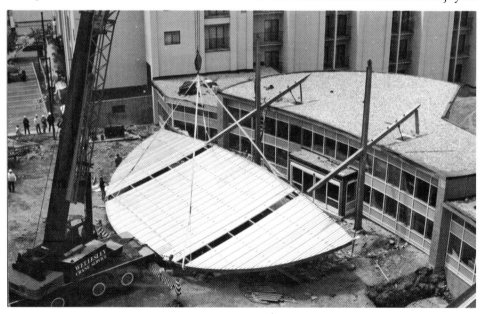

As part of a project for John Moriarty & Associates, an 80-foot wide, 16 ton canopy is hoisted into place at the Embassy Suites hotel in Marlboro, Massachusetts.

Shortly after opening, Doherty bid on a project with a client he had cultivated for Mill City. Moriarty and Associates of Winchester, Massachusetts, which has since grown into one of the leading contracting firms in the country, gave Diamond Ironworks its first big break. Doherty successfully outbid Mill City for the $500,000 job. The project was for the corporate headquarters for Stride Rite in Lexington and included the fabrication and installation of large, circular steel stairs for the building's lobby, a steel atrium, and hundreds of feet of railings. Diamond successfully completed the job and still counts Moriarty and Associates among its major clients.

During that project Doherty hired his first employees. He made a plan early on to keep his shop employees, the majority of whom were welders and fabricators, solely in the shop environment. He then decided to subcontract union ironworkers for the actual installations, an innovative idea that has proven to be highly cost-efficient.

Diamond's next big project was for Spaulding and Slye of Boston. The firm invited Doherty to bid on a major addition for Varian, a large electronics firm in Gloucester. Doherty's work on the Varian project earned him a repu-

Workers erect steel, with the use of a helicopter, for an addition at the Varian Corporation headquarters in Gloucester.

A sweeping, circular staircase with handrails that was built at a Westford office building for John Moriarty & Associates.

tation for finding creative solutions to difficult jobs. It involved adding an addition to a large existing structure, which would have involved the use of a massive and costly crane for several days. Doherty realized the job could be done with the use of two helicopters, and successfully completed the aerial installation in one 15-hour day.

In 1998 Doherty moved the business to a large property with an existing 7,500 square feet of shop space. It was there that he constructed a new facility, adding an additional 7,500 square feet of work space. The new structure also had 1,500 square feet of office space

and a five-ton overhead crane that carried parts and equipment from one part of the building to the other.

Today Diamond Ironworks brings in more than $6 million in annual commercial business. It has worked on 111 Huntington Avenue, one of the biggest high-rises in Boston, a graduate dormitory building on the MIT campus, and a high-rise for the Suffolk University School of Law. Forty percent of Diamond's work is structural (interior or hidden) with 60 percent being decorative work such as staircases, railings, and other visible steel pieces.

Doherty is at the top of his field, but he hasn't forgotten his days in the shop. He strives to make the working environment one that is relaxed, and yet focused. He believes that alot of his success is due to surrounding himself with good employees who enjoy their work and are willing to put in long hours for the rewards the job offers. And his reputation for giving his clients the best work for the most reasonable price has assured him of solid business relationships that have continued to grow for more than a decade.

LOWELL GENERAL HOSPITAL

For more than a century, Lowell General Hospital has developed a heritage of dedicated medical innovation and compassionate commitment to the needs of the Greater Lowell community. Built for the people and by the people of Lowell, the history of the hospital is intricately interwoven with the history of the city and its residents.

Throughout the 1800s the city of Lowell's industrial textile mills attracted immigrants from across the globe—intent on capturing their share of the "American Dream." However, by 1890, the same mills that had garnered prosperity and accolades for Lowell earlier had severely degenerated. Mill owners exploited immigrants as a source of cheap labor and were responsible for crowded working and living conditions that offered a ripe breeding ground for the transmission of disease.

Although two hospitals existed in Lowell, none served the entire community. St. John's Hospital had deep roots in Catholicism and charged fees, while Lowell Corporation Hospital was a private facility intended for industrial and

Graduates of the Lowell General Hospital Training School for Nurses made integral contributions to the development of the hospital. Photo, circa 1970.

Past and present coexist in Lowell General Hospital's eclectic architectural design and long-standing commitment to community service.

mill workers only. Outraged after being reprimanded by Lowell Corporation Hospital for treating a non-employee, physician and surgeon Lorenzo S. Fox decided it was time to create a new hospital that would serve the entire community.

To explore the idea of creating a charitable public medical facility, Fox joined forces with Larkin Thorndyke Trull, a prominent Lowell attorney, and 50 other local doctors and philanthropic-minded citizens. They formed an organization called the Lowell Free Hospital Association, which ultimately became Lowell General Hospital Corporation.

On July 16, 1891 prominent Lowell businessman James K. Fellows was inspired to purchase the 12.5-acre estate of the Samuel Fay family, in the Pawtucketville section of Lowell, for the sum of $30,000. This parcel of land was donated to the Lowell General Hospital Corporation and is the primary location of the facility to the present day.

Lowell General Hospital opened its doors to patients on July 20, 1893. Hospital records show that the first building housed "patients, nurses' quarters, operating rooms, executive offices, and

all other activities." The Lowell General Hospital Training School for Nurses opened that same year. Comprised of eight students, the first nursing class represented the best and brightest women in the area.

While Dr. Lorenzo Fox did not live to see the opening of Lowell General Hospital, his efforts initiated a cycle of commitment to community and philanthropy that remains to this day. Larkin Thorndyke Trull, however, continued to be involved with the hospital as an active, loyal member of the board of trustees for more than 40 years, until his death in 1941.

Since the beginning, Lowell General Hospital has fostered a spirit of service and dedication. In 1926 a student nurse wrote, "We worked 12 or more hours a day, from 7 a.m. to 7 p.m., except Sunday. For all we might have been exploited, we didn't think so and it was a very satisfactory experience."

Although Lowell General Hospital Training School for Nurses closed its doors in the 1980s, individuals who graduated from the school played a pivotal role in the development of the hospital and continue to serve as valued, long-term employees.

Throughout the years, with the generous efforts of local philanthropists, dedicated staff members and devoted volunteers, Lowell General Hospital has continued to grow and change to meet the needs of the community. Whether holding steadfast during the shortages of World War II, providing invigorating hydrotherapy to polio victims in the 1950s, or assembling a team of certified trauma surgeons to save the lives of accident victims, Lowell General Hospital continues to be there for the people of Greater Lowell.

Currently the hospital consists of 10 buildings on the original site, serving newborns to seniors. The Hanchett Building, donated in 1937 by Frank Hanchett, contains the hospital's Sleep Lab and Neurodiagnostic Center. The Mansfield Pavilion, completed in 1974, houses many clinical areas, including cardiology and radiology services, while the medical/surgical building encompasses surgical and emergency patients, among others.

The maternity/pediatrics building houses The Children's Place, a family-centered inpatient unit for children and adolescents, as well as The Birthplace. With more than 2,000 deliveries every year, The Birthplace is the area's most trusted birthing facility. It has received a prestigious five star rating, ranking Lowell General Hospital's maternity care among the best in the nation. The Special Care Nursery at The Birthplace, affiliated with the renowned New England Medical Center, features the only Level II neonatal care unit in the Greater Lowell area, so babies can get the special attention they need close to home.

The 1990s saw the addition of The Cancer Center, a cutting-edge treatment facility that has brought advanced outpatient care, hope, and support to area patients living with cancer. In 2002, The Cancer Center introduced positron emission tomography (PET), bringing the premier technology for diagnosing cancer to the people of Greater Lowell.

Lowell General Hospital is committed to leading the way in cardiac care services for the Merrimack Valley. In 1991 the hospital opened the area's first

With more than 2,000 deliveries a year, The Birthplace at Lowell General Hospital provides the most trusted maternity care in the area and is ranked among the best birthing centers in the nation.

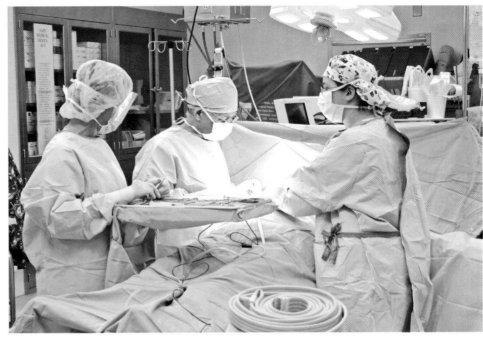

Lowell General Hospital brings the latest in medical and surgical technology to the people of Merrimack Valley.

cardiac catheterization laboratory. New hope was brought to area cardiac patients in 2003 with the implementation of enhanced external counterpulsation (EECP) therapy, providing non-surgical treatment for relief of angina and circulatory conditions. In 2004 Lowell General Hospital offered life-saving, emergency cardiac care to over 250,000 residents as they became the first facility to provide primary angioplasty services in Greater Lowell.

The area's newest state-of-the-art Endoscopy Center opened at Lowell General Hospital in 2003. Using endoscopy, physicians can make a visual examination of areas inside the body, without invasive surgery. Among other vital uses, endoscopy can help detect and screen for colon cancer, and diagnose and treat stomach and gastrointestinal problems.

The hospital also includes two satellite locations in Chelmsford. Lowell General at Drum Hill houses The Surgery Center and Patient Service Center and provides a modern, comfortable setting for outpatient surgery and diagnostic testing. The Women's Imaging Centers of Lowell General, with locations in Chelmsford and at the main Lowell campus, provide a peaceful

environment where women can have annual mammograms, bone density testing, and other diagnostics specific to women.

During the more than 100 years that Lowell General Hospital has served the Merrimack Valley, many things have changed. However, the commitment to provide quality, comprehensive, compassionate medical care to all the people of the community remains the constant factor in the continuing legacy of Lowell General Hospital. One of the hospital's original fact sheets summarizes the essence of its mission: "Lowell General Hospital is a place where no one except death is ever turned away. Where life enters timidly, and is coaxed to remain. Where men and women spend their lives saving the lives of people they never saw before. This is a hospital—and when you leave you may forget all about it. But it never forgets you. It stands there ready, day and night, to help whoever needs help."

Then, as now, the core mission of Lowell General Hospital stands strong and unwavering for the community it serves.

MERRIMACK VALLEY HOSPITAL

Merrimack Valley Hospital provides healthcare with a personal touch to the people of northeastern Massachusetts. Although the name of the 120-bed state-of-the-art facility is relatively new, the hospital has been a long-standing and well-respected institution, serving the people of Merrimack Valley for more than a century.

The hospital opened its doors as Haverhill City Hospital in 1887 due to the vision and financial gifts of a town leader, the Honorable Ezekial J.M. Hale. In the late 1800s Hale put into motion a plan for the area's first public hospital. He purchased a large parcel of land between Kent and Moore streets to be the potential home for the growing community's new hospital. Unfortunately, Hale passed away before construction began; however, he generously bequeathed $50,000 for construction and operating expenses.

Although the location was eventually found to be unsuitable for the facility, Hale's mission was carried out. In 1886 James H. Carleton donated a house situated on seven acres of farmland overlooking a lake on Kenoza Avenue. Haverhill City Hospital opened its doors on December 29, 1887.

The staff was comprised of a superintendent, matron, head nurse, assistant

The first hospital opened in a mansion in 1887.

Ezekial J.M. Hale.

nurse, cook, laundress, and extra help as needed for nursing and domestic services. During the first year of operation, according to the report of the trustees, more than 100 patients were treated at the facility. The farm proved to be beneficial, providing fruit, vegetables, and housing a modest amount of livestock.

Twelve years later, the hospital's name was changed to The Hale Hospital, in honor of its esteemed founder. It continued to operate true to Hale's original vision: "to the high and holy purposes of ministration to the unfortunate and suffering in our midst."

Since those early years of establishing and maintaining a facility dedicated to public healthcare, the hospital has evolved through relocations, many expansions, and the 1931 ownership takeover by the city of Haverhill. It also has kept pace with the ever-chang-

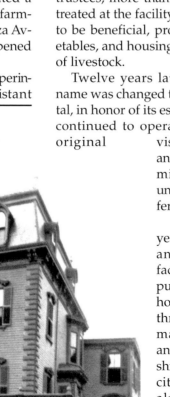

ing climate of healthcare and technology.

Privatization of healthcare institutions became commonplace over the past decade, as a way of survival. Hale Hospital was the last remaining municipal hospital in Massachusetts and operating the institution was a financial strain on Haverhill. In 2000 the city was faced with the choice of either selling or closing Hale Hospital, leaving the area without its much needed services.

On September 1, 2001 Essent Healthcare, a Nashville-based company dedicated to growing essential community hospitals, purchased The Hale Hospital. With its successful operational experience, Essent recognized the potential for Hale and knew keeping its doors open was the right thing to do for the community.

"The Hale Hospital has been saved and a public health crisis averted," said James A. Rurak, Haverhill's mayor at the time of the sale. "Essent Healthcare is a true partner to this community. They were here for us when it counted. They will be running a hospital that will serve our entire region."

Essent Healthcare respected the 100-plus years of commitment shared by the community and its hospital, so the company chose to let the people of the area have a voice in renaming their new healthcare facility. A resident of Haverhill won the "Name Your Hospital" contest and in November of 2001, Merrimack Valley Hospital (MVH) was introduced.

After one year of operation as Merrimack Valley Hospital, *The Haverhill Gazette* stated in an editorial "The old Hale, for all of its virtues, did little to build public trust or plead its case. You will see no such lackadaisical behavior at Merrimack Valley Hospital. It will not be seen as a backwater of healthcare, but as the best community hospital it possibly can be and the hub of medical services in Haverhill. Little more than a year ago we feared we might lose our hospital. Now, under new management, its future looks bright."

Since operating under the name of Merrimack Valley Hospital (MVH), many great changes have occurred. In December 2001 a new chief executive officer, chief financial officer, and director of nursing were appointed. In April 2002 a new board of trustees was established. In April 2003 MVH's emergency room nursing team was recognized as number one in New England in *ADVANCE by Nurses* magazine. And new doctors and specialists joined the MVH team, bringing further strength and stability to the new hospital.

Positive changes to the facility have occurred as well. With a $5.3 million investment in outpatient services renovations, MVH offers more healthcare options than ever. In October of 2002 the Adult Behavioral Medicine Unit was opened. In conjunction with New England Geriatrics, the unit offers the best psychiatric care possible with the goal to restore good mental health and activities of daily living to older patients.

In June 2003 MVH introduced a new state-of-the-art MRI suite, as well as an Oncology/Hematology Center with Commonwealth Hematology-Oncology. This center provides individualized care and a full range of services including diagnosis and staging, chemotherapy, coordination of radiation therapy, immunologic therapy, biologic therapy, and experimental treatments.

MVH continued its expansion of outpatient care in the fall of '03 with the opening of The Sleep Center and The Pain Management Center, and the expansion of outpatient surgery and endoscopy. In addition, PET scanning was added through New England PET. In December of that same year, the

The new Hale Hospital on Lincoln Avenue opened in 1984. This facility became Merrimack Valley Hospital in 2001.

hospital opened RiverSong Plastic Surgery, providing comprehensive care for all aspects of cosmetic and reconstructive plastic surgery.

Essent Healthcare and Merrimack Valley Hospital place a significant emphasis on giving back to the community. MVH values its role as an integral part of northeastern Massachusetts, providing a partnership through volunteerism and support. MVH staff members are involved in many local and civic boards including the Chamber of Commerce, Rotary, Kiwanis, Merrimack Valley Workforce Investment Board, Haverhill Pride, and the Northern Essex Community College Foundation.

Awareness is also a tool that MVH uses to create a better way of life for residents. The hospital's professional staff offers informative seminars on various helpful topics such as insurance options, smoking cessation, and CPR education.

MVH has overcome obstacles that have presented real challenges and has created changes that have provided catalysts for a better way of life for people in Merrimack Valley. After more than 117 years, Merrimack Valley Hospital continues to grow and serve a noble purpose—just as Ezekial Hale had planned.

In 2004 the new main entrance to the Merrimack Valley Hospital was dedicated.

NORTHERN ESSEX COMMUNITY COLLEGE

Northern Essex Community College (NECC) opened its doors in 1961 to 186 students in the former Greenleaf Elementary School. Since that humble beginning, a picturesque, 106-acre campus in Haverhill was built in 1971. Later, in 1991, the college added an inner-city Lawrence campus, which was donated by Prudential Insurance Company.

Today, Northern Essex is one of the largest community colleges in Massachusetts, enrolling close to 15,000 students annually. The school offers over 70 associate degree and certificate programs, as well as hundreds of non-credit courses designed for workforce development and personal enrichment.

The inspired leadership of the college's three presidents, Harold Bentley (1961 to 1975), John R. Dimitry (1975-1996), and David Hartleb (1996 to the present), has been the driving force behind NECC's remarkable growth and prosperity.

Like his predecessors, President Hartleb demonstrates his passion for the community college mission. NECC is committed to insuring that all residents of the Merrimack Valley have access to an education and the ability to use learning to change their lives in positive ways.

"Our students come from a wide variety of ethnic, economic, and academic backgrounds, which gives us

The new Haverhill campus Technology Center is proof that public and private partnerships work.

vibrancy and vitality," says President Hartleb. "Whether it's an 18-year-old first generation college student, a 37-year-old returning to school to make herself more valuable in the workplace, or a retiree taking classes to continue a lifelong intellectual journey, we have a fascinating student body and a stimulating mission."

During his tenure, Hartleb has effectively delivered the community college message, forging innovative partnerships with Merrimack Valley educators, businesses, and government leaders. His devotion and inspiration has created a clear and compelling vision for the college and the students it serves.

Shortly after coming to NECC, David Hartleb brought the entire institution together to create a five-year strategic plan—the college's first. Considered a success, this process was recreated in 2003 and a second strategic plan was developed. A decision was made to create a "living/evolving" plan that focused on one college-wide priority—student success. "The number one priority of everyone at this college is to assist our students in setting and achieving their educational goals, whatever they may be," says President Hartleb.

Having support services available to

NECC's registered nurses work hard in local hospitals.

students is one of the best ways to insure student success. In the summer of 2002, NECC was awarded a $2.2 million federal grant from the U.S. Department of Education's Title V Developing Hispanic-Serving Institutions Program. The college, which is the only educational institution in New England to receive the federal designation of a Hispanic-serving institution, has a student population that is 45 percent Hispanic at the Lawrence Campus and 22 percent Hispanic overall. "This grant has given us the resources to help insure success for our Latino students," says Hartleb. "We want to create the personal bonds and develop the support services that are going to keep these students in college."

Believing that Northern Essex has a role that extends far beyond granting degrees, President Hartleb considers literacy and developmental programs an important part of what the college does. "Many people in the Merrimack Valley, especially non-native English speakers, are underemployed or unemployed because of a lack of basic skills," according to Hartleb. "We want to raise their skills in English, writing, reading, and math and then enroll them in college programs which lead to jobs."

The college works closely with local literacy programs to deliver basic education in the Amesbury and Lawrence communities. Graduates of these programs are strongly encouraged to continue their education, and the college has aggressively pursued grants to help them achieve this goal.

The college also works hard to open doors for students who wish to transfer after attending NECC. In the fall of 2004 transfer articulation reached a new level when Salem State College began offering bachelor's degree completion programs on the college's Haverhill and Lawrence campuses.

Understanding that it's important for NECC to stay on top of constantly evolving workforce training needs, Hartleb serves as a member of the state and regional workforce investment boards. His own workforce development expertise, complemented by advice from the business and industry leaders who serve on the college's many Advisory Boards, enhances NECC's ability to keep its program offerings current and relevant.

On-site customized training is provided primarily by the college's Center for Business & Industry. Since the state's workforce training fund was created in 1999, over 40 area companies have partnered with the college to access approximately $2.5 million in funds. The businesses have then turned to the college to deliver the training their employees need to remain competitive.

NECC President Hartleb (right) hosted an economic development summit with a national legislative delegation, including Representative John Tierney, Representative Martin Meehan, and Senator Edward Kennedy.

Today's NECC graduates inspire tomorrow's students.

As state budget cuts have put a strain on already limited resources, NECC has been extremely proactive in developing solutions. Soon after coming to the college, Hartleb recognized the importance of seeking alternative sources of funding and expanded the institutional advancement function at the college.

The wisdom of this approach was celebrated in November of 2003 when the college broke ground on a technology center on the college's Haverhill campus. The center was funded by a combination of $2 million in privately donated funds and $7.5 million from the state of Massachusetts. "Northern Essex has been a leader in the technology area," says President Hartleb. "We've developed innovative programs in response to changing needs and invested heavily in computer classrooms."

Another construction project that was funded almost entirely by private donations is the Ourania Behrakis Student Center. The newly renovated one-stop center will locate all student services in one place, an approach that has been closely connected with increasing student retention. This $2.9 million project was funded in part by a generous initial donation from George Behrakis of Lowell to honor his late sister, Ourania, a former member of NECC's board of trustees.

Northern Essex Community College is about much more than just new buildings, new programs, and increasing enrollments. The faculty and staff at NECC are passionate about serving students and developing people. "At Northern Essex it's not about us as a college, it's about the students," says President Hartleb. "We have a responsibility to each and every resident of the Lower Merrimack Valley who might benefit from higher education. We want to be sure that a lack of education is not preventing anyone from reaching their full potential."

PEPSI-COLA BOTTLERS FOR THE MERRIMACK VALLEY

In 1941 the Pepsi-Cola Company was in its forty-third year of business and its stock first began trading on the New York Stock Exchange. That year, residents of Merrimack Valley were first introduced to the soft drink when George and Florence "Dixie" Robertson completed construction of the area's first Pepsi-Cola bottling plant on Broadway in Methuen, Massachusetts. Robertson and her son, Clyde Fore, managed the company until 1957 when they sold it to Michael J. Lattif of Syracuse, New York.

Meanwhile, David R. Coffman was slowly making his way into the beverage industry. A native of Chicago, who grew up in Cleveland, Coffman began working as a salesman for the Coca-Cola Company in Lansing, Michigan in 1938. He was called away to serve in the Navy during World War II, and upon his return he worked for General Motors. He was soon called back to serve in the Korean War and while on duty he met a former business acquaintance, who had since become an executive for the Pepsi-Cola Company. He offered Coffman a job and Coffman accepted. That began a relationship

David and Barbara Coffman.

with Pepsi that would last the rest of his life. He worked in sales for Pepsi from 1953 to 1959. Through his experience he soon realized that the benefits of the business would culminate with owning a franchise.

Coffman found the opportunity he was looking for in 1959. That year, familiar as he had become with the territory through his sales position, he decided to buy the Methuen franchise from Lattif. Two key employees stayed on at Coffman's Pepsi-Cola Methuen

Bottlers Incorporated—Robert Allen, who had worked there since 1941, became his production manager and Thomas DiMauro, involved in sales since 1949, became general manager. Eventually DiMauro retired and Allen passed away, but both were instrumental in helping Coffman realize his plans for growth in those early days.

Coffman quickly recognized that substantial development was possible for the plant just through the application of new business practices. At the time, the plant was a bottling operation where concentrate was distributed to bottlers who were responsible for the finished product and would, in turn, sell it by the case to hundreds of retail outlets. Coffman made quality his number one concern and began adding to his sales department, hiring driver/salespersons to work directly for him rather than subcontracting through independent distributors. He increased productivity and imposed quality control measures. Hundreds of thousands of gallons of Pepsi were bottled at the plant in its more than forty years of operation.

Coffman dreamed of developing the company as a family business and appointed his son-in-law, Donald H. Sorrie, as assistant general manager. Sorrie would later become general manager and vice president, and retired in 2003. He remains a member of the board.

Donald's son, David A. Sorrie, represents the third generation to enter the business. 'Starting work for the company's redemption center as a youth, he entered the business full-time in 1993 and was groomed to become the next general manager of the franchise. He officially took on the title in 2000. Coffman remains chairman of the board, treasurer, president, and CEO—positions he has held since 1959.

The business, says Sorrie, is constantly evolving, even in name. It became Pepsi-Cola Bottlers for the Merrimack Valley when it moved to a new facility on Neck Road in Haverhill,

David Coffman (right), president, and Donald Sorrie, board member, of Pepsi-Cola of the Merrimack Valley.

Right to left: Joe Scott; Donald Sorrie; Patricia Sorrie; Barbara Coffman; David Coffman; James A. Rurak, former mayor of Haverhill; and friends.

Massachusetts in 1997. Though the company bottled product until 1983, today it is strictly a sales and distribution center. Production is handled by a production cooperative based in Ayer, Massachusetts. That allows Pepsi-Cola Bottlers for the Merrimack Valley to take advantage of the production efficiency afforded them by developments in machinery and equipment in the early 1990s, as well as the cooperative's increased buying power and economies of scale.

Product offerings have adjusted to cover all Pepsi-Cola variations as well as Mountain Dew, Sierra Mist, Orange Crush, Schweppes products, Aquafina, and Poland Springs brands of bottled water, SoBe products, Mug Root Beer, Gatorade, and Dole juice products. The large majority of products are bottled in plastic or cans, but soon the company will reintroduce 12-ounce glass Pepsi bottles to meet consumer demand. Sorrie says his company delivers all products directly to its customers, including vending machines, coolers, fountain equipment, signs, and promotional materials. Running about fifteen trucks on any given day, the company maintains its own high standards of customer service.

Though the staff is smaller than it was in 1959, Coffman is proud of the fact that he was able to shrink it by attrition—with absolutely no layoffs. In turn, the company has boosted its sales force and added more supervisors, with around seventy employees on the payroll. According to Coffman, Managing expansion has been the biggest challenge. Expansion has been rapid, especially as the Pepsi-Cola Company has risen to challenge its main rival, the Coca-Cola Company, and has given its franchisees many opportunities to grow. That includes dealing with new channels in a world populated less often by small, locally owned, mom-and-pop type shops and more national chain outlets and superstores, such as Wal-Mart and Super Stop & Shop.

During the last decade Sorrie has focused on learning as much as he can about the beverage industry, making sure he'll have the experience to bring the business into the future. His sons, at ten and twelve, are a little young to participate, but he'll welcome them into the company if they choose that path. Sorrie agrees with Coffman, his mentor, who says, "We are in the beverage business to stay. We take advantage of every new thought that comes along, and we have benefited from being a part of the Pepsi-Cola family."

DANA F. PERKINS, INC.

Come to the New England area to buy a home and most likely the home's plans will bear the name "Dana F. Perkins, Inc." Take a look at the plans for local roads, industrial complexes, subdivisions, even golf courses dating back to the 1800s and chances are the same name will be prominently displayed. That's because Dana F. Perkins Inc., one of the most trusted land surveying companies in the New England area, has been in business since 1882. Since then, the firm has grown from a simple land surveying company into an industry leader in civil and environmental engineering, land management, and land surveying satellite technology.

Currently in the hands of fourth and fifth generation family members, it got its start when Dana Edson Perkins graduated from Massachusetts Agricultural College (now University of Massachusetts, Amherst) as a civil and hydraulic engineer in 1882. Soon after graduation, the young man got his first job working on a survey of the Mississippi River for the United States government. He loved the work so much he decided to go into private practice. In late 1882 he founded the Dana E.

W.A. Mason & Son was bought out by Dana F. Perkins in 1947.

A 1722 plan for "The Town of Boston."

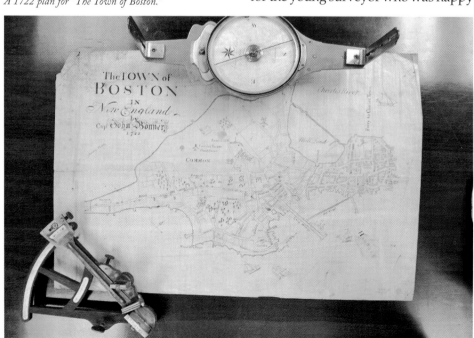

Perkins Company and began working from his residence at 20 North Street in Wakefield, Massachusetts.

At the time, the state of Massachusetts was experiencing tremendous growth with homes springing up all over the place, new roads being built, and old roads being upgraded. That translated into a steady stream of work for the young surveyor who was happy if he earned $10 or $20 a week in those early days. Before the turn of the century, $100 a month was considered a wonderful salary for a good surveyor.

Dana E. worked from home for about a year before moving his business to a location in Medford where it remained until the 1940s. Essentially a one-man operation, the hard worker did get some assistance from his family. He had nine children, including four boys, who pitched in to help their father starting as early as age 10.

In a *Boston Post Magazine* article that appeared March 18, 1951, his oldest son Dana F. recalled those early days working with his father. "Dad and I sometimes rode to work on a tandem bike, a two-seater," he said. "He'd strap his transit across the handlebars and tie the rod and a bundle of stakes on the back end. The tapes and our lunch we'd carry in a bag. We'd have to start at 5 a.m. to peddle from Medford to Bedford. That transit was an awful heavy thing."

When Dana E. first launched his business, the tools of the trade also in-office. There, he would calculate the information and plot it manually into a drawing, which he would draft by hand.

The trade required painstaking precision in every step of the process with accuracy to a hundredth of an inch. Surveyors in Dana E.'s time were men of science and highly intelligent. They were very well-respected within the community, and people called them "Esquire" as a sign of that esteem. Dana E.'s journals reveal that not only was he a fine surveyor, he was also an inventor and held patents on several inventions, including a water wheel.

Although society held surveyors in high regard, property owners had a different view of them altogether. In the late 1800s land surveying could be a particularly dangerous trade. Property owners resented surveyors nosing around their properties with their measuring tools and often ordered them off the premises with a shotgun. For protection, surveyors often slipped a gun in their hip pocket before heading out on a job.

By 1912 when his son Dana F. was 25 and started his own surveying business, things weren't nearly as dangerous. "Occasionally some fresh kid

Dana Edson Perkins, March 16, 1886.

Dana Fielding Perkins in 1962.

cluded compasses, sextants, and links. Links were a cumbersome bundle with each metal link measuring eight inches long. A whole set of chains measured 66 feet. On surveying jobs, Dana E. would set up his transit, measure distances with the links and place stakes to mark the distances. He would then write down his findings in a field book, which he would bring back to his

might dash by and aim a kick at your tripod, or a housewife would douse you with dishwater. But the life of a surveyor today is tame, by comparison, to the problems those old-timers faced," Dana F. once said.

Dana F. learned everything he knew about surveying from working with his father. According to the elder Perkins' journals, he continued to mentor the younger Perkins when he began his own company. Dana F. maintained the business philosophies his father had drilled into him over the years. One of Dana E.'s favorite sayings that would be passed on to future generations of surveyors was: "Don't take the noose off your client's neck and put it on yours." This refers to clients who may want a surveyor to "move a wetlands line over to get an extra lot" or to be less than honest in dealing with governmental agencies. Dana E.'s basic philosophy of honesty, accuracy, and reputation has been carried on by each generation of Perkins.

When Dana E. died in 1934 at the age of 73, Dana F. combined the two businesses and took possession of all of his father's records, including land plans

Advertisement for Dana F. Perkins, circa 1940.

and field notebooks. During the next 28 years, he expanded the business greatly, buying out some 20 other engineering and surveying firms. With those purchases came 500 field notebooks and about 200,000 land plans—the oldest of which dates back to 1725. From the early 1800s there are plans dating back to when the Back Bay in Boston was still underwater. Other documents include plans for the Merrimack Canal and the Cape Cod Canal.

When Dana F. incorporated his father's company into his own, he also made sure to retain all of his dad's historical tools of the trade. Dana F. kept a set of links his father used back in the late 1800s, along with a sextant and a compass that are both more than 150 years old now. In the 1950s Dana F. marveled that the compass was still accurate. The younger Perkins also held on to an English dumpy level, a short telescope fixed rigidly to a horizontally rotating table, which was used by his father along the Mississippi River. All this historic equipment, as well as the field notebooks and land plans, is still in the possession of the company today.

Present-day field men with modern equipment. Pictured from left to right: John D. Lougee, Stephen Surette, Mark Hussey, and Gregory R. Corcoran, PLS.

An advertisement for W. A. Mason & Son, which was purchased by Dana F. Perkins in 1947.

During Dana F.'s time as leader of the company that bears his name, it cost approximately $1,000 to equip a surveying party with all the necessary equipment. Since then, those costs have skyrocketed. Today, with increasingly sophisticated tools and vehicles, it can easily cost tens of thousands of dollars to equip just one surveying team.

Dana F. was the only one of Dana E.'s sons to follow in his father's trade. However, with Dana F. at the helm, several other family members joined the business. Representing the third generation of Perkins surveyors were Dana F.'s own sons Dana R. and Willard. Like his father before him, Dana F. continued working until his death in 1962. Dana R. had died as a young man, so it was Willard who took the reins when his father passed away.

Willard had started working full-time for his father following a stint in the U.S. Navy in World War II. The period following the war proved to be one of rapid growth for the land surveying company, which moved to the town of Reading in the 1940s. As veterans returned to their families, there simply weren't enough homes to go around. That created a massive housing boom in the 1940s and 1950s with homes going up at a record pace. When new homes and housing tracts are built, surveyors are the first people on the scene. As the demand for surveyors grew, the company had to expand with additional help.

The firm experienced its greatest growth with Willard as president. With

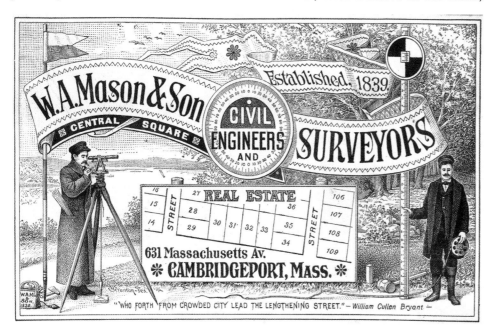

an eye toward the future, he decided to diversify the company. As a complement to civil engineering and land surveying, he added land development and environmental engineering to the core business. These new services brought in new business, but that wasn't the only reason behind the company's success. During the 1980s the New England area experienced such tremendous growth that it helped bring the company to new heights. Under his leadership, the company grew from 20 employees to 60 at its peak.

Under Willard's watch, new state-of-the-art equipment dramatically changed the way surveyors do business. Just like his father and grandfather before him, Willard was determined to stay ahead of the curve with the latest technology. Dana F. Perkins Inc. was one of the first land surveying companies to use computers in its offices. New field equipment included electronic distance meters (EDM), which were introduced in the 1970s. EDMs shoot a light beam to a reflector allowing surveyors to measure distances horizontally.

Also in the mid-1980s, data collectors were introduced. Data collectors interface with the instruments in the field, electronically recording the data. The data collector creates an electronic field book that records angles, distances, and elevations. At the end of the day when surveyors return to the office, all they have to do is plug the data collector into the computer and watch as it transfers the raw data and converts it to a format suitable for use with a computer. Then it transfers the points into the electronic drawing.

During this period, hand drafting became a thing of the past. Today, 99 percent of drafting is done via computer. Other operations have followed a similar course. Surveyors in the 19th century had to possess excellent mathematics skills and use logarithm books to look up trigonometry functions. That eventually gave way to the advent of

A plan by Dana Edson Perkins and some of his field equipment.

the handheld calculator and subsequently to the desktop computers of today.

While Willard was intent on looking to the future in terms of technology, he never stopped looking to the past for guidance. He strictly adhered to the philosophy of "honesty, accuracy, and reputation" set in place by his grandfather. His belief in the power of honesty was so strong, Willard used to say, "If you don't lie to begin with, you never have to struggle to remember what you said."

Following in the family tradition, Willard's daughter Janet couldn't wait to start working for her father. "When I was little, my father would come home from work and sit in the kitchen with my mother and tell her about his day," recalls Janet Perkins Lougee, the president of Dana F. Perkins Inc. since 1991. "I just loved it. I loved hearing all his stories. They were so fascinating. I just couldn't wait until I turned 14 and could get my working papers."

As soon as she reached her 14th birthday she started going to the office after school and began learning the ropes. Lougee really wanted to go into the field with the surveyors, but her father wouldn't allow it. "Back in those days," she says, "women didn't really go out into the field, so I learned office work." Lougee's path to the presidency also included acting as her father's secretary and eventually becoming chief bookkeeper. By the time her father retired in 1991, she had already been working at the company for 25 years.

As president, Lougee has continued to follow the company tradition of staying ahead of the game in terms of technology and equipment. In the 1990s she made a major investment in the future of the business with the purchase of a Global Positioning System (GPS) for about $100,000. GPS is a state-of-the-art technology that uses satellite signals in space and allows a surveyor to pinpoint any position on the face of the planet to centimeter-level accuracy. With this acquisition, Dana F. Perkins Inc. became the first company in the New England area—and one of only five in the United States—to possess the new technology.

Another technological break-through arrived with the introduction of AutoCAD, a software program for design. With AutoCAD there is no need for hand-drafting, as all the contouring for plans is generated by the computer. For instance, roadway profiles show cross sections and grades of road, underground utilities, and more.

Technology isn't the only thing that's changed about the industry since Dana E. first ventured out as a land surveyor. In her father's, grandfather's, and great-grandfather's day, there was plenty of work to go around. Today, however, it's become a very competitive market. Add to that the economic setbacks following 9/11 and Lougee was forced to make some changes to remain viable. Whereas her father bulked up the business to 60 employees, Lougee currently operates with a leaner crew of 12.

Lougee is quick to point out that having a smaller number of employees hasn't put the firm at a disadvantage. According to the fourth-generation president, even though the business is relatively small now, its state-of-the-art technology enables it to execute large-scale projects. She explains that most firms their size aren't equipped to undertake such major endeavors.

Adapting to a changing market-place is part of the reason why Dana F. Perkins Inc. has survived for so long. Over the years, the company has had to keep up with other changes as well. For instance, the engineering and sur-

John D. Lougee, fifth generation, using a global positioning system (GPS) in the field.

veying profession has become more and more regulated, making it increasingly difficult to become licensed. To become a surveyor, candidates need years of education and the testing is rigorous. Regulations such as environmental protection laws and zoning laws change frequently and new regulations are often being introduced. To stay current, surveyors need ongoing education. That's why the company sends its surveyors and engineers to seminars and courses on a regular basis.

The company's ability to shift with the changing times is only part of the reason it remains so successful. What has kept clients coming back for decades is Dana F. Perkins Inc.'s reputation for accuracy and outstanding professional service. Title examiners, lawyers, other surveyors, and engineers have all accessed the company's knowledge and services on a wide range of surveying issues because they know that they can trust their product. Thanks to its extensive plan archives,

field notes, and records, the company has become one of the area's leading experts in solving complex land surveying problems.

More than 100 years after its founding, Dana F. Perkins Inc. remains an industry leader. Although it currently offers an array of services, land surveying still accounts for the bulk of its overall business, representing approximately 60 percent of revenues. Surveying services include land subdivision plans and title insurance surveys, in addition to topographic, property line, as-built, land court, and GPS surveys.

Other services include civil and environmental engineering design services. Commercial and industrial site design, roadway, and subdivision design and golf course design all fall under this realm. The firm also designs storm-water runoff control systems, sewage lift stations, and commercial and industrial sewage disposal systems. The company can design virtually any project based on a customer's specifications and it can guide customers through a plan from start to finish. That includes creating construction plans, obtaining wetlands permitting, overseeing stormwater management, conducting hydrological analysis, assisting with permit acquisition, and conducting feasibility studies.

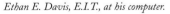

Ethan E. Davis, E.I.T., at his computer.

With its reputation for outstanding service and accuracy, you'd think the walls of the firm's office would be lined with awards. But Lougee explains that she and her ancestors have never applied for any awards. It's not that they don't think they're worthy of them. It's just that they aren't interested in making a big splash about their accomplishments. According to Lougee, "We like to keep quiet about what we do. We're not seeking attention."

The same holds true for the company's involvement with the community. The Massachusetts firm, which moved into its new headquarters in Tewksbury in 2003, volunteers its services to charitable organizations on a regular basis. For instance, the staff members at Dana F. Perkins Inc. have helped with surveying for various buildings and they've been involved with numerous civic groups over the years. But again, Lougee doesn't advertise their efforts. Instead, she prefers to offer these services quietly and confidentially.

Like her ancestors before her, Lougee is committed to staying ahead of the curve in terms of equipment, technology, and regulatory concerns. However, also like her ancestors, she

vows to keep the business firmly rooted in the past and especially in the philosophy created by her great-grandfather. In fact, she often refers to Dana E.'s old journals for inspiration.

"When I read his journals, I am always pleased to see that his philosophy is still the one we maintain today," she says. "He worked long and hard and kept his nose to the grindstone. We don't take shortcuts. We make sure that we maintain standard practice procedures and methodology that were instilled in us from the previous generations. Although the instruments have changed over the years, we still do things the same way—checking and

Janet Perkins Lougee studies a record of a survey made by her great-grandfather. On the wall is a portrait of her father, Willard F. Perkins.

re-checking to lessen any possibilities of error."

It's a philosophy she saw her father put into action, and it's one she tries to impart to her own children. Two of Lougee's three children currently work in the family business. Jennifer, 29, runs the business end, and her brother John, 25, does design with AutoCAD. They now represent the family's fifth generation in the business.

Lougee's brother, Willard Dana "Bill" Perkins, a registered civil engineer in Massachusetts and New Hampshire, left the firm in 1996 to establish his own real estate and land development company. His very successful company, Hearthstone Realty Corp., operates in Andover, Massachusetts.

"Dana Edson instilled good, strong values to his son Dana F. who instilled them to his son Willard F. who instilled them in me," she explains. "Hopefully, I have done my part to teach my children the values of hard work, honesty, and accuracy and that tradition will continue." If history is any indication, that tradition, as well as the firm of Dana F. Perkins Inc., will continue for decades if not centuries to come.

Jennifer E. Lougee, fifth generation.

SAINTS MEMORIAL MEDICAL CENTER

Two stone figures greet patients, visitors, and employees in the foyer of Saints Memorial Medical Center (SMMC) in Lowell, Massachusetts. However, the sculpture of St. John and St. Joseph symbolizes more than the mission of the Roman Catholic institution to "provide comprehensive holistic health service to all people." The statues from Rome are also a tangible reminder of the recent creation of SMMC from the union of two of Lowell's oldest institutions, St. Joseph's Hospital, Inc. and St. John's Hospital.

With more than 165 years of history, SMMC is the largest healthcare provider in the Merrimack Valley. An emphasis on providing top-quality care for patients, continuous training for employees, and serving all who need care makes Saints Memorial one of the top community hospitals in the northeast region. The 1,300 employees at Saints are led by Thom Clark, the hospital's chief executive officer, who holds a nursing degree, as do most of the top administrators.

"We are proud to be one of the top-rated hospitals in Massachusetts," Clark says. The Joint Commission on Accreditation of Healthcare Organizations awarded SMMC an exceptional 95 percent overall score during its 2002 accreditation survey. Treating approximately 50,000 to 55,000 patients per year, SMMC is also one of the few community hospitals in Massachusetts on solid financial footing.

SMMC recently received another award that holds great meaning for Clark, who is a former medical corpsman in the U.S. Navy. Joining an elite group of 15 businesses which includes American Express, Bank One, Sprint, and Wal-Mart, Saints Memorial received the 2004 Freedom Award from the National Committee for Employer Support of the Guard and Reserve. SMMC has supplemented the paychecks of 25 employees who have served in the National Guard or Naval Reserve. Staff and administrators have also sent 1,000 pounds of personal care items to servicemen and women overseas.

The creation of Saints Memorial Medical Center in 1992 evolved from the merger of two distinct hospital traditions. Lowell Corporation Hospital, which later became St. Joseph's, was founded in 1839 by area textile mill owners to care for mill workers. As the first industrial hospital in the United States, it was housed in the mansion of the late Kirk Boott, owner of Boott Mills of Lowell. Employees paid for their care at the rate of $3 a week for women and $4 a week for men. Mill owners paid for services that employees could not afford and no one was turned away for lack of funds. In 1840 the first children's ward was opened in the facility.

As thousands of immigrants flooded to work in the textile mills, the need for healthcare expanded. A flood of Irish immigrants led to the establishment of several new parishes in Lowell. The pastor of St. Patrick's, Father John O'Brien, worked with Sister Emerentiana, who was mother superior of the Sisters of Charity, St. Vincent de Paul at St. Peter's Church. In 1867 they established St. John's Hospital on Livermore Street to care for the Irish who were ineligible for treatment at Lowell Corporation Hospital.

Another notable year for Massachusetts healthcare was 1891 when Sara A. Williams, M.D. became the first female physician appointed to the staff of Lowell Corporation Hospital. Prior to the merger in the 1990s, the Congregation of St. Martha, a

Operating room, circa 1900.

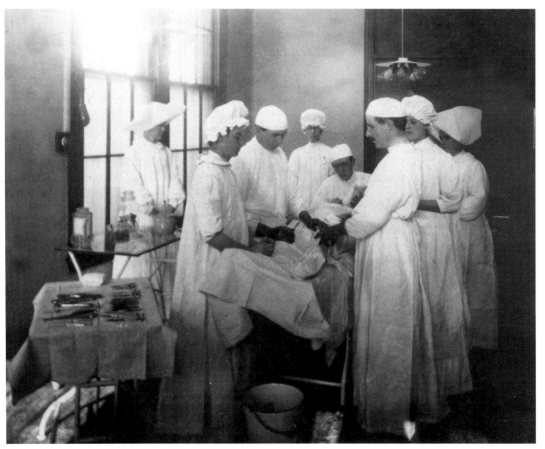

Roman Catholic order of sisters based in Nova Scotia, managed St. John's. However, one of the founders of St. John's Hospital is known for more than just the legacy of the hospital. He is also known as the man who discovered a tonic for respiratory distress that is still manufactured today.

Although several different versions exist about how "Father John's Medicine" originated, the popularity of the medicine recommended by Father John O'Brien is well-documented. One version recounts that Father O'Brien visited the Lowell apothecary of Carleton and Hovey on Merrimack Street for relief from a cough. The tonic he was given contained cod liver oil flavored with licorice. It contained no alcohol, unlike many of the "medicines" of the time. When Father O'Brien had good results with the tonic, he sent people with a similar complaint to the apothecary to ask for "Father John's Medicine."

The shop began packaging "Father John's Medicine" with his picture on the label. It was advertised as alleviating "consumption, grip, croup, whooping cough, and other diseases of the throat." Demand for the medicine grew and the apothecary reorganized as the Father John's Medicine Company.

The factory building on Market Street housed manufacturing, bottling, packaging, shipping, and advertising facilities. The company was sold in the 1970s and the factory that once produced the tonic was transformed into housing for the elderly.

Although Father John's Medicine is no longer manufactured in Lowell, it is still made in the United States and remains a popular tonic for respiratory ailments. The bright orange box, featuring his picture, is still available in the cough and cold remedies in pharmacies and stores throughout the United States and Canada. The recipe has remained unchanged, with the exception of one ingredient, from the days when Father John sent his parishioners to pick up "Father John's Medicine" free of charge.

Saints Memorial Medical Center.

As economic difficulties befell the New England textile mills in the 1920s, the Lowell Corporation Hospital declined. On November 1, 1930 the Oblate Fathers of St. Joseph's Parish took over the facility, which became known as St. Joseph's Hospital of Lowell. For their expertise in hospital management, the Oblate Fathers called upon the Grey Nuns of the Cross of Ottawa (now called the Sisters of Charity of Ottawa) to manage St. Joseph's in the French tradition.

The first superior was Sister St. Alphonse Rodriguez, who received a rather chilly welcome from the staff. After assuring employees that their jobs were not in jeopardy, the staff and sisters undertook the task of rehabilitating the neglected facility. In the book, *A Call to Care: The Women Who Built Catholic Healthcare in America* by Suzy

Farren, Dr. Marshall Alling recalls a story about the enterprising Sister St. Alphonse:

"It became known to Sister St. Alphonse that one of the mills in the Merrimack Mill yard was being torn down. This served a golden opportunity to build a laundry...She called the office... and was referred to the agent. To him the bricks were a nuisance, so he told her to take all she wanted—70,000 or 80,000. She contracted several trucking firms, but all wanted $4 per thousand to transfer them to the hospital yard. Her perseverance paid off, however, for the last one promised to deliver them at no cost, if she was in no hurry.

She sent out a shower of postal cards to many who owed bills to the hospital which they had been unable to pay, asking if they might be willing to work out the bill (by) cleaning and stacking bricks. The answer was quick and generous, and in a short time 70,000 to 80,000 bricks were cleaned and neatly stacked in the yard."

Although Sister. St. Alphonse determined that it was more practical to keep sending the laundry out, the bricks were used to build the backyard boiler house at St. Joseph's Hospital. With the merger of St. John's and St. Joseph's in the 1990s, St. Joseph's was closed and the nine-acre facilities at St. John's became the main campus for Saints Memorial.

Ambulance, circa 1900.

The board members and administrators of the two institutions initiated the merger to offer a broader array of services and to improve efficiency and fiscal health. The Saints Memorial Medical Center Foundation was incorporated in 1995 to provide fundraising and community outreach services. The foundation raised $3.5 million from 1990 to 1995. It now oversees assets of more than $15 million.

The merger became effective in 1992, and was completed in 1995, the year that Clark arrived. Clark notes that his administrative team faced a few challenges combining hospital traditions and staff members. He was well-suited to the task and brought with him his clinical nursing background and extensive experience in hospital administration, with stints in Atlanta, Toronto,

Buffalo, Fort Worth, and Dorchester, Massachusetts.

Clark praises the staff and the boards of trustees at both hospitals for making a smooth transition to create the nurturing and welcoming environment that defines Saints Memorial. Through reinforcing the concerns of staff while focusing on quality of care, Saints has become the most technologically advanced community hospital in Massachusetts. "We are committed to using the very latest technology available at Saints Memorial," Clark says.

By listening to what physicians, nurses, and technicians need to best treat their patients, the administrators at Saints have expanded or added services which include a vascular center that opened in 2002. The center now has the second-highest treatment

CEO Thom Clark, surrounded by members of the Saints Memorial Medical Center team.

volume of abdominal aortic aneurysms in the greater Boston area. Plans are underway to further expand treatment options for patients with vascular disease.

Other new services include digital mammography, stereotactic breast biopsy, minimally invasive total knee replacements, and image-guided frontal sinus surgery. Saints Memorial also offers comprehensive dialysis and predialysis services at several locations in the Merrimack Valley. The Orthopedic Clinic, the Sleep Disorders Center, the Pain Management Center, the Oncology Care Center, the Family Birth Unit, the Weight Management Center, and other facilities are housed at Lowell's main campus.

Clark and his team continue to make listening a top priority at Saints. He meets with every new employee to help them succeed in the challenging world of healthcare. His team also strives for continuous quality improvement in patient care, and measures that im-

provement in every area through multi-disciplinary teams.

SMMC participated in the groundbreaking Statewide Patient Survey Project that was conducted by the Massachusetts Healthcare Quality Partnership in 1998. This "snapshot" of patient care in Massachusetts was taken by an independent coalition of healthcare providers, payers, and purchasers. "Year to year, the hospital experiences an overall improvement of almost 20 percent in scores on the Picker survey (MHQP project) by refocusing on issues that patients identify as being most important," Clark says.

Having nurses at the top—including Clark; Judith Casagrande, SMMC's chief operating officer; and Julie Granger, the vice president for patient care services—makes SMMC a unique institution. Even the legal counsel, Marjorie Boldt, came to Saints Memorial with a background in nursing, as well as law. Shirley Albert-Pressman, vice president for managed care and business development, also began her career as a nurse before earning her MBA.

Janice Stecchi, former chairman of the board of trustees who is also a

nurse, notes that the nursing connection has paid off by creating a nurturing and supportive atmosphere at the 225-bed medical center. "The culture of the institution is very caring," Stecchi says. "The administrators take that nursing focus of caring and apply it to everything they do."

Just as the boards and staff members of St. Joseph's and St. John's looked toward the future to create Saints Memorial, Thom Clark and the current administration are again hoping to create a new vision of healthcare for the greater Lowell area. Clark would like to see SMMC join with Lowell General Hospital to create one health system and provide even more comprehensive care for Merrimack Valley residents.

"My focus is on cooperation and collaboration to increase the quality of care for our patients and benefits to our employees," Clark says. Although the prospects of a merger with Lowell General are uncertain, one thing remains very clear about the future of SMMC "We will continue to carry out our mission to provide holistic, clinical, surgical, and medical services to all members of society." Clark proudly says.

THERAFIT, INCORPORATED

Therafit, located at 176 Walker Street in Lowell, Massachusetts, is more than a fitness center; it is a physical therapy clinic and total health gym combined. Therafit's physical therapists specialize in rehabilitation and sports and orthopedic injuries. Their objective is to get their clients functional and keep them physically fit.

The fitness portion of the facility, called Therafit Plus, has the state-of-the-art equipment and specialty classes one would find at any complete gym. What is different is its clientele. The average age of a Therafit client is 50 to 55. Most have suffered an injury or are in need of some sort of physical rehabilitation. Many older clients are intimidated by the glitz and glamour of some centers—Therafit Plus was designed to help them overcome that fear and exercise for good health in a relaxed atmosphere. The specialists at Therafit enable their patients to complete prescribed physical therapy, help them strengthen injured areas, and maintain overall health.

The unique two-step physical therapy and gym workout approach

Gym equipment at Therafit's fitness center.

was born out of necessity. "I was sick and tired of seeing patients walk out the door and not be as well as they should be," says Sue LaRoche, one of the original founders of the corporation. She was frustrated that patients were limited to their prescribed physical therapy sessions due to restrictive insurance guidelines. It was at her insistence that a warm water pool and gym be added to Therafit so patients could continue exercising and work

Left to right: Nicole McCarthy, Darin McCarthy, and Sue LaRoche.

toward complete rehabilitation. But this addition was a long time coming for the company which began over 20 years ago.

Sue LaRoche learned by experience how important it is to have complete rehabilitation after an injury. In the early 1980s LaRoche tore a ligament while she was playing competitive tennis for The University of New Hampshire (UNH). Her injuries were career threatening and so extensive that she had to give up playing the sport competitively. Both a curse and a blessing, this injury is what piqued her interest in the medical world and sports rehabilitation. During her two years at UNH, she interned in the athletic training field, in hopes of working for a sports team one day.

Financial considerations finally brought LaRoche back to her hometown of Lowell. She shifted focus slightly and, while continuing her athletic training internship, worked toward a degree in physical therapy at the University of Lowell. With the combination of her athletic training background and her practical degree in physical therapy, LaRoche had a great opportunity for potential work.

Before she could seek employment, though, she had to pass the required exams to become board certified. She took the American Physical Therapy Association exam and the National Athletic Trainers Association exam, passed both, and then received corresponding licenses for each.

The two certifications gave LaRoche options. She could work for a sports team or in a medical facility's rehabilitation department. Making her future even more interesting was a third choice—opening her own business.

In October of 1985, just a few short months after LaRoche graduated, two physicians and the head athletic trainer from the school approached her about opening an independent physical therapy clinic. The 22-year-old LaRoche was newly engaged and hesitant to embark upon such a venture. However, one thing weighing in favor of the business proposition was the shared philosophy of patient care.

"We all believed that the patients and their goals came first," LaRoche recalls. "If we made a little money along the way, fine, but we all believed that we had to do everything in our power to get them better." So, with encouragement from her fiancé and family and her fellow business partners, LaRoche decided to accept the offer. Greater Lowell Fitness and Physical Therapy soon opened in a small 800-square-foot building located at 16 Pine Street in Lowell.

"It was birth by fire," says LaRoche of those early days. Because she had no business degree, and was brand new to the professional world of physical therapy, she was unsure about her contributions to the growth of the company. However, one thing LaRoche had to offer was a real plus—she was a hometown girl who was born and raised in the community.

When the doors opened, many people in town knew who she was and were willing to support her new endeavor. She was also respected as a star player from her high school days.

Therafit's warm water pool.

She had been captain of both the basketball and tennis teams at Lowell High School and her reputation was still intact. This, coupled with her other partners' expertise, allowed for immediate growth. Within a year, the company expanded and moved into a 1,900-square-foot medical office.

By 1988 the nation's fitness craze was in full swing. More people were involved in sports activities than ever before, and with more involvement came more injuries. The company, now called Therafit, was one of the only independent physical therapy clinics in the area. The demand for outpatient therapy had become so large that

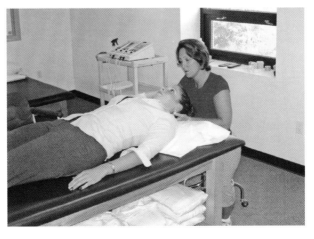

Sue LaRoche treats one of Therafit's patients.

LaRoche and her partners opened a satellite facility, called Therafit II, in a local hospital.

A third facility was opened later that year with a new program called "Back to Work." Its main function was to serve workers compensation patients, instructing them in back safety and giving them ergonomic assessments and physical therapy. Three more full-time physical therapists were hired to accommodate the growth, along with additional administrative personnel and several aids.

The business flourished throughout the '90s and LaRoche, now sole owner of the company, decided to bring all locations together under one roof. In 1999 the company expanded to its current location where it houses the clinic in its 9,500-square-foot space and employs about 25 people.

In 2003 LaRoche made a monumental decision regarding the ownership of her company. She decided to sell it to Nicole McCarthy, one of her trusted employees and an expert physical therapist. Her family's growing needs made the decision easy for LaRoche, as did McCarthy's commitment to Therafit's patients.

"I was approached by several larger rehabilitation corporations to buy Therafit, but I knew I had to sell to someone who shared my philosophy— and that was Nicole," LaRoche says. Today, the company continues to put patients' goals first and remains dedicated to enhancing their total fitness. Still true to its beginnings, Therafit has indeed made a significant difference in the lives of many Lowell residents.

UNIVERSITY OF MASSACHUSETTS LOWELL

The Lowell Normal School, a two-year teachers' college—the first of two progenitors of today's UMass Lowell—was created by a vote of the Massachusetts legislature on May 8, 1894. Its sister institution, the Lowell Textile School, conceived separately and—for the next 80 years—independently, as an antidote to the deepening distress of the state's textile industry, was brought into being by the same state body 13 months later.

The first conceived was the second to open. The Normal School, under the direction of former Lowell High School principal Frank F. Coburn, began in four rooms in an unfinished building at the corner of Broadway and Wilder—what would later be Coburn Hall—with hammered nails as coat hooks, in October 1897. There were 108 students enrolled, all but three of them women. Tuition was free to residents of Massachusetts, $30 for others. Those who didn't arrive on foot came by way of the Boston and Maine Railroad or on the city's electric trolley, which stopped at the end of the Normal School's front walk.

The school, its teachings augmented at the nearby Bartlett Training School (dedicated to the "observation and practice" of kindergarten and ele-

Coburn Hall at the Lowell Normal School, circa 1899.

mentary-school education), featured courses in English, chemistry, geography, psychology, music, figure-drawing, and nature study. The school's model was distinctly British: formal morning assemblies, daily phys ed classes in middy blouse and calf-length bloomers, rigorously monitored attendance, group chorales of "Onward Christian Soldiers," and readings from the book of Psalms.

The Textile School, meanwhile, had opened its doors in rented rooms on Lowell's Middle Street eight months earlier. Its initial day-school enrollment of 40 students—38 of them

male—chose among four curricula: cotton manufacture, wool manufacture, textile design and textile chemistry. The school also offered evening classes, free of charge, to local textile workers who could exhibit an understanding of English and simple arithmetic.

The school was conceived around the vision of its founder, James T. Smith, the one-time secretary of the Lowell board of trade. In Smith's view, it was futile to continue to compete with the low-wage mills in the South over production of cheap goods. Instead, he argued, the goal should be the training of skilled workers and the gradual acquiring of modern technology—which together, by undercutting the prices of European producers for higher-grade Swiss muslin, for example, would position the U.S. for competition in the world textile market.

The early years were hard. Budget hardships and political infighting were almost incessant; between 1899 and 1906 the Textile School graduated an average of 11 students per year. In 1903, due largely to Smith's energies and the generosity of a New York City family

A geography classroom at Lowell Normal School in the early 1900s.

with local connections, the board of trustees dedicated an ambitious new yellow-brick building across the river from downtown—what would be South-wick, Falmouth, and Kitson halls—with an arching entryway leading onto a courtyard, elaborate cornice-work, and carved Italian marble slabs.

It was an extraordinary architectural achievement, with a venue for every textile trade: cotton yarn in Kitson, weaving yarn in Falmouth, chemistry labs in Southwick, with space enough for stockrooms, knitting, dyeing and finishing, wool scouring, classrooms, and offices. The interior rooms were vast—mill-sized—with high ceilings, cast-iron posts, broad wooden beams, and six-foot windows that flooded the rooms with light. Years later, as the school grew and other sciences took over the curriculum, electrical engineering morphed out of weaving yarn, wool scouring gave way to mechanical engineering, and the top floor of Southwick eventually became a gym.

The Textile School gradually found its place alongside New England's established institutions. A fledgling program of pick-up baseball and basketball had led, by the early 1900s, to a schedule that included games with Boston University, St. Anselm's, and Phillips Exeter. By 1920, the baseball season included contests against the

The class of 1900 at Lowell Textile School.

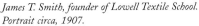

University of New Hampshire, Colby, BU, and MIT.

Early fiscal problems mushroomed with the coming of war. In the spring of 1917, a campus recruiter enlisted 24 people—more than 15 percent of the enrollment—in a single afternoon. Faculty left to join the Quartermasters' Corps; night-school attendance fell by half. As the textile mills boomed with wartime production, the Textile School, at least briefly, was on the verge of almost certain bankruptcy.

President Smith, by then in his 80th year, turned his energies to a final, political saving gesture—a state takeover of the school. In 1918, overriding the governor's veto, the Massachusetts Legislature voted to accept the transfer of the property. A board of trustees was appointed, $50,000 was set aside, and textile education in Lowell was given an extended lease on life. With the outcome certain and the school's future once again secure, Smith retired.

Meanwhile, across the river, the Normal School's founder, Frank Coburn, had succumbed to ill health and retired. His first successor had served eight years, then died prematurely. The next man chosen for the job, in 1916, filled it for four years, took a two-year leave of absence, then left for a job at BU.

By the time Clarence Weed took over, in the fall of 1922, the school was in urgent need of direction. Weed was a scientist—an entomologist, with a passion for butterflies—whose exactitude was legendary. He set rigorous standards for the faculty, from whom he demanded a loyalty he only sometimes received.

In 1932, the Normal School was reconstituted as Lowell Teachers' College, offering four-year bachelor of science programs in elementary education and music. Teachers of both were expected to set a certain standard. By 1936, the college, though still facing declining enrollments, had a solid faculty, a respected curriculum, and a growing, loyal alumni. The new president, James Dugan, replaced the harsh strictures of the Weed administration with a freer, more experimental style—the class of 1939 was the last to wear middy blouses and assemblies were no longer required. He replaced retiring faculty members with younger ones, allowed a loosening of the curriculum

The first principal of the Lowell Normal School, Frank F. Coburn, led the school from 1897 to 1907.

James T. Smith, founder of Lowell Textile School. Portrait circa, 1907.

and welcomed student expression, even dissent.

When a new austerity measure in the late 1930s called for the closing of four state teachers' colleges, including Lowell, as a method of fiscal "retrenchment," the opposition was led by a teachers' college student committee, which received support and advice from the president himself. The group collected 16,000 signatures, then broadcast its challenge on local radio: "Would you spend what it costs to buy a pack of cigarettes to keep the teachers' college open?" The public's answer was yes. The legislature rejected the governor's position and voted to fund the colleges.

The war came soon after, followed by the postwar population boom that created demand for teachers everywhere. The class of 1950 included nine men on the GI Bill among its total of 69 graduates. James Dugan retired that same year. His replacement, Marguerite Gourville, one of his newest, youngest faculty members, already had introduced student singing to the ritual of graduation, created a yearly "ethnic festival," and transformed the tradition of the annual spring dance.

In 1928 the Lowell Textile School, by order of the state legislature, became the Lowell Textile Institute (LTI). While the change in name was largely symbolic, it had been backed strongly by the students and championed by the campus newspaper, *The Text*. Under President Charles Eames, more students were recruited, as well as more faculty; the curriculum was broadened and admissions requirements were made more rigorous.

Throughout the 1920s and 1930s, the demographics of the student body widened markedly. No longer confined largely to the Lowell—or even Boston—metropolitan area, incoming freshmen increasingly came from New York, New Jersey, Pennsylvania, even the South. Foreign students became more common. As one Ecuadorian undergraduate said at the time, he knew of only three institutions of higher learn-

Above: The UMass Lowell campus overlooks the Merrimack River.

Right: Southwick Hall at UMass Lowell.

ing in the U.S.—Harvard, Yale, and the Lowell Textile Institute. There was also, during this time, a marked increase in the number of women students.

With the increased out-of-state enrollment, coupled with the higher tuition rates for non-Massachusetts students (up to double for foreign enrollees), there were more dollars available for faculty hiring. By 1921—with roughly 350 students enrolled—the faculty included eight full-time professors and 24 instructors.

The attack on Pearl Harbor in December 1941 shook the foundations of the institute, nearly undoing the progress of the previous decade and a half. The student body was decimated by enlistments; renewed production in Lowell's still-surviving mills drew off the night students. The school's enrollment, at its nadir in 1943, reached the almost unthinkable level of 70 students.

By war's end two years later, the institute was on the edge of bankruptcy. Charles Eames had announced his retirement. His replacement, Kenneth R. Fox, had some serious choices to make. Fox was young—under 30—a Lowell native and alumnus, an assistant MIT professor with a young man's energy and a local understanding of the school. At the time of his hiring in 1945, he was the youngest college president in the U.S.

By early 1946, the institute's wartime decline had been reversed. A tidal wave of veterans, released by the GI Bill, flooded the campus, overwhelming its resources while filling its coffers almost too quickly to take account. The school, which had been struggling to keep classrooms open, began to turn away nine out of ten applicants. Faced with this windfall, the legislature gave Fox what he needed to add faculty, staff, a library, dorms, and an administration building.

A professor of textile technology himself, Fox saw the opportunity, for the industry as well as the institute, that lay in new technology. A protege of MIT's Edward R. Schwarz—who predicted at the 1946 graduation that "the future will belong to manmade fibers"—Fox steered the school toward this vision, adding new courses in business and labor relations, as well as master's degrees in engineering and textile chemistry. Before his second year was over, he had secured the commitment of the New England Textile Foundation to augment the salaries of LTI faculty, provide undergraduate scholarships, and launch a $250,000 fund-raising campaign for new research equipment to benefit New England's textile schools.

At the 1950 graduation, Fox, only 34 and with less than five full years on the job, announced he had accepted another offer. The trustees quickly hired yet another 32 year-old, Martin J. Lydon, LTI's dean of students and an early advocate of Fox's vision.

In late 1950 Dr. Daniel H. O'Leary was hired to lead Lowell Teachers' College, succeeding the successful Marguerite Gourville as acting president. A former Boston high school

Students research online at UMass Lowell's O'Leary Library. The digital library at the school offers more than 10,000 journals, most U.S. newspapers, and wide-ranging, multidisciplinary reference works.

teacher, O'Leary had served as chair of the history department at Boston Teacher's College. He sought to transform the college into a liberal arts institution with an education program. He brought in younger faculty such as Mary McGauvran, whom he hired as director of admissions in 1952, and Patricia Goler, the first African American with a Ph.D in the state college system, who chaired the history de-partment and later was dean of liberal arts.

With the postwar baby boom; the nation was hungry for teachers. By 1955, freshman enrollment at the school was close to 500—115 of them men— the largest number in the history of the school. O'Leary and others successfully lobbied the state to expand the scope of teacher-training schools—they were now qualified as liberal-arts colleges, and could confer bachelor of arts and music degrees.

By 1965, the campus, as we know it today, was more or less in place. Twenty-six acres of newly acquired land provided space for a new classroom building, power plant, science building, and 300-student dorm. The academic curriculum now included majors in history, English, secondary education, nursing, and liberal arts.

Campus life revolved around student formals; the literary magazine and student government still mattered deeply and team sports pulled large crowds. And in the Little Theatre and the "music cubicles" in Mahoney, later in Dugan and Allen halls and finally, overlooking the river in Durgin Hall, students in one of the finest collegiate music programs in New England played long into the night.

In 1953, Lowell Textile became Lowell Technological, a bow to the school's commitment to new directions in the sciences. The late 1950s and early 1960s were a boom time for higher education. This was the time of the birthing of plastics engineering—which, under Dr. Russell W. Ehlers, took up residence in Ball Hall—and general engineering, which began as a four-year bachelor's program in the fall of 1956. Electronics (later electrical engineering) also saw an expansion, while chemistry and physics widened their reach to offer LTI's first doctorates.

By the mid-1960s, the campus was feeling some of the radical energies of the nation's college youth. A peace vigil at Lowell State in 1967 joined the students of the two schools in a shared protest against the undeclared war in Vietnam. A policy of dormitory room searches and a prohibition on alcohol brought the censure of the student newspaper a year later.

Social tensions had largely been defused by 1971. Martin Lydon had announced his retirement, and Lowell State's President O'Leary had broken the news of an imminent merger of the Lowell campuses. LTI president Everett Olsen began the reshuffling that would precede the merger. He created three degree-granting colleges—pure and applied sciences, business management, and engineering—as well as the graduate school. The new dean of engineering was a faculty member and former engineer named William T. Hogan.

The merger of Lowell State College and the Lowell Technological Institute, the subject of at least six years of meetings, feasibility studies, public hearings, and preliminary legislation, was formally approved by the Massa-

Among UMass Lowell's research specialties are nanomanufacturing, biotechnology, advanced materials, and medical devices. The average annual expenditure on research is $25 million. UMass Lowell is nationally ranked by the Carnegie Foundation as a Doctoral/ Research University–Intensive. The American Association of University Professors ranks the Lowell campus in its highest category.

Chancellor William T. Hogan, University of Massachusetts Lowell. A Lowell native who earned advanced degrees at M.I.T., Chancellor Hogan joined the mechanical engineering faculty at Lowell in 1963. He served as dean of engineering and vice president for academic affairs before being named to lead the University in 1983.

chusetts House and Senate in 1973. The first president of the new University of Lowell, John B. Duff, former provost at Seton Hall University in New Jersey, was installed in October 1976. When Duff left in 1983, the university had more students and faculty and a larger budget, but his legacy also included less tangible results. His creation of the ULowell Foundation, designed to enhance the city's cultural image, and his leadership of the Lowell Historic Preservation Commission, a federal agency supporting the development of Lowell's new national park, exemplified the kind of community outreach that would come to define the school's regional role.

Duff's successor, William T. Hogan, has maintained and expanded on that role. Both through his partnership with the city in the creation of the Tsongas Arena and LeLacheur Park, and through his continuing commitment to the city's many needs and causes, he has been a living symbol of the contributions of both schools, as well as validation of an old truth—that the whole is often greater than the sum of its parts.

More significantly, Dr. Hogan has sharpened UMass Lowell's focus to provide the maximum benefits to its students and the state. *

Upon joining the University of Massachusetts system in 1991, the Lowell campus was given a special charge by the university's trustees: to provide to students an affordable education of high quality and to focus some of its scholarship and public service on assisting sustainable regional economic and social development.

Northeastern Massachusetts was the cradle of the nation's industrial development. Through the years, the region has been a real-world laboratory of complex issues, ranging from technological innovation and its environmental impact to the dynamics of multi-cultural communities and public health challenges. Lowell is recognized worldwide as a premier model of a revitalized industrial city.

"In Massachusetts, we have learned that economic strength and social vitality flow from innovation. Ours is a knowledge-based economy," says Chancellor William T. Hogan. "As UMass Lowell seeks to create more opportunities for people in our region and state, we focus on understanding how a particular area can renew itself—how it can flourish and reflourish. We intend to be recognized widely as a model within higher education, a model that demonstrates how a public university providing excellent, affordable programs for students, and operating in the fine tradition of land-grant institutions can assist sustainable regional development in a global economy."

What makes a sustainable region? Examples of failures abound—regions that have depleted natural resources, depend on a single industry with absentee owners, or have apathetic citizenry. But a region is more than the sum of its assets, whether tangible, ed-ucational, or economic. It relies on the ingenuity and creativity of its people.

Vitality and quality of life grow out of varied options for work; a living wage for most and a safety net for the few; education that is accessible regardless of wealth; freedom from fear of violence; clean air and water and reliable power; places of refreshment and beauty; invention and creativity; and a grass-roots democratic process. Social and economic problems are part of human existence. However, a sustainable region offers effective settings for managing change, from discussions over coffee cups in diners and church basements, to meetings of police leaders with community groups, to research forums in universities, to committees of state leaders and legislators. These problems and conditions offer a continuing set of challenges for a university seeking to serve its community.

In research, UMass Lowell is moving forward with a center for nanomanufacturing research, building on its strengths in plastics engineering, advanced materials, and relationships with industry. This enabling technology, which cuts across product sectors, offers UMass Lowell a chance to establish a competitive niche among research institutions.

Konarka Technologies, located in Lowell, is an example of growing an idea from basic research into a commercial entity. Konarka's nanoscale technology produces flexible, lightweight, and low-cost solar "fabric." The company has secured more than $32 million in venture capital, as well as a $1.5 million loan from the state's renewable energy trust fund. The company now has 40 employees, and UMass Lowell holds a 7 percent equity interest.

Teaching initiatives include new general education requirements, an annual student research symposium, and a project funded by the National Science Foundation to integrate service learning throughout the engineering curriculum. The new School of Health and Environment and the department of Regional Economic and Social Development (RESD) are dramatic ex-

The Paul E. Tsongas Arena was built as a joint project of UMass Lowell and the city of Lowell. The arena, which hosts concerts, conventions, and conferences, is the home of UMass Lowell River Hawks Division I ice hockey and the Lowell Lock Monsters of the American Hockey League. Courtesy, James Higgins.

amples of reconfigured education. The new school, combining the College of Health Professions with the department of Work Environment, promotes health and development that enables people to live in safe and productive communities and environmentally sustainable economies. RESD is interdisciplinary, drawing from economics, history, political science, psychology, sociology, and urban planning.

Outreach is a longstanding commitment at UMass Lowell. Extensive relationships with area public schools are fostered by the center for field services and studies (CFSS). The Francis College of Engineering pioneered programs to improve the pipeline of science and engineering majors.

The Center for Family, Work and Community (CFWC) serves as a portal to the city. The recent Scenarios Project is one example of fostering the informed public discourse that is vital to the social development of a region: CFWC collaborated with the city planners to organize a planning workshop in which residents developed their visions for Lowell's future.

UMass Lowell is an evolving community, one that grows and adapts in response to changing times and conditions. As Provost John Wooding has said, "The larger question here, the question that goes to the core of our role in the region, is this: What is the broadest interpretation of sustainability, concerning both UMass Lowell and the region, that can meaningfully be applied? This means technological advances, the support and encouragement of economic development, the provision of skills to our students to enable them to get jobs and careers. But, more than this, it means the generation of thoughtful and compassionate human beings who can help build vibrant communities."

* This account draws on the facts and narrative in *To Enrich and To Serve: The Centennial History of the University of Massachusetts Lowell* by historian and Professor Emeritus Mary H. Blewett, with Christine Dunlap, executive director of communications and marketing at UMass Lowell.

ESSEX COMPANY

The Essex Company is responsible for creating Lawrence, Massachusetts. Influenced by the success enjoyed by Lowell some 11 miles upstream, a group of local entrepreneurs set out to once again harness the power of the Merrimack River. The project attracted a group of Boston investors who visited Bodwells Falls on the Merrimack River in 1845 and found the site surrounded by farmland and woodlots. With a drop of only five feet, it became clear that a dam of impressive, perhaps even unprecedented, size would be required to raise the fall of the river to a usable height of 30 feet. Undeterred, Abbott and Samuel Lawrence, Nathan Appleton, Charles Storrow, and the other founders of the Essex Company, set out to create a "New City on the Merrimack."

The heart of the venture was the construction of the Great Stone Dam. No dam of comparable size existed across a river with the characteristics of the Merrimack in either Europe or the United States. As such, there were not good examples nor abundant theories for Charles Storrow, the chief engineer, or his assistant, Charles Bigelow, to

The water that once provided the mechanical power to the mills of Lawrence is now used to generate electrical power. The process utilizes a 15 MW hydroelectric plant that the Essex Company constructed and opened in 1981. The Great Stone Dam is visible on the right.

follow as they undertook their task. After much study, Storrow settled on a slightly arched, masonry, gravity dam. The first stone was laid on September 19, 1845 and the final crest stone was set exactly three years later in 1848. Though many speculated about the

dam's strength, nerves were calmed and Storrow's solid design and workmanship were confirmed when it withstood the fury of the great flood of 1936. The storm raised the water nearly 14 feet of water over the dam's crest, and the dam stood strong—and remains essentially unaltered today.

If the dam was the heart of the operation the canals were the veins, delivering water to power the industry that eventually defined Lawrence. The North Canal was completed a few months prior to the dam and the smaller South Canal was built in 1896. The Essex Company sold water rights, known as "mill powers," to mills, which used them to turn turbines. The largest mills were located on the North Canal, which at its peak had a capacity from 10,000 to 13,000 horsepower. The South Canal was home to smaller mills that were able to use its 2,000 horsepower.

Although it was seen primarily as a power supplier, a sizable portion of the firm's activities and revenues came from other ventures. For ex-

Engineers, draftsmen, and clerks hard at work inside the company's Essex Street office, circa 1898.

ample, the Essex Company contracted to build mills and equip them with machinery from the Essex-owned Lawrence Machine Shop. Land holdings also were profitable. At the outset, firm officials bought about 2,000 acres on each side of the Merrimack. The growth of the city and the resulting transformation of marginal farmland into prime industrial space, brought about an explosion in the value of the firm's land holdings.

Even after it sold parcels of acreage, the organization retained tight control over its use through restrictions and covenants that were written into each deed specifying the number and type of buildings that would be permitted. Similarly, control of public services such as sewer, water, and street paving helped Essex Company officials enforce its image of an ideal industrial community. Company influence in Lawrence's internal affairs waned as the city developed independent social and political communities.

By the mid-20th century the textile industry's migration out of New England and lower-priced alternatives to mechanical water power combined to threaten the firm's well-being. A radical increase in oil prices during the 1970s made water power, at this time hydroelectric power, economically attractive once again. In the mid-1970s the Lawrence Hydroelectric Associates, a partnership intent on a major redevelopment of the Merrimack's power potential, purchased controlling interest in the Essex Company. By 1979, the firm had secured private financing, reacquired water rights from mill owners and received the necessary state and federal permits to begin construction on a new $28-million power plant at the south end of the Great Stone Dam.

The redevelopment of Lawrence's valuable water resource from mechanical to hydroelectric power was once again historic. The project was one of the first commercial redevelopments of an existing low-head dam for power production in the United States.

A runner is lowered into the new Lawrence hydroelectric project's powerhouse in December 1980. The 7.5 MW was the first bulb, turbine generator unit made and installed in the U.S.

It also marked the first time that American-made bulb-type turbines were used. Furthermore, it was the first project certified under new federal regulations designed to facilitate the development of alternative energy sources. From an ecological standpoint, the project restored fish passage to the river through the construction of a fish elevator.

Without disturbing the historic Great Stone Dam, the Essex Company placed the project into operation in 1981 with enough generating capacity to meet one-third of the electricity needs of a city the size of Lawrence at that time. At the August 16, 1981 dedication, the Commonwealth of Massachusetts' Governor Edward King praised the project for putting Massachusetts "at the head of the pack in renewable energy technology and ingenuity."

Through the application of new technology to maximize a historically valuable resource, the Essex Company has made an ongoing contribution and a lasting commitment to the city that it spawned. Today, the public can get a glimpse of the history of the Essex Company by viewing many of the firm's early records, photographs, designs, and journals housed in the Essex Company Collection at the Lawrence History Center.

The Lawrence Hydro Facility and Essex Company continue to operate today as affiliates of Enel North America, Inc., a leading owner and operator of renewable energy in the United States.

A unique picture of the Great Stone Dam, likely taken in the early 1960s, shows the workmanship and size of this historical example of civil engineering.

A TIMELINE OF LOWER MERRIMACK HISTORY

70,000-18,000 B.C.
The Wisconsin Glacier, the most recent glaciation, spread over a large portion of North America, including the northeast region of the modern United States down to Long Island and parts of Pennsylvania.

15,000-10000 B.C.
The recession of the Wisconsin Glacier created the present day topography of the Merrimack watershed and redirected the river to its present course, away from Massachusetts Bay.

9,200-8,700 B.C.
The first human inhabitants arrive in the Valley.

9,000-300 B.C.
Human populations in the Valley moved, by stages, from being nomadic people that hunted caribou and other game, and came to adopt an economy of agricultural communities.

1613 A.D.
Explorer Samuel de Champlain published a map that showed the Merrimack, although under a different name. The river and the watershed were then opened to European settlement and exploitation.

1629
King Charles I incorporates "the Company and Governor of Massachusetts Bay in New England," and puts the bounds of the company three miles north of the Merrimack. Uncertainty about the course of the river made for future boundary disputes.

1635
The General Court of Massachusetts incorporated the town of Newbury. The first English settlement was established on the Merrimack.

1640
The towns of Haverhill and Salisbury were incorporated.

1646
Andover was incorporated.

1647
John Eliot, "Apostle to the Indians," made his first visit to the Native Americans on the Merrimack. Eliot established praying villages throughout the Massachusetts land-grant where he

Samuel Osgood was the first postmaster general under George Washington. Painting by Jonathan Trumbull Studio, courtesy, North Andover Historical Society.

preached the Christian gospels in Algonquian

1655
Chelmsford and Billerica, which is now the site of present-day Lowell, were incorporated by the General Court.

1655
Paul White built the first authorized wharf on the Merrimack.

1660
Papisseconewa (or Passaconaway), leader of the Pennacook tribes, made a farewell address to his people.

1668
The town of Amesbury was incorporated.

1672
The town of Dunstable was incorporated.

1683
After decades of existence as "Rowley Village on the Merrimack," the settlement opposite Haverhill was incorporated as the town of Bradford.

1692
The witch trials at Andover were overshadowed by the infamous trials at Salem in the same year. However, there were more accusations of witchcraft, arrests, and confessions at Andover than any other town in New England. More children were involved, as well, and the public uproar lasted from early July into October. Governor Phipps intervened and put an end to witch trials throughout Massachusetts when his wife was accused. By that time, three Andover residents had been convicted and hanged—Martha Carrier, Mary Parker, and Sam Wardwell. Widow Ann Foster, age 72, was also convicted, but died in prison while awaiting execution.

1697
Hannah Duston was captured at Haverhill by marauding natives. She and two accomplices later escaped after killing 10 of the Indians and scalping them. Duston became an instant heroine —and collected a bounty for the scalps that she had brought back with her.

1701
The town of Dracut was incorporated.

1708
The last raid on a Merrimack town by French and their native allies.

1726
The town of Methuen was incorporated

1734
The northern stretch of Billerica, that touched the Concord River, was separated and incorporated as the town of Tewksbury.

1739
The king's Privy Council settled the long-standing boundary dispute between New Hampshire and Massachusetts, naming Pawtucket Falls as the pivotal marker.

1763
Dummer Academy in Newbury became the first independent boarding school in Massachusetts. The more famous Phillips Academy at Andover followed in 1778.

1764
Merchants and traders at Newbury successfully petitioned the General

Court for a separation, arguing incompatible differences with the farming interest at the other end of town. Newburyport was incorporated.

1775

Hundreds of minutemen, from the Merrimack towns, march to Charlestown and join others to confront British troops at Breed's Hill and Bunker Hill.

1778-1781

Privateers, privately owned vessels that were licensed by Congress and had been operating out of Newburyport and Salisbury, joined in the war at sea against Britain's Royal Navy—at that time the most powerful armed force in the world.

1788

Massachusetts ratified the new federal Constitution. Samuel Osgood of Andover became the first postmaster general of the United States.

1789

The birth of Amos Kendall at Dunstable (later Tyngsborough). When Andrew Jackson was elected president in 1828, Kendall was a member of the notorious 'kitchen cabinet,' and is often credited with writing the president's veto of the Bank Bill in 1832. He also served as postmaster general in Jackson's second administration, a post he retained under President Martin Van Buren. Kendall also helped to transform the idea of the telegraph into a national enterprise. He died in 1869.

1790-1799

The first bridges were constructed across the Merrimack at Chelmsford, Haverhill, and Newburyport.

1792-1796

Merchants at Newburyport incorporated "the proprietors of the Locks & Canals on Merrimack River," which built the Pawtucket Canal to circumvent the Falls at Chelmsford.

1797

Merchants in Boston began building the Middlesex Canal a few miles upstream from the Pawtucket at Chelmsford. A stunning technological achievement for its time, the Canal ran 27 miles to Boston harbor by the time it was complete in 1803.

1811

The town of Tyngsborough was incorporated.

1819

The town of West Newbury was incorporated.

1821

Nathan Appleton and his friends, known as the Boston Associates, made their famous perambulation at Pawtucket Falls (Chelmsford), and decided to locate their next textile operations there. The "Associates" acquired the power rights to the Falls by buying "the Proprietors of Locks and Canals," and morphing a transportation business

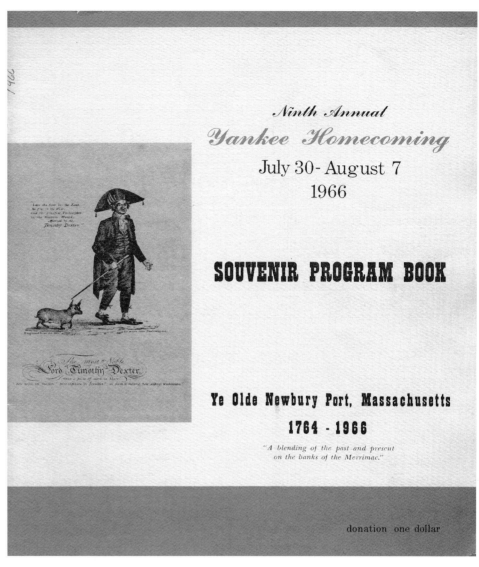

Cover of the program for the ninth annual Yankee Homecoming in 1966. Courtesy, Newburyport Public Library.

into a power company. They also incorporated The Merrimack Manufacturing Company (1822) and the Lowell Machine Shop (1825).

1826

The town of Lowell was incorporated.

1834

James McNeal Whistler was born. George Washington Whistler, the painter's father, was superintendent of the Lowell Machine Shop at the time, and the family occupied the house built by the company.

1840

The first issue of *The Lowell Offering* was published, a journal that featured the poems and stories of the city's single, female workers.

1845-1848

The construction of "the Great Stone Dam" by the Essex Company demonstrated the vital role the enterprises played on the Merrimack in the development of American engineering.

1847

The town of Lawrence was incorporated. Known for two years as the "New City on the Merrimack," the legal name honored the Lawrence brothers—Amos, Abbott, Luther, and William—who had been principal investors in the Essex Company in 1845, which had developed the site as a planned industrial community. The Lawrence brothers were the sons of a Groton farmer and had left the farming life to become successful merchants in Boston.

1849

Henry David Thoreau published *A Week on the Concord and Merrimack Rivers* at his own expense. Four years later he wrote in his journal that 706 copies of the original run of 1,000 had been returned to him at Concord. He noted, "I now have a library of nearly 900 volumes, over 700 of which I wrote myself."

1855

The town of North Andover was incorporated.

1876

The town of Merrimac was incorporated.

1892

Robert Frost shared valedictorian honors with Elinor White at their Lawrence High School graduation. The two were married in 1895.

1899

The American Woolen Company was founded at Lawrence under the leadership of William Wood.

1905-1911

The construction of vast, steam-driven mills was undertaken on the south side of the Merrimack at Lawrence. The city's workforce nearly doubled in less than a decade, largely by the wholesale importation of foreign labor.

1912

A spontaneous walk-out by workers at the American Woolen Company in

February quickly spread to other mills in the city. Soon the involvement of the Industrial Workers of the World (IWW) brought international attention to Lawrence's labor struggle. In addition to organizing the effort, the IWW leadership ran a brilliant newspaper campaign to foster sympathy for the strikers. When, at the end of the strike in March, the workers gained a pay raise, Lawrence became a symbol of American labor's vindication.

1913

A great fire at Salisbury Beach destroyed most of the existing structures at the resort, including the Cushing Hotel.

1922

The birth of Jack Kerouac at Lowell. Known worldwide as "The King of the Beats" and the author of *On the Road* (1957), Kerouac maintained ties to his hometown until his death in 1969.

1936

Cities and towns along the Merrimack were inundated by the worst flooding since 1852.

1947

Merrimack College was founded in North Andover for the specific benefit of low-income families in the Greater Lawrence area.

1978

Federal legislation established the Lowell National Historical Park, the first urban national park in the nation.

1984

The first annual Bread and Roses Festival was held on the Lawrence Common.

1990

The Lowell Parks and Conservation Trust was founded with a mission to improve the quality of life of Lowellians "through the creation, conservation, and preservation of parks, open spaces, and special places."

1995

The fire that destroyed Malden Mills became an international story when Aaron M. Feuerstein, president of the company, immediately announced his decision to rebuild. Feuerstein showed

an unusual level of corporate responsibility to his workforce, keeping them on the payroll and insured during the rebuilding.

2001

John Ogonowski of Dracut, the pilot of American Airlines Flight 11, crashed into the north tower of the World Trade Center on September 11. Betty Ong of Andover was also a member of the flight crew. Among the 92 passengers on board, six were from the lower Merrimack: Peter Gay and Peter Hashem of Tewksbury, Robert Hayes of Amesbury, Mildred Naiman of Andover, Jane M. Orth of Haverhill, and Kenneth Waldie of Methuen. There were also two passengers from the region on American Airlines Flight 175, which crashed into the south tower of the World Trade Center: Douglas A. Gowell of Methuen and Brian Kinney of Lowell. David W. Bernard of Chelmsford died later, in December, from injuries he sustained when he was struck by falling debris when he was walking to a meeting at the Trade Center on the morning of 9/11.

Lowell's Southeast Asian Water Festival, which attracts participants from the local Cambodian and Laotian communities, offers boat races, music, dancing, and food. The event, which takes place along the Merrimack River, mirrors the traditional festival along the Mekong River in Lao. Courtesy, James Higgins.

Suggested Reading

Bailey, Sarah Loring. *Historical Sketches of Andover (comprising the present towns of North Andover and Andover), Massachusetts.* Boston, 1880 (reprint 1974).

Barber, Russell. *The Wheeler's Site: A Specialized Shellfish Processing Station on the Merrimack River.* Cambridge, 1982.

Chase, George Wingate. *The History of Haverhill, Massachusetts, From Its First Settlement in 1640 to the Year 1860.* Haverhill, 1861.

Coburn, Frederick. *History of Lowell and Its People.* 3 vols. New York, 1920.

Cole, Donald. *Immigrant City: Lawrence, Massachusetts, 1845-1921.* Chapel Hill, North Carolina, 1963 (reprint 1980).

Currier, John J. *History of Newbury, Massachusetts (1635-1902).* Boston, 1902.

————. *History of Newburyport, Massachusetts.* Boston, 1905 (1977 reprint).

Dublin, Thomas (ed.). *Farm to Factory: Women's Letters, 1830-1860.* New York, 1981.

Dublin, Thomas. *Women at Work: The Transformation of Work and Community in Lowell, Massachusetts, 1826-1860.* New York, 1979.

Eno, Arthur L., Jr. (ed.). *Cotton Was King: A History of Lowell, Massachusetts.* Somersworth, New Hampshire, 1976.

Fuess, Claude M. *Andover, Symbol of New England: The Evolution of a Town.* The Andovers, 1959.

Greenslet, Ferris. *The Lowells and Their Seven Worlds.* Boston, 1946.

Gregory, Frances W. *Nathan Appleton, Merchant and Entrepreneur, 1779-1861.* Charlottesville, Virginia, 1975.

Hazen, Henry A. *History of Billerica, Massachusetts with a Geneological Register.* Boston, 1883.

Holden, Raymond P. *The Merrimack.* New York, 1958.

Hurd, D. Hamilton (ed.). *History of Essex County, Massachusetts, with Biographical Sketches of Many of its Pioneers and Prominent Men.* 3 vols. Philadelphia, 1888.

————. *History of Middlesex County, Massachusetts with Biographical Sketches of Many of its Pioneers and Prominent Men.* 3 vols. Philadelphia, 1890.

Josephson, Hannah. *The Golden Threads: New England's Mill Girls and Magnates.* New York, 1949.

Labaree, Benjamin W. *Patriots and Partisans: The Merchants of Newburyport, 1764-1815.* Cambridge, Massachusetts, 1962 (paperback 1975).

Massachusetts Historical Committee. *An Archaeological Survey and Documentary History of the Shattuck Farm, Andover, Massachusetts.* Boston, 1981.

Meader, J.W. *The Merrimack River; Its Sources and Its Tributaries.* Boston, 1869.

Merrill, Joseph. *History of Amesbury, including the First Seventeen Years of Salisbury, to the Separation in 1654; and Merrimac, From its Incorporation in 1876.* Haverhill, 1880.

Moorehead, Warren King. *The Merrimack Archaeological Survey: A Preliminary Paper.* Salem, Massachusetts, 1931.

Nason, Elias. *A History of the Town of Dunstable, Massachusetts from its Earliest Settlement to the Year of Our Lord, 1873.* Boston, 1877.

Perry, Gardner. *History of Bradford, Massachusetts.* Haverhill, 1820.

Roberts, John L. *The Glacial Geologic History of North Andover and the Surrounding Area.* North Andover, Massachusetts, 1977.

Robinson, Harriet H. *Loom & Spindle or Life Among the Early Mill Girls.* Boston, 1898 (reprint 1976).

Roddy, Edward G. *Mills, Mansions and Mergers: The Life of William M. Wood.* North Andover, Massachusetts, 1982.

Sears, John Herny. *The Physical Geography, Geology, Mineralogy and Paleontology of Essex County, Massachusetts.* Salem, Massachusetts, 1905.

Stevens, Horace Nathaniel. *Nathaniel Stevens, 1786-1865. An Account of His Life and the Business he Founded.* North Andover, Massachusetts, 1946.

Walters, Ronald G. *American Reformers, 1815-1860.* New York, 1978.

Waters, Wilson. *The History of Chelmsford, Massachusetts.* Lowell, 1917.

Index

GENERAL INDEX